THE OCTOBER HORSES

GENEVIEVE MCKAY

StonePony Studios

Chapter One

M y new life began, as is so often the way, with an abrupt ending.

There's that old saying about when one door closes another opens. Well, in my case, that door slammed shut on my life with an explosive, earth-shattering, bang that ended everything. That nearly ended *me*.

I found out later that I'd been dead for five minutes. They'd almost stopped trying to resuscitate me by that point, and it was only at the frantic urging of my mother that they kept going.

Nobody, besides my mother, would have blamed them for stopping. I'd been languishing away at the Shady Grove Palliative Care facility for the last six months and my inevitable death was a foregone conclusion.

Even I didn't care by that point.

It happened on a Wednesday afternoon, although I didn't know that at the time, and I had spent my morning before the event mindlessly watching a lone finger of sunlight inch across the wall of my room.

Back when I had been in the middle of treatment, one of the hospital nurses had shown me how to do simple Tai Chi exercises to control my breathing and stay calm. It helped me deal with the pain and panic that would often take control of me.

I'd started off being able to do the exercises standing, and then had been stuck weakly doing them from the confines of my hospital bed. Eventually, I had been only able to do the breath-work without the movements; inhale through my nose, hold for six seconds, exhale through my mouth and hold for six seconds. Over and over in a gentle, relaxing rhythm. At some point, my lungs had stopped working and I'd been hooked up to a ventilator to control my breathing, but I still clung to the routine in my head.

Inhale, hold, exhale, hold. My eyelids flickered peacefully shut and when I mentally exhaled, there was a sudden shifting feeling in my stomach. Then I was inexplicably standing in a rolling green meadow.

This is it, I thought, feeling strangely disappointed. *I've finally died and this is some sort of weird heaven or an end-of-life hallucination.* But I didn't feel dead. I felt amazing; better than I had in a very long time. My exhausted body felt refreshed and full of energy. I looked around with interest at the meadow wondering what I was supposed to do next.

It was the most vibrant, *alive* place I'd ever seen in my life. The colours of the grass, the flowers and the sky were so *saturated* that it was like I'd been transported to another dimension or something. It wasn't like a normal dream. I wasn't just watching the scene; I could *feel* the light wind on my face and the grass was soft and cool under my bare feet. Nearby, bees buzzed busily over a clump of fragrant wildflowers. I inhaled deeply, revelling in how well my broken lungs now worked, and tilted my head backward so I could see the rich blue sky overhead. It was so beautiful I could barely look at it.

There was a sharp snorting sound behind me and I turned, again marvelling at how well my body obeyed me in this new world, to look over my shoulder.

There, unexpectedly, was a horse.

Let me just say here that I had never, in all my life up until that very moment, been remotely interested in horses. In fact, I sort of resented them.

When I was nine years old, my little sister Angelika had somehow conned our cash-strapped parents into hiring a low-budget painted clown named Cowgirl-Annie for her seventh birthday party. The clown arrived with a defeated looking brown pony in tow that all the kids took turns being led around on.

I'd had no interest in getting on the pony but then, of course, Angelika had said that I was a chicken unless I did it and that had made me climb on just out of pride.

I don't think the pony had enough energy to be mean but when I clambered aboard it took two steps and tripped over a tuft of grass that sent me flying over its shoulder onto the ground. I cried, probably more with embarrassment than hurt, but it was enough to make Angelika and all her annoying little second grade friends laugh at me for the next year or so. They'd given me the name Chubby Chicken because I was round enough to bring down a pony and scared enough to cry.

That had been the beginning and the end of my relationship with horses, so it was no wonder that finding a horse in my life-altering dream came as such a shocker.

This animal was no defeated pony.

I spun around to face him fully, then stood frozen from a mixture of awe and fear, not daring to move. He was the most beautiful, terrifying thing I'd ever seen. He towered over me; I had to tilt my head back to see him fully. His black coat glistened so darkly that it shimmered with purples and greens, like the iridescent summer feathers of a raven. His mane and tail trailed sideways in the breeze but other than that, he stood motionless, watching me.

My breath caught in my throat as I gazed into his fathomless eyes. I couldn't remember what real horse eyes looked like, but I was pretty sure they weren't this potent mixture of reds and blues swirling together as if it was living colour trapped under glass.

I couldn't say how long we stared at each other, it could have been seconds or years, but while I was trapped, motionless in that gaze, something was happening inside of me.

Looking into his dark, steady eyes was like staring into the center of the universe. I was flooded with feelings of fierce love, not the paltry love I'd thought I'd felt for my ex-boyfriend Duncan, but an overwhelming love that was so much bigger than me. It was mixed with a deep sadness too and a sort of infinite knowing. I still can't properly describe it but, to this day, every time I see a lush rolling field under a cloudless blue sky, I'm transported back to that pivotal moment where everything changed. The moment I got my second chance.

I woke up fighting. Gasping and wheezing for air, I flailed out, my hand connecting solidly against something soft and fleshy. I opened my eyes to see that I was surrounded by a team of nurses all working over me frantically. Someone in the background was shouting. I shut my eyes to block out the noise, beeping, and chaos. Somewhere, somebody was crying. And then everything went black.

Chapter Two

Most people would probably divide their lives into the time before illness and the time after illness, since nearly dying is a pretty life-altering event. But from that moment onward, I divided my life into the time before the dream and the time after the dream. Because it wasn't until after the dream that my real life, *my important life*, truly began.

For my entire last year, I'd been the center of a maelstrom of doctors, specialists, and urgent appointments. Instead of finishing my first term at University, there had been radiation, surgery, and experimental treatments. There had been drug trials and surgical trials, diagnostics, chemicals, and so much medication. And there had been unending pain and nausea.

During the last part of my illness, my non-religious mom had resorted to fervent prayers and had even hired an over-the-phone faith healer from South Africa in a last-ditch attempt to save me.

Nothing had worked. And after a year of all that turmoil, I was bone-tired.

I was actually a little relieved when everyone gave up on me.

After all the chaos, the palliative care facility had been a cocoon of blessed silence. The heavy doses of medication kept the pain at bay. I pretty much slept for the next few months, getting steadily weaker and day by day, losing my tenuous grip on life.

My parents had visited every night after work, but during the day there was just the quiet beeping of machines, the shuffling of the gentle palliative care nurses making their rounds, and my own drug-muddled thoughts.

I mostly drifted in and out of consciousness, only aware of the gentle rhythm of the respirator, my slowing heartbeat and the sunlight drifting peacefully across the wall.

That's all there was. Until I had the dream.

Chapter Three

When I opened my eyes again, the first thing I noticed was how quiet everything was. It took me a moment to figure out that it was the hissing, ticking sound of my ventilator that was missing.

I reached up weakly to touch the tube that ran to the port in my throat to help me breathe. It had been there for months but now it was inexplicably empty; a square bandage in its place.

What the heck? I ran my fingers gently over the bandage, trying to comprehend that I was somehow breathing on my own. How long had I been asleep?

"Are you awake, honey?" Racheal, my favourite nurse looked down at me worriedly and touched my forehead gently with the tips of her fingers. "You've had quite the time here."

"What happened?" I croaked, wincing at the pain in my throat. My voice sounded rough and strange to my ears. Speaking around the ventilator tube was awkward so most of the time I didn't bother. How long had it been since I'd spoken out loud?

"Well, you crashed and we were pretty sure that we'd lost you. You've been out for two solid weeks."

I stared at the ceiling, digesting that information. I felt strange, like I'd been away from my body for a long, long time and had just arrived back. It was not a very comfortable fit. My unused muscles felt weak and sore, and my throat and tongue burned.

"And in that time, you somehow started breathing on your own again. Dr. Harrison doesn't know what to make of it."

I nodded slowly and focused on the novel feeling of my own breathing. The steady inhale-exhale that I'd spent the first nineteen years of my life taking for granted. It hurt a little but in a good way.

"It might be a remission," Racheal said cautiously, "but of course, it's too soon to tell."

"Water?"

"Yes," she said slowly, "a little bit should be fine."

When she came back carrying a little paper cup, she pressed a button at the side of my bed and raised the back so I was in more of a sitting position. Then she held the cup to my lips so I could drink.

The water was cold and soothing on my dry mouth and throat. I had gotten out of the habit of drinking since I had IVs and a gastric feeding tube that supplied me with most of my nutrients, but now I realized how much I'd missed the sensation.

"Take it slow," Racheal said. Her voice sounded far away all of a sudden and had taken on a mournful, musical quality, and I knew that one of my IV drugs had kicked in.

It sounds like when Angelika sings, I thought muzzily. As much as I made it a rule to dislike everything about my sister, her voice was something else. Every note that poured from her mouth made her sound like a divine angel. It's one of the things that made everyone love her and forgive her for having the most shockingly awful personality.

I don't want to think about Angelika, I thought sleepily. *I want to go and visit that horse again.*

My eyes blinked shut and when I opened them again, Racheal was gone and the night sky outside my window was black and full of stars.

I didn't remember having any dreams but my thoughts didn't feel as fuzzy as they had earlier. I felt more aware of myself and my surroundings than I had in a long time. I turned my head a few inches to the right and looked around my room for the first time in forever.

My parents were not at all rich and the private insurance my dad had through his work did not cover a private room, even if Shady Grove had had those on offer; which they didn't. I was in one of a dozen narrow rooms and I shared the space with two other beds. And I say beds and not residents because, as a rule, no one who checked in stayed very long.

There were thin, blue curtains that could be pulled between patients for privacy but hardly anyone used them. The only window was at my end of the room and it overlooked the front lawn and a small corner of the parking lot. It was placed just right to catch the morning sun, and in the afternoon the light filtered through a big maple tree outside. Everyone wanted to look out the window so we generally kept the curtains between us open.

I turned my head slowly to see that at some point over the last few weeks the bed beside me had become occupied by a tiny, little old lady. Her equally ancient husband had pulled up a chair beside her bed and was leaning over her attentively, telling her something in a low, soothing voice.

They didn't notice me watching and I half-shut my eyes and carefully slid my pillow down so I could spy on them undetected.

The woman had grey hair that hung to her shoulders and soft blue eyes. She must have been in her late nineties but her face looked younger and well, sort of preserved. Her skin was tanned and she had sun-spots on her hands that spoke of hours spent outdoors.

I bet she's a gardener like my gran was, I thought idly.

The man had fallen silent and I shifted my gaze to the framed photos on her bedside table. A younger version of herself standing proudly beside a big red horse that had his muzzle stretched out to touch her cheek. Another of her on a brown horse leaping a jump. And yet another of a smaller girl riding a fluffy white pony.

Horses. I drew back, startled, the memory of my dream washing over me so strongly that I could almost feel the lush, green grass under my feet.

"Do you remember Top Hat?" the man said suddenly, his lilting voice startling me.

"He bucked me off in the middle of the Nation's Cup," she whispered back slowly, her voice paper-thin. "I hated him that day."

"You loved him every day," the man said with a smile, leaning closer. "What about Aristocrat?"

"He threw a shoe at a water jump at Badminton, and it flung up and knocked out that reporter and broke his camera."

"I remember that, we were nearly sued."

She smiled at him gently and patted his hand. Then her head nodded off to one side and she was asleep. At least, I hoped she was asleep; in here you never could tell.

The man didn't look up and I studied his weathered face uninterrupted. He was as nut-brown tanned as she was and wore a grey-checked cap like golfers wore. He was dressed in brown pants and a blue polo shirt and his arms were ropy with muscle like he'd worked out every day when he was young. Maybe he still did for all I knew.

He stared down at her with such love in his eyes that it made my heart constrict painfully. I wished that someone, just once, had looked at me like that while there had still been a chance. Maybe before I was bald, emaciated, and terminal. Duncan had been nice enough, before his ultimate betrayal, but I didn't think he'd been capable of deep, passionate gazes.

I didn't feel sorry for myself very often but watching these two old people together made my eyes sting and I finally had to look away.

"We've had a long road together, Gretta," I heard him say. "A long, good road. We've had some fine adventures and I wouldn't change a single, solitary thing."

He paused and I waited, listening hard, hardly daring to breathe until he spoke again.

I must have waited a long time, and I guess the meds still flowing through my system kicked in, because when I woke up it was dark inside the room, though light still filtered in from the hall, and the chair beside the old lady's bed was empty.

I looked over at the woman, Gretta, to find her wide awake and staring at me in the semi-darkness, her eyes shining.

"Hello," she said quietly, "you must be Breanna. I heard your mother call you that and I thought at the time that it was such a beautiful name."

"Bree," I wheezed, the word hissing across my dry mouth like sandpaper. I wished I had another glass of water.

We were silent for a few minutes and then my gaze drifted to the photo of her and the red horse. I could just make out the images in the dim light.

"That chestnut was Ripple," she said, following my gaze. "The bay horse in the other photo was Atticus, and the little girl is my great-granddaughter, Sally, on her pony, Sundae."

I nodded, staring at the photos one by one. When you're in palliative care, time stretches out and nobody expects you to do things quickly, so you're free to answer at your leisure.

"I dreamt of a horse," I said finally, clearing my throat. "He was ... amazing."

"Was it a black one?" She asked eagerly. "A big horse on the beach?"

"A black horse in a green field," I said, shaking my head. "His eyes ..."

"Oh yes, I know. Like he could see to the bottom of your soul.

I dream about him nearly every night. He's coming to take me home. Is he coming to take you home, too?"

Her eyes were fixed on me glassily, too bright in the dim light of the room, and I could make out the flushed patches on her cheeks.

Probably a fever, I thought, worriedly. *She's hallucinating.*

"Well, is he?"

"Er, I'm not sure," I said, wondering if I should buzz the night nurse.

"No, I don't think he is coming for you yet." She dropped her voice down to a conspiratorial whisper. "Do you want to know why?"

"Um, not really ..."

"It's because there's something important you have to do first," she said insistently, half-sitting up in bed. "Your life's purpose is calling."

"I have no purpose," I said flatly, suddenly realized how depressingly true that was.

"Oh, but you do," she said, her eyes blazing. "He told me that you are going to take care of my horses. You're the one who will look after my October horses. You're a rider, too, aren't you?"

"Uh, I've never ..." I broke off, looking at the hopeful expression on her face. What harm would it do to humour her if it made her happy? She was clearly rambling. She probably wouldn't even remember any of this in the morning.

"Sure, I ride. I like horses." At least the second part wasn't a lie. I liked *one* horse. The horse from my dream.

"I knew it. That's what he told me. And he told me to tell you that this is your second chance. So don't waste it."

And then before I could respond her head dropped abruptly to the side and she began to snore.

Well, that was bizarre, I thought in astonishment. *She doesn't know anything about my future or my life's purpose. She's just a crazy old lady.*

But inside of me, a seed of hope began to stir.

Chapter Four

I can admit now that before I got sick I had been one of those people who just sort of floated through life.

I think I had a happy childhood. I had friends, although maybe not *best* friends. I was marginally good in school, lukewarm at sports, average in art, and terrible at music, much to Angelika's delight. I liked to read books but didn't have any particular favourites, and I never stuck with anything long enough to have a true hobby.

I graduated in the middle of my class and enrolled in my first year of university in a field I didn't care about because I couldn't think of anything better to do. I met my first real boyfriend, Duncan, who was nice but not thrilling, and then I became sick. End of story. That was my whole life before the dream in a nutshell.

One day I was too under the weather to go to class and the next, I'd collapsed on the floor of Duncan's dorm room, hardly able to breathe, and was rushed to Emergency by ambulance. At first, they thought it was just a bad case of pneumonia, but then there were tests and more tests, and the doctors were saying things like *surgery, chemotherapy,* and *guarded prognosis.*

My life sped up exponentially after that.

I was in and out of the hospital non-stop, whisked out of my dorm room and back at home, sleeping in my old childhood bed. Then there were months at the hospital, moving floors so often that I hardly knew where I was on any given day.

Finally, there was nothing more anyone could do for me and I was transferred to what was supposed to be my final resting spot, Shady Grove. The last station on the train ride.

I glanced over at the photo of Gretta and the big red horse. Wondering what made one person live their lives full-tilt toward a series of never-ending goals and another person just let life sort of happen.

I had never had a burning passion to *do* anything like my sister had. Even as a very little kid she'd thrown her heart and soul into every new hobby as if her life depended on it. When she'd discovered music, it was like she'd untapped a gift that was already inside of her, just waiting to get out.

It made me a little jealous, honestly. It didn't seem fair that the universe had gifted her with yet another talent when I'd had nothing. But, as much as I'd spent my life really disliking her, I had to admit that she'd worked her tail off to make her dreams a reality. Nobody could fault her for that.

I hadn't had an all-encompassing hobby like my dad, who was a literature and history fanatic, and had filled the basement of our childhood home with dozens of little table-top dioramas of famous battles and historically significant moments. He'd even become sort of famous for them in some circles. Not my cup of tea, but clearly a passion that he'd devoted a good part of his life toward.

My mom was crazy about cooking. She spent all of her free time in the kitchen creating spectacular desserts and dinners. The second she got home from her nine-hour work shift she'd disappear into the kitchen to unwind. She'd pour a glass of wine and play some cooking show on the little portable television and just create things until it was time to go to bed.

I could see, from listening to them, that that unquenchable zest for life, that desire to *make things happen*, was inside Gretta and Lorne, too.

"Do you remember how it all began?" Lorne said, startling me out of my thoughts.

Gretta had been sleeping a lot that morning. She hadn't mentioned our conversation from the night before and had seemed more tired than usual. She kept drifting off in the middle of her conversations with Lorne and I could tell that it was upsetting him.

"You said to me, *Lorne, I'm going to the Olympics*, just like that, one day over breakfast. And low and behold if you didn't start training for it like it was a done deal. Of course, we didn't have any money, sponsors, or a horse. You didn't care though, you said, *Lorne, I'm going to buy a racehorse that's going to take us to the Olympics.*

"I never knew how you pulled these crazy ideas out of thin air, but I was always happy enough to go along with it. Of course, we had no idea what we were getting into."

He broke off, his eyes shining as he replayed some long-ago memory.

I stared dreamily at his face, but my medication must have kicked in and, the next thing I knew I'd blinked, and there I was dreaming of horses again.

This time I wasn't alone. Gretta was beside me, her two frail hands clutching my arm. We stood at the edges of a rain-soaked muddy track, caught in the middle of a pelting storm, thunder rolling overhead and the ground vibrating with the raw power of a dozen oncoming horses.

They approached us like a freight train, bodies so slick with grey mud that they were all the same colour, like they'd broken free from the earth in some primal eruption. The ground shuddered as they ran past. My teeth rattled in my head and I felt the breath squeeze out of me, my heart pounding to the overwhelming rhythm of their hooves.

"See," Gretta said, squeezing my hand, "see?"

The rain had slicked her grey hair down against her skull and mud from the horse's hooves had spattered her cheekbones but her eyes shone and she looked more like a little girl than like an old woman.

A horse neighed nearby; a clear clarion call that went right through me. I woke up with the sound still echoing in my ears.

I sat straight up in bed, gasping for breath, my partially-amputated lung struggling to keep up.

What was happening to me? As far as I knew I'd never seen a horse-race in my life. I hadn't even bothered to watch one on television. But this dream had been so heart-wrenchingly real, and so, so beautiful, that tears were streaming down my face.

Both Lorne and Gretta were staring at me with very different expressions. Lorne looked alarmed and like he was debating whether to buzz for the nurse, and Gretta was beaming and nodding at me like she'd been on the race track with me the whole time.

At that moment, it seemed quite possible that we *had* stood side by side on that track and shared the same dream.

I took another rasping breath and fumbled weakly for the button that would raise my bed into a sitting position.

"See," Gretta said, touching Lorne's arm gently. "She's just like us."

Lorne muttered something under his breath and looked away, his jaw set in a stubborn line.

"Don't be like that, go on," Gretta said, laughing, "just humour me, I know what I'm doing."

He sighed as pulled himself slowly to his feet and moved stiffly toward my bed, holding something in one hand.

"Gretta wants you to have this," he said grudgingly as he came closer. He limped as he walked, though the rest of him looked incredibly strong for a man of his age. His fingertips were calloused when he carefully dropped a little necklace into my hand.

It was a simple silver chain with a charm. A racehorse running with its neck outstretched, ears flattened, every carved inch of it saying *forward*. The rider crouched low on its back, only a passenger on an unstoppable missile. Again, I heard the thunder of hooves.

Lorne stared at me hard as he turned back to Gretta and I knew it belonged to her, that it had been an important part of her, and that he didn't want to give it up.

I promise to give it back to you as soon as she passes, I thought, but to Gretta I said, "thank you, you don't have to give me this. But it's beautiful."

"I want someone to carry on my work," Gretta said, beaming at me encouragingly, *"our* work. I think you understand."

I didn't, but one sharp look from Lorne and I knew enough to just smile, nod, and humour her.

"Of course, thank you."

Lorne sat back down at his card table and began to deal out another round with only the little *thwack, thwack, thwack* sounds to convey his disapproval.

"It began with a horse," Gretta said, smiling over at the photos on her dresser, "a big, red horse."

"Ripple," I said and Lorne looked up at me with a flash of surprise.

"Yes, that was our boy. He was training when we got there. The sun was hardly up and he blazed down that track like a comet, fire trailing in his wake. We thought he was the fastest thing we'd ever seen."

"Turns out he wasn't fast for a racehorse," Lorne said, coming out of his sulk. "And he was clumsy, too. He didn't know where to put his feet. They couldn't wait to sell him to us."

"He was still growing." Gretta smiled. "He was only two then.

By the time he was four he was over 17 hands high and wide as a house."

"A monster," Lorne said.

"Our beautiful monster." Gretta gazed at her husband with so much love in her face that I felt like an intruder watching them. I had to look away.

I stared at the maple tree swaying in the breeze outside, the little, silver racehorse clutched in my hand so hard that I felt its tiny hooves digging into my palm.

Chapter Five

Gretta lived for three more days.

Each morning, Lorne would arrive to visit before the sun came up. He'd pull the little side-table against Gretta's bed and play endless games of Solitaire.

When Gretta was awake they'd speak quietly together and when she drifted off it was only the flap, flap sound of the cards slapping quietly against the table in a purposeful rhythm.

I lay there, too exhausted from using my lungs all on my own to do much more than stare at the ceiling and think.

Way back, during the treatment phase of my illness, the upper lobe of my left lung had been cut out and I'd never really had a chance to adapt to the loss before the raging infection that had started my abrupt, downward spiral kicked in.

It's not like you even need two good lungs anyway, Angelika had said, *you're not an athlete or a musician. You don't need that much air to read books.*

She'd been trying to be funny, to lighten the situation, but it came out sounding mean as heck and my dad had told her that maybe she should go home.

I had actually been starting to enjoy her visits. We hadn't

spent much time together voluntarily since we were little kids and I had forgotten how funny and sarcastic she could be. It was a good antidote to all the tears and anxious worry my parents showered down on me.

It's okay, she can stay, I wanted to say. But the tube in my throat wouldn't let me get the words out and she'd flounced out without a backward glance.

She'd gotten her revenge that afternoon by finding my hapless boyfriend wandering the hallways and dragging him back to our childhood home to have her way with him. Actually, it turned out, they'd been sleeping together for a couple of weeks, but that was the day they got caught.

"You're having another good day," my mother said in surprise, sinking tiredly into the chair beside me. She was still in her hotel uniform and she pulled her shoes off as soon as she sat down, wincing as she rubbed her feet. I knew she saved money by taking the bus from The Whitley Hotel where she worked as a front desk manager and then walking the four blocks from the bus to the hospital. This was after a full shift of working standing up; they were only allowed to sit down on their half-hour lunch break.

My parents had decided to go down to one car at some point and my dad was always lugging home books and student papers from the university so he was the one who usually got to drive.

Being in palliative wasn't at all like the movies where your friends and family live at your bedside the entire time. Many illnesses stretch out for weeks or months, or even years in their final stages. Even well-meaning, loving family has to go back to work and resume their lives at some point. They still have to eat and pay the bills.

"There's my girl," Dad said, striding into the room a few minutes behind Mom. He'd spent the summer attempting to grow a beard to look distinguished enough to impress his students, but so far it was looking pretty patchy.

We were all pretending that this partial remission thing was our new normal even though I could see the deep worry-lines around my dad's eyes and the defeated sag of my mom's shoulders. In some ways, this illness was harder on them than it was on me.

"All right, let's hear it," I wheezed, "I want to know all about your day. Tell me what's happening outside."

It wasn't something I'd ever dreamed of saying to my parents before I was sick. I would have rarely given a second thought about how their days had gone. But now I loved hearing about the world outside of Shady Grove, and all those minute, boring details that made up a normal person's life. A late bus, a homeless person feeding pigeons, being caught in a summer rainstorm without a coat; all those tiny, beautiful, insignificant details that, when combined, made up such a rich and vibrant tapestry.

My parents were great storytellers and they could make any bad situation seem hilarious with just a few carefully placed words. Maybe not a sick daughter type of situation but everything else.

"Hey, what's this?" my dad asks, zeroing in on the chain I'd wrapped around my wrist.

I hesitated, glancing over to make sure Gretta was still asleep and Lorne hadn't come back from the cafeteria. I didn't know if Gretta would even remember giving me the charm; old people forgot things all the time.

"Just a present," I said quickly, covering it with my other hand.

"Nice." He pulled up a chair beside my mom and sat down, opening his multi-level lunch box. It was the metal kind that kept his home-made meal hot and packed enough for two. Even though my mom was the cook in the family she had to work longer hours. So, every day, dad rushed home from his summer-school classes so he could cook healthy food for the two of them and then come visit me.

Today, he had rice and steamed vegetables smothered in some sort of delicious-looking sauce.

My stomach rumbled loudly in response to the food, taking us all by surprise.

Usually, I had to focus on something else while they ate because the smells and sounds of food being swallowed made my overly-sensitive stomach heave. But that day I could smell the nutty undertones of the rice, the tang of lightly steamed vegetables and the sweetness of the sauce. For the first time in forever I wanted food.

I squeezed the little racehorse between my fingers, remembering the steady gaze the black horse in my dream had given me, and wondered what was happening to me.

Chapter Six

On the next day, Gretta didn't wake up very much.

I lay there listening to Lorne's steady voice as he murmured on and on, reminding her of every last detail of the life they'd had together. He didn't seem to be able to stop talking, even when she started snoring and he couldn't pretend that she was paying attention to him anymore.

Finally, he drifted into silence and I glanced over from where I'd been staring out the window. The look on his face was shattered, so broken and vulnerable that I gasped out loud.

His eyes flicked upward, meeting mine and for a moment I was imprisoned in his gaze, unable to look away.

"How did you two meet?" I blurted, saying the first thing that came to my mind. Anything to get him to stop staring at me in that haunted way.

He sighed heavily and rubbed a hand across his eyes, looking down at Gretta's sleeping form again.

"We"—he cleared his throat a couple of times—"we both worked at the same barn when we met. We hit it off right away; we had the same philosophies when it came to training and handling horses, and we shared the same dreams of one day being able to make our living riding. We also shared an appalling lack of money. We had champagne tastes on a ramen noodle budget, I'm afraid.

"Gretta loved Eventing and she knew that if she was going to succeed that she needed an unstoppable horse. Not a good horse, but a great horse. One with endless bravery, strength, and stamina. And most of all, it had to have heart.

"The trainer we worked for bred warmbloods, but she'd also had some success in retraining young thoroughbreds fresh off the track.

"Gretta and I went to that racetrack for the first time not knowing a thing, except that we thought we needed a horse. That visit led to a love-affair with thoroughbreds that spanned our whole lives."

"That was the day you came home with Ripple," I reminded him.

"Yes," he said, his eyes widening in surprise. "How did you remember that?"

"I have nothing else to do but lie here and remember things," I said and then flinched because it sounded like I was feeling sorry for myself when really I wasn't.

"This is a good place to reflect on life, isn't it? And death."

I nodded and looked over at Ripple's picture again, suddenly hit with an unfamiliar pang of regret. I'd come to be quite accepting of my fate, but right then I wished that I had spent time with real-life horses when I'd had the chance. What had I been doing with my life, anyway?

That morning, I'd woken up feeling hungry for the first time in ages. The feeding tube in my stomach gave me the nutrients I needed at regular intervals but suddenly I desperately wanted real food.

"A hamburger?" Racheal said, raising her eyebrows into her hairline. "Really?"

"With extra cheese," I said, smiling at her hopefully. "And pickles."

"I'll talk to Dr. Harrison," she said, shaking her head.

When she came back an hour later, she handed me a kid-sized fruit popsicle.

"See how that goes down and we'll work on your hamburger order in the future."

It was just a plain old orange popsicle but I swear it was the best thing I'd ever tasted. I was only able to eat half of it, but when I lay back in my bed, I felt completely satisfied for the first time in a long time.

"We'll have the doctor look in on you today," Racheal said when she came in to check on me. She withdrew the silicone thermometer from under my tongue and raised her eyebrows again. "Probably time to re-do some bloodwork."

I made a face. Despite having been poked about one gazillion times with a variety of sharp implements, I hadn't lost my squeamishness. If anything, I'd become *more* sensitive rather than less.

I looked over to see that Lorne sat silently by Gretta's bedside, one of her frail hands clasped tightly in both of his. I could see that he'd been crying.

"Okay," I told Racheal, "whatever you need to do."

I resumed my usual staring out the window, but for the first time in a long time, I felt bored and restless.

"Would you like to read these?" Lorne appeared at the side of my bed with a small stack of magazines clutched between his calloused fingers. He set them down in the space between the bed rail and my legs without waiting for an answer, fanning them out so I could see the titles. Eventing, Horse and Hound, Dressage Today. "I brought them for Gretta but, well, she's not feeling quite up to reading, today."

They looked like they'd been well-read already. The Eventing ones were at least ten years old and all the covers were creased and sun-faded. Bits of paper stuck out of the tops where someone had probably marked out interesting articles.

"Yes, please," I said, "thank you."

He didn't move and I realized that he was staring down at the racehorse chain wrapped carefully around my wrist. He had that far-away expression on his face like he'd been caught in a distant memory.

"I can give it back," I said quietly, glancing over to make sure Gretta was still asleep. "I can keep it for you until ... um, until you need it again."

"No," he cleared his throat a few times. "No, she wanted you to have it so you should keep it. The thing is she always meant to pass it down to our daughters."

I reached over to undo the chain. There was no way I wanted to get caught up in a family drama. I was pretty sure I could go on Amazon and find my own racehorse chain just like it in about two minutes.

"No," he said again, covering my hand with his own, "I mean she wanted to hand it down to someone who loved horses as much as we did. Our daughters are good girls, and they love all animals but they don't have that burning, unquenchable passion for horses that marks a true horseperson. It's something that gets deep in your soul and doesn't let go."

"Oh," I said, thinking about the black horse in my dream.

"She must have seen that in you."

I froze, feeling like a complete imposter. I wasn't sure how Gretta had mistaken me for some sort of horse person who could carry on whatever mission she had in life. But this also didn't seem like the best time to clear things up. After she passed away, I'd tell Lorne the truth and give the charm back to him.

I picked up a magazine to cover my confusion and pretended to read, waiting for Lorne to limp back to Gretta's side.

It took me all morning to go through the magazines one by

one, carefully studying the pictures and reading the articles. I understood only about a third of it. It was like reading a manual of technical terms and I wished I had my tablet handy so I could look things up. I made a mental note to find out where it had been stashed away and plug it in to charge.

In the old Eventing magazines, there were jumps so big that they would tower over my head if I stood beside them. And yet there the horses were, springing happily over them like they hadn't a care in the world. Their riders sat poised, crouched in just the right spot so they could guide the horse without interfering. I wondered what it would be like to be up there.

It's probably not as peaceful as it looks, I thought, *you would only stay suspended in space for that one perfect moment. All the rest would probably be aching muscles and noise, sweat, mud, and fear. It would be wind and rain in your face and thundering hooves like in my dream about the racetrack.*

I sighed and when I looked up again, Gretta was awake and both she and Lorne were staring at me.

Gretta flashed me her brilliant smile and patted her husband's arm.

Chapter Seven

At lunch, I was surprised to see my dad walk in.

"It isn't Saturday," I said as he pulled up a chair beside my bed. "Don't you have class?"

My dad taught classes during the regular terms at the University. But he also taught summer school to make some extra money.

"No, but it was test day today so I was able to sneak away early." He set a box down on the table and I could see that it was our old game, Chinese Checkers, one of my childhood favourites.

"Where did you dig this up from?"

"The storage room in the basement. I remembered how much you loved this when you were a kid."

Whenever my mom had been busy ferrying Angelika around to one class or another, my dad and I would always make popcorn and hot chocolate and play board games together until they got home. Those were some of the best memories I had. Angelika would always be furious when she got home and found out that we'd played without her. Come to think of it, I couldn't remember a time when she'd played with us at all.

"Do you feel up to playing one or two rounds?"

"Yes, of course." I pushed the button to raise myself into a sitting position while my dad pulled up the little end table and set up the board.

This is nice, I thought, *it's a little like being a kid again.*

We played for a while in companionable silence and I didn't look up until Lorne's chair scooted back and he stood up and stretched with a groan.

"Would you like to join us?" my dad asked politely but Lorne merely shook his head and muttered something about going to the cafeteria. I wondered if we should have invited him sooner.

"So, Dad," I said, glancing over to make sure that Gretta was asleep. "Did we have any people who rode horses in our family? Like a great grandparent or something?"

"Not that I know of," he said, looking confused, "but, oh wait, your grandma on your mom's side had a horse when she was young. I remember seeing the old photos in her picture album."

"What colour was he?" I asked.

"I have no idea. I mean, it was a really old photo so it was in black and white. Maybe a dark brown? She jumped it in shows, I think."

"Was it a thoroughbred like this?" I opened the magazine next to me and pointed to one of the photos I liked best.

"Honey, all I know is it had four legs and a tail. Why all this sudden interest in horses?"

"Oh, I don't know. I've been having these strange dreams."

Dad frowned, looking concerned all of a sudden. "Did you tell the nurses or Dr. Harrison? You're supposed to let us know if any changes are going on. You do look a little flushed."

"Yes, Dad," I said patiently, even though I realized that I hadn't. We were supposed to tell our palliative team whenever something in our bodies, or our minds, changed because it might be a sign of a drug-reaction or of some internal process that couldn't be detected from the outside. "It's nothing bad. I'm just dreaming about horses is all."

"I hear that's very dangerous," he said, suddenly trying not to smile. "Horse dreams are a gateway to wanting to ride actual horses ... and they're more expensive than street drugs."

"Ha ha. How would you even know?"

"Oh, there are some horsey students in my classes. You can pick them out by the mud on their boots and the bits of hay that fall off of them. And the dark circles under their eyes. They have the aura of people who live on tomato soup and crackers while they pay six hundred dollars a month in horse board."

"Six hundred dollars?" I asked in astonishment. "Is that really how much it costs to keep a horse?"

"I'm just going by what I've overheard. Maybe that's for luxury accommodations."

"Hmm." I was strangely disappointed. Having my own horse had been a nice fantasy to distract myself over the last couple of days. I'd allowed myself to imagine that, if things had been different and I hadn't gotten sick, that a healthier version of myself could have maybe had a horse like Ripple. A beautiful, mystical animal that would let me brush its hair, leap over jumps, and be my best friend. Not at six hundred dollars a month, though. The old me would have had to work three full-time jobs to afford that and still eat.

"I don't think you have to own a horse though, one of my students just takes lessons at a barn. I think she even does manual labour to help pay for it."

Now that was more like it.

"Dad, do you think you could find out what barn she rides at so I could look it up on the internet? Oh, and do you know where my tablet is? I want to charge it up."

He looked at me with a strange expression on his face as if he were seeing me for the first time.

"Sure, honey," he said. "I'll find your tablet as soon as I get back. But, right now I'm just going to go talk to the nurses for a minute. You rest here and I'll be right back."

Later, I found out that my innocent question had sent my dad into a spiralling panic. He'd assumed that I had a fever or was hallucinating or something. It's a strange phenomenon that sometimes a dying person will feel really good right before they pass over. They'll be able to talk and laugh and understand everything, and their relatives will think that it's a miraculous sign they're getting better. But then they'll die in the next few hours instead. That's what my dad thought was happening to me.

As a result, Dr. Harrison came bustling in, taking all my vital signs and directing the nurse to draw multiple vials of blood from me. He shook his head as soon as we were done and scuttled out of the room as fast as he could. He was always in a hurry and he rarely spoke to the patients or even made eye contact. I never minded him or thought him cold, though, like some of the other patients did; he just seemed to always be in his own world. I liked to think it was the sign of a genius.

Anyway, Racheal came in right afterward to calm my dad down and to bring me a minuscule bowl of applesauce that I practically inhaled. I caught my dad watching me with wide-eyed wonder at least a dozen times.

"I'm just eating a snack, Dad," I said impatiently, "not growing a second head. Are we going to play another round or not?"

Usually, I fell asleep at least a couple of times when my parents visited but today, I not only stayed up but hardly felt tired at all.

"You'd better not be letting me win," I warned, squinting at him suspiciously when I beat him for the second time.

"No, never. Look, I've got to run home now, but I'll be back tonight with your mother. You have someone call us if there are any changes."

"Yep," I said, rolling my eyes. *I'll let you know if I'm about to die.* I didn't say that out loud though, it wasn't fair to even joke about that with him. My parents had been amazing through all this and I hated that I'd basically destroyed their lives for the last year. I could see the worry lines that had been permanently etched into my mom's face and that my dad had aged about ten years since I'd gotten sick.

As much as I loved visiting with him, it was nice to be able to relax without him hovering over me worrying. I could go back to reading my magazines in peace.

Chapter Eight

By the afternoon, things were not looking good for Gretta. In the late afternoon, her heart and respiratory rate had plummeted and there was a flurry of activity around her until she was stable again. She had slept through the whole drama, but poor Lorne had gone white as a sheet and the nurses made him lie down on the far bed, which was currently empty. Dr. Harrison put a hand on Lorne's shoulder and gave it a brief, sympathetic squeeze, which was the most emotion I'd ever seen from him.

The nurses fussed over Gretta even though she was asleep and laid warm blankets over her and made sure her pillow was positioned just right. They really were the best people; it took an incredibly special person to work with the dying and they always went that extra mile to make sure the patients were comfortable.

"Here, I'll just shut this, Lorne, to give you more privacy," the afternoon-nurse, Janet, said, pulling the curtain across the space between my bed and Gretta's.

I felt a strange panic in my chest when I was all alone, which was silly because I barely even knew these people. Still, they felt a little like family to me now.

"No," Lorne said abruptly, "Gretta loves the sun. She loves the sun, the rain, the wind, and the wide blue sky over her head. She could be outside in any weather and never complain."

"Well, if you're sure," Janet said doubtfully, pulling the curtain back again. She gave me a sympathetic smile.

I did my part to give Lorne and Gretta their privacy by making myself as unobtrusive as possible.

I burrowed down under the covers and fired up my long-neglected tablet. It had spent a few hours charging already and seemed to be in working order. I went through all the old book titles that I'd stored on my *Kindle* app, smiling as I saw my long-forgotten favourites again and then settled down to do some research.

"Ripple Running" was the first thing I typed. Even though he'd been famous over fifty years ago, dozens of old photos of him popped up right away. There he was, soaring over jumps or galloping through water or powering around a sand arena, his mane braided and his neck proudly arched.

In many photos he just stood posed, staring regally into the distance, with Lorne or Gretta or sometimes both of them standing beside him.

There was one that popped up over and over that was really stunning. He stood on a windswept hillside with Gretta, looking about twelve years old even though she'd been in her late twenties, standing beside him. She was wind-blown, and exhilarated with her hand on his big shoulder, eyes shining up at him with a look of pure love.

I didn't know why that photo spoke to me so much but I closed my eyes, suddenly awash with regret and longing.

I've wasted my entire existence, I thought miserably, *Gretta and Lorne were about the same age as me when they started out. Why wasn't I out there doing interesting things while I had the chance? Now it's too late, I'm broken and ...*

"He was a good horse," a rough voice said beside me and I jerked sideways, my eyes snapping open.

Lorne stood beside my bed looking down at the tablet I'd let slip from my fingers. He reached out and ran a finger across Gretta's photo and then jerked back when the picture enlarged at his touch. "Damn, I'll never get used to this newfangled technology."

Despite being sunk in self-pity, I had to smile at the baffled expression on his face. I touched the screen again and the photo went back to normal.

"It's like magic," he said. "Are you doing all right, kid?"

"Yes," I lied. He didn't need to hear about my problems when the love of his life was fading away in front of him.

"Hmm." He narrowed his eyes at me and his mustache bristled. I realized that he was waiting for me to keep talking.

"I'm being childish," I said, "it's just that I wish ..." I broke off, looking down at the photo again with a sigh. "I wish I had done something like *this* with my life. Something that made me look as happy as Gretta did in this picture."

"Gretta was a force to be reckoned with," he said, looking fondly down at the photo again, "she still is. She made her own destiny, that's for sure. She was always one to know exactly what she wanted and to go after it like a bulldog. You want to work with horses?"

"Oh, er, well, I do like them," I said, thinking again of the horse in my dream and the photos of Ripple. I didn't know if *like* was the right word since I didn't know anything about them. The horses in my dreams had sure caught my imagination, though. And the connection that Gretta had had with Ripple. "I guess I wish I'd done *more* is all."

"Well, if you're bored, you could go watch the horse show in a couple of weekends. It's a dressage show, which I think is about as exciting as watching paint dry, but there will be plenty of horses for you to look at. It's right in town so if you were feeling well enough maybe your family could take you."

"Really?" I said with a sudden flash of interest. But my mood fell again when I remembered my situation. "I can't leave," I said flatly, "I'm not strong enough."

"Suit yourself," he said gruffly, turning abruptly away, "you look well enough to me."

Do I? I wondered as I watched him limp back to Gretta's bedside. I hadn't seen myself in a mirror in months so I had no idea what I looked like. Leaving Shady Grove to watch a horse show was impossible, though. I was still hooked up to my IV pole and all these monitors. I had a gastric tube. I hadn't walked in months. It was an effort just to pick up my tablet to use it. Of course, it was impossible. Lorne didn't know what he's talking about.

That afternoon Gretta and Lorne's daughters flew in from the other side of the world. They arrived in a flurry of tears and hurried movements and broken-hearted wailing and completely disturbed the peaceful atmosphere we'd had going on.

There were the two grown daughters and their husbands plus a thirteen-year-old girl who belonged to one of them and two young boys who belonged to the other. No matter how quiet and respectful people are trying to be, it's hard to not be noisy when you've crammed ten people into one tiny area.

One of the daughters gave me a harried look and abruptly pulled the curtain across.

I tried not to be offended. In all the months I'd been here, I'd seen my share of deaths and I knew that everyone grieved differently. Some people got angry, some people cried, and some stayed locked in silence. Some people joked their way through it and some people grew very kind and peaceful. Some people demanded constant attention from the nurses and doctor, and some people moved about like shadows.

Still, I'd grown attached to Lorne and Gretta and it had come to feel a little like *I* was their family and now that these loud, fluttering people had intruded it was hard not to be irritated.

I scrounged around until I found my headphones and plugged them into my tablet so I could both drown out the sound of my neighbours and watch some videos.

Racehorses, I typed in first and then waited expectantly.

The next few hours went by in a blur. Horses thundered by on the screen, their churning hooves amplified in my headphones until it felt like I was right there at the track, in the arena, on the cross country course, in the barn. Their alien snorts, whuffles, and ragged breaths becoming more familiar by the second.

When the curtain was pulled back abruptly and my parents appeared at my bedside, I jerked backward, nearly startled out of my skin.

I pulled the headphones from my ears and stared up at them, taking a moment to remember where I was.

"Oh, honey, are you okay?" my mom whispered, glancing over her shoulder at where Lorne and Gretta's families were still huddled on the other side of the curtain.

It was quieter now but there were still a few low murmurings and muffled sobs.

"Yeah," I said quietly, "it's no big deal."

It was. It was a very big deal. But there wasn't much any of us could do about it.

By the time my parents had to leave, the crowd around Gretta's beside had thinned. It was only Lorne, one of his daughters, and the pale-faced granddaughter who stared at me with wide eyes when the curtain drifted aside for a moment. She looked lost and overwhelmed, and I didn't blame her. Death is a little over the top the first dozen times you encounter it. Even after that, it's still unsettling.

It was just after midnight when I woke up again. The curtain had been pulled back between Gretta's bed and mine, and the moon shining in from my window cast the whole tableau in an other-worldly light.

Lorne and one of his daughters were sleeping in their chairs side by side, the daughter leaning heavily on her dad's shoulder.

The other daughter and the teenage girl were asleep in the empty bed.

They're like statues, I thought, watching the way their skin glowed white in the moonlight. It looked like one of those art installations of sculptures of people doing everyday things. Life becomes art.

"Breanna." The word was so soft that at first I thought I'd imagined it. "Breanna, come here."

I swivelled around to find Gretta watching me calmly, looking fully alert and not like she was dying at all. She glanced at Lorne and her daughter, and edged herself slowly upright a few inches, careful not to disturb them.

"Come here," she whispered again, smiling at me encouragingly and beckoning with one hand. "I have something to tell you."

"I can't," I whispered back. I couldn't remember the last time I'd stood on my own. I needed help with nearly everything now.

"You can." She said it with such confidence and the moonlight cast everything in such a magical glow that somehow I found myself believing her.

Shaking and wheezing with effort, I pulled myself into a sitting position and pried at my shrunken legs one by one until they hung over the side of the bed.

I can't believe I'm doing this, I thought, feeling both reckless and afraid at the same time.

I inched forward until my bare toes touched the floor, pausing to take in the almost-forgotten sensation.

"You're almost there," Gretta said, but I clung to the bed, not ready to trust my wobbling legs.

Finally, ever so slowly, I stood up, swaying like a new-born fawn on its feet for the first time. Still, it had worked. I was upright. I went from holding the bed to holding the dresser. I reached over and snagged my IV bag off the overhead hook and held it clutched against my chest.

My last few steps felt steadier and I was able to carefully lower myself onto the edge of Gretta's bed and let her take my hand. Her grip was surprisingly strong, almost painful, and I had to resist the urge to pull away.

"The horse is here to take me home," she said calmly.

"Wha ... what do you mean?" I asked, gulping. I knew exactly what she meant and a hard shiver ran down my spine.

"He has a message for you."

"For me?" I squeaked.

Her face looked so different in the moonlight. Every second I stared at her she seemed younger and younger and her skin had taken on a shimmery sort of glow. I couldn't look away.

"You're to take over where I left off. See to my October horses. Lorne will help you when you get stuck."

"I don't understand what you—"

"Follow the path where it leads you and everything will fall into place. I have complete faith in you."

"In me? Oh, but you shouldn't. I'm—"

"I wish I could be here to see all the great things you accomplish," she broke in softly, "but I'm afraid I have to go now. This life was a beautiful ride. I wouldn't have changed a thing. Good-night, Breanna."

She patted my hand and shut her eyes, a gentle smile on her face.

I sat frozen, worried for a second that she'd passed away right there in front of me, but soon I could hear her gentle breathing and I fumbled my way back to bed.

My body shook hard with effort and it was all I could do to

hang up my IV bag and climb under the covers, panting and trembling, my eyes stinging with tears.

I knew it was probably the last time I'd talk to Gretta. What she had told me made no sense at all, but it had been so sweet and magical at the same time.

Another thought hit me. *I walked. If I can walk and sit on my own, I can sit in a wheelchair. And if I can sit in a wheelchair, I can go to a horse show.*

I felt the strangest sense of hope wash over me. What if I did get to walk out of here someday? What if somehow one of the experimental drugs had kicked in at the last minute, or one of the faith healers my mom hired had actually worked? What if I'd defied all the doctor's predictions and I was going to get a second chance?

I pushed the dangerous thoughts away. I'd been down this hopeful path too many times in the past year. Sure, it was a nice daydream to think that I had a future, a path to follow, but I knew reality would come crashing back in the morning.

Maybe I'll just believe for tonight, I thought sleepily, *one night won't hurt. Someday I'll walk out of here and never look back. And maybe there's even a horse out there waiting for me, too.*

I closed my eyes and dreamt of Ripple, of that first day they'd seen him at the racetrack. How he'd shone like fire in the morning light, full of promise.

Chapter Nine

✿✿✿

W hen I woke, the curtain beside my bed was drawn and the air was, once again, heavy with muffled sobs.

Gretta is gone, I realized sadly, *poor Lorne.*

I'd lost quite a few roommates during my stay here. The first one had been an awful shock, especially since she'd only been a few years older than me with a husband and a baby of her own and everything. After that, it had gotten easier, but that day Gretta's death hit me like that first one all over again.

There was no place to escape to. I kept my headphones plugged in and my eyes resolutely fixed on the screen. I'd found a playlist of horse movies to watch, although it turned out that most horse movies were basically created to make you cry.

I sobbed my way through Dreamer, Seabiscuit, and Wild Hearts Can't be Broken, and had just started on The Black Stallion when the curtain drew back and my mother was there wrapping me in one of her tight, warm hugs.

"Oh, sweetheart, I'm so sorry," she said, her eyes bright with tears. "I wish we could afford a private room for you. I hate that you have to go through this over and over again."

My dad was behind her, looking sad and anxious.

I glanced over at Gretta's bed but it was empty. Down at the far end of the room, the curtain over the third bed had been partially pulled, but I could see that another, white-haired woman was sleeping quietly where Lorne's daughter and granddaughter had slept the night before. She was hooked up to oxygen and the machines beeped quietly at her side.

I sighed heavily and looked away.

"It's okay, you guys," I said to them. I squeezed my mom's hand. The last thing I wanted was to make them feel guilty about not having money. They'd almost had to re-mortgage their house because of me. If it hadn't been for Angelika throwing a last-minute fundraiser they might have lost everything. If anyone should feel guilty it was *me* for having an expensive, unconventional illness that dragged on endlessly.

"I'm glad I met Lorne and Gretta. I just ... I just really liked her. She was sort of special."

"I know, honey, she seemed like a really nice person. They both did. And their family, too."

I nodded, privately adding that if I hadn't been staying in here, I wouldn't have known about Ripple either, and about horses in general. It had opened up a whole new world for me, if only for a short time.

"Hey, do you think ... do you think we could try moving my bed to the day room for a few hours? I wouldn't mind a change of scenery."

My parents looked at each other with wide eyes, doing that near-telepathy thing they did over my head. As if I didn't know what they were thinking.

"Sure," my dad said slowly, "if you're feeling up to it. Are you sure?"

"Yeah, I am. I've been feeling pretty good for the last few days."

"We noticed," my mom said, hope and fear warring in her eyes. "Okay, let's see if we can find a nurse."

Because not many of the patients at Shady Grove could walk, the beds were mobile enough to be moved from room to room or pushed to the dayroom or out into the garden on nice days. They'd even made the paths in the garden extra-wide enough to accommodate them, which I thought was a nice touch.

As soon as the nurses weren't busy, they helped to roll my bed out into the hall and down to the windowed dayroom that looked over the garden. It was a nice area with a bunch of comfortable couches for guests, a tea-station and a small library. They parked my bed by the big window in front of the bird feeder.

"Can you raise it up, please?" I asked so that my bed was more like an armchair. I was sick of lying flat for so long.

"You look flushed," my dad said anxiously, "are you sure you feel well enough to be up?"

"Yes, I'm sure." I smiled as a fat black and tan bird landed on the feeder. His weight rocked the whole thing from side to side but he clung firmly to the edge, stuffing seeds into his beak as fast as he could.

"We need to have the doctor see you tomorrow. Something's changed in your condition. We don't know what to think. We nearly lost you and now ..."

"You have to stop fussing, Mom," I said, "I'm fine at the moment." I actually felt really good, but I knew things could change at any second. Gretta had seemed great last night when I'd talked to her too, and now where was she?

I suddenly remembered something Lorne had told me earlier. I had dismissed it at the time but now I wondered.

"Actually, I might have a favour to ask you guys."

"What? Ask anything," my mom said anxiously.

"Lorne mentioned to me that there is this horse show happening nearby in a few weeks' time. If Dr. Harrison says it's okay, do you think we could try and go out for a few hours to see it?"

There was a long silence while they both stared at me.

"Wow, honey, I don't know. I don't think—I mean, how would we get you there? I'm not sure that—" She broke off helplessly and looked at my dad.

"The thing is," my dad said, clearing his throat, "is that we're not quite sure what we're dealing with here, Bree. You were, well, very sick just a short time ago and we wouldn't want to have you do too much too soon."

"It's not far," I said quickly. "And maybe if I could sit up in a wheelchair it would be okay."

I had to admit that the whole thing must seem pretty strange from their point of view. A couple of weeks ago I was literally on death's doorstep, and now here I was eating popsicles and talking about horse shows.

"You really should just be concentrating on resting and getting better," my mom said, reaching over to place her palm against my forehead, that time-tested mom trick of seeing if I had a fever.

"I know, but I'm sick of resting. What if Dr. Harrison said it was okay? Would you take me then?"

They looked at each other again in bewilderment and I sighed inwardly, struggling for patience.

I could understand their confusion. I had never been what you'd call an outdoorsy girl and I'd never pushed hard to have a pet like Angelika had. She'd begged to have a dog or cat of her own but my mom had worried about allergies, shedding hair and the cost of vet care so my sister had had to make do with fish and a lonely hermit crab.

"It's okay, guys," I said finally, "If it's too much trouble—"

"No, honey, it's no trouble at all," Mom interrupted quickly, "of course, we can do whatever you like. It just took us by surprise after all. We didn't expect that you'd be able—"

They looked at each other and my dad patted first her arm and then mine. "If Doctor Harrison says it's okay with him then it's okay with us. Don't get your hopes up though, okay?"

"Right," I say, "of course not." But secretly, my hopes were already up. Something inside of me had changed in the last few weeks. It felt like I'd been a dormant tree after a long, cold winter that had suddenly woken up and all that life-giving sap was flowing through me again.

I stayed out there watching the birds in the garden until dusk fell and it was time to go back to my room.

It seemed so much emptier and lonelier without Lorne or Gretta. The woman in the end bed didn't look like she'd wake up any time soon.

"Breanna, Lorne left a present for you," the dark-haired night-nurse Janet said, after she'd helped to push my bed back into place. "He told me to give it to you as soon as I got on shift tonight."

"Oh, wow, he didn't have to do that."

"He said Gretta wanted you to have it."

"That was nice of him," my dad said, looking down at the small square package in my lap.

I peeled back the paper with trembling fingers, already guessing what I'd find.

"It's Gretta and Ripple," I said, tears stinging my eyes as I looked down at the faded photo in the beautiful wooden frame.

"What a lovely photo." My mom reached out and brushed a finger across the top of the frame. "Was Gretta the one who started all this sudden interest in horses?"

"Yes, well, sort of. Actually I had a dream about a horse before I'd even met Gretta properly, but she and Lorne loaned me the magazines and told me all about their thoroughbreds."

"We'll talk to Dr. Harrison," my dad said after a long silence. "If there's any way to get you to this horse show without compromising your health then we'll do it."

"Thanks, Dad," I said, "that means a lot."

That night, as soon as the many residents of Shady Grove had mostly fallen asleep, I began to put my burgeoning plan into action.

The memory of my last conversation with Gretta, when I'd stumbled my way to her bedside, still sat with me strongly. Everything had just seemed so magical and otherworldly the night before, like I could have done anything, so walking after having been bedridden for months hadn't seemed so impossible.

If I could walk last night then surely I could do it again. I had to know that it wasn't just a one-time thing.

Right, you can do this, I told myself, pulling my body upright with a surge of effort.

I thought that maybe it felt a little easier than it had the day before; maybe I was just a tiny bit stronger.

I stared down at my painfully thin legs, wondering how such thin toothpicks would ever hold me upright. How on earth had I lost so much muscle over such a short time? I had almost wasted away into nothing.

You did it last night, I reminded myself firmly, *just make it happen*.

The floor was cold against my bare toes but I relished the feeling because it meant that I was standing on my own without my parents or nurses hovering near me.

I stood until my legs began to shake and then sat down to recover and catch my breath. And as soon as I was able, I stood again.

For some reason, I remembered one of the tai-chi movements a long-ago nurse had taught me. What had her name been? Eileen? Ellen. The memory of her lessons had stayed with me even if I couldn't remember her name.

"It's called Parting the Wild Horse's Mane," she'd told me, demonstrating how her fingers flowed downward through the tendrils of an imaginary mane.

The name hadn't meant much to me at the time but now I suddenly felt like I understood. Balancing carefully, I let my fingers glide through the air, curving in soft arcs, remembering how the individual strands of my dream horse's mane had risen off his neck in the slight wind.

A feeling of contentment washed over me.

I stood there as long as I could, until my legs wobbled with exhaustion, and then I slid back under the covers and slept, dreaming about horses, Gretta, and wide, endless fields of rolling green.

Chapter Ten

"I'll wheel you down to the dayroom so you can get a change of scenery if you like," Racheal said the next morning. "You shouldn't be sitting in here on your own all day."

I wasn't exactly alone, but the nameless woman in the third bed wasn't going to wake up and she didn't have any visitors to break up the monotony. The big room felt empty and lonely without Gretta and Lorne so I was glad to let her cap my IV line so I didn't have to stay attached to that pole, and push me out into the hall. The wheels slid smoothly across the white, tiled floor and I tilted my head to the side, glancing in the open doorways all the way down to the dayroom. Most people were still sleeping even though it was after ten o'clock and only the light chatter from the nurse's station broke up the quiet.

Racheal parked my bed over by the window with a view of the bird feeder. "I'll be back to check on you or you can wave someone down if you need anything. Can't have you getting bored."

"Thanks, I'm fine," I said, waving a hand to the tablet and magazines I'd piled on my bed. "Although I am a little hungry."

She'd already half-turned away but now she swivelled back and looked at me closely. "Hungry, really? I can bring you a popsicle for now and I'll make sure to get Dr. Harrison to take a quick look at you before we decide on more food."

"Sure, fine."

The rest of the morning was pretty peaceful. I ate the juice-popsicles and applesauce Racheal brought me. I alternated between reading and watching the birds fight over the feeder outside. I napped, thought about Lorne and Gretta, and all the while I felt this new strange restlessness flowing inside me. Like a horse at the starting gate, staring straight down that endless dirt track, every muscle coiled and ready to explode. Only my muscles were about one million times weaker than a racehorse's.

I was in the middle of watching a video when Dr. Harrison came to check my vital signs. "We need to run more bloodwork," he said to Racheal, not to me, "and a repeat X-ray of those lungs. How has she been feeling overall?"

"You can ask her," Racheal said, rolling her eyes a little and waving a hand in my direction, "she's right there."

"Oh, er, right. You've been feeling brighter, I presume?" the doctor said, glancing at me quickly without making eye contact.

"I think I am," I said slowly. "I don't know what it means but I'm hungry, and restless. I don't want to stay in bed anymore."

"Huh," the doctor said thoughtfully. "Well, you don't have to. You can get up and do whatever you're able to do as long as you keep in mind your body's limitations. You can eat with the feeding tube in but you'll have to take it slow. If you can hold that down for a few days we'll see about adding in more food. Let me know how it goes."

He smiled at me briefly and then swept out of the room without a backward glance.

"I'm just going to borrow a bit more blood from you," Racheal said, smiling at the lame joke she must have told hundreds of times by now.

I looked away when the needle poked into my skin and

concentrated on the wind blowing through the trees outside. The bird feeder swayed back and forth, dropping bits of seed to the pathway below. I wondered if maybe I could go out there. I hadn't been outside in what felt like forever.

"There, all done," she said, plopping a cotton ball on my arm and sticking a Band-Aid over it to cover the little hole the needle had made. "You rest here and I'll see what I can rustle up for you in the kitchen."

I didn't feel like resting, though. The doctor's words had made me more determined to get up than ever. I looked around the room and set my sights on a guest couch on the wall opposite me. It would still have a view of the garden and it looked comfortable enough.

I looked around furtively to make sure none of the nurses were in sight and then I sat up and swung my legs over the side of the bed. I had slippers on this time and they buffered me a little from the cold floor.

Just like last night, I told myself, rising firmly upward. I kept one hand on the wall for support and the other on my tablet as I made my way slowly toward the couch on shaky legs. It took me a long time but I didn't waver or fall. I sank gratefully onto the couch and leaned my head against the window, panting to catch my breath, weak but oh, so proud of myself.

"Oh, boy," Racheal said when she found me sitting there. "Here, let me get you a blanket. She wrapped one blanket around my shoulders and another one over my lap and set my applesauce bowl on the table beside me.

"You are stronger," Racheal said thoughtfully, once I was settled. "I heard your dad talking about you wanting to go out for a few hours in a couple of weeks."

"To a horse show," I told her, "if I feel well enough."

"Be patient with yourself and your body. We don't want to rush things. I do hope you end up going. Horses are great. I used to ride a lot as a kid."

"You did?" I said, suddenly interested.

"I did. I barrel raced and did games and things."

I didn't know what that meant but it sounded fun.

"Hey, Racheal, do you know what an October horse is?"

"No, never heard of that. There are some weird breeds out there, though. Why?"

"Oh, just something Gretta said before ... well, you know."

"Hmm, that sounds like something to ask the internet. I have a bunch more patients to visit right now but I'll come back to check on you later."

As soon as she was gone, I pulled out my tablet.

October Horses, I typed in but what came up wasn't what I'd expected.

In Roman times, the October Horse, or Equus October, was sacrificed to the ancient God, Mars, during a horse-racing festival held on October 15th.

"Oh, gross," I said out loud. This couldn't be what Gretta had meant. She'd loved horses, she could never be involved with something like this.

The right-hand horse in a two-horse chariot was considered the strongest animal and it was this horse, from the winning chariot, who was chosen to be sacrificed since he was the best offering to the God. He would be stabbed with a spear and then his head would be—

Nope, I flicked back to the search engine as fast as I could, I did not need to read about that.

But nothing else came up when I searched, just a few books about Roman times and some references to Julius Caesar.

Huh, I thought, maybe if I ever saw Lorne again I could ask him.

Outside the sun was out and the little garden was full of life. Birds flew everywhere, pecking busily at the ground and flitting from tree to tree.

They have a purpose, I thought, *they are full of living every moment of the day.*

"I'm going outside," I said to nobody in particular. I set my blanket aside and fixed my slippers more firmly on my feet. Leaning on the wall for support, I slowly made my way to the garden door. For a long time, I just stood on the cement pathway, marvelling at all the things happening in such a small space. The wind blew, ruffling my hair and setting all the branches over my head to moving back and forth like waves. If I closed my eyes, it sounded just like the ocean; something I hadn't seen with my own eyes in as long as I could remember.

The birds weren't afraid of me, they were used to the residents coming out here and knew nobody would dream of chasing them or hurting them. So they boldly flew to the path at my trembling feet, staring up at me with their little heads tilted to one side, hoping I had breadcrumbs for them.

"Sorry, birds, I'll bring you something next time."

The path was wide and smooth, made for unsteady feet, wheelchairs or even beds when the nurses had time to push the patients outside.

It led straight through the middle of the fenced garden to a picnic table under a large old maple tree, and I sat down, looking around with interest. I hadn't been outside since I'd been admitted here and I sat very still, relishing the sounds and smells of summer. The air was warm, bees buzzed everywhere, and the tree branches shook with birds. A little patch of earth nearby had been recently dug up and the freshly turned soil smelled rich and fragrant. I inhaled deeply, that good air filling my lungs and then whooshing out again.

I do feel better, I thought, hardly daring to believe it. I felt a thrill of excitement.

If I truly am in remission and I'm able to get strong enough then I'm going to see if I can ride. Even just one time. That's all I want. I closed my eyes and listened to the world around me, all the birds and insects and trees full of life. *Please God, or Universe or whatever, if you're out there, just let me ride one time.*

I had never prayed before, I'd never wanted anything bad enough to make bargains with the universe or a higher power, not even to live on this planet a little longer. But that day I did, fervently, over and over, *please let me ride a horse*.

There wasn't a lightning bolt from the sky or an angel descending or anything but, as I made my way back to my bed, I was filled with the most calm, peaceful feeling. It wasn't an answer or a promise, but I was struck by a sudden certainty.

I will ride a horse, I told myself silently, *I know it*.

Chapter Eleven

The blood test results came back surprisingly positive, and the next day I was hustled over to the hospital for X-rays, a CT scan and finally, an MRI.

"It's early days," Dr. Harrison said gruffly. "We need to monitor you closely for changes. It's too soon to make any long-term decisions."

Yeah, yeah. I'd heard all that before. It was doctor-speak for *we don't know what to do with you.*

"I don't understand, though," my mom broke in, always ready to search out answers like a bloodhound. "Why is she feeling better all of a sudden? Is it a ... a remission of sorts? Was it one of the drug trials? Why is this happening?" Her cheeks were flushed and her dark hair had partly come free of its braid, the strands straggling across her forehead.

"As I said, it's too early to talk about remission or causes," Dr. Harrison said, looking irritated. I knew he wasn't really mad at us; he was the type of person who liked to have practical, scientific answers to things so unexplained remissions would feel like a personal affront. "We just have to take things day by day."

"But …" I could tell my mom wasn't going to let this go without an intervention.

"There's a horse show next week," I interrupted quickly, "and I'd like to go watch it for a little while. I could sit in a wheelchair if you'd let us borrow one and I'd make sure not to overdo it."

"Horse show?" Dr. Harrison looked at me as if he'd never heard of such a thing.

"Yes, a dressage show, it's not far from here. I just want to watch a bit of it."

"Oh, I see. Well, as long as nothing about your condition changes then I don't see why not. If you're able to sit comfortably in the car and the wheelchair for an hour or so then a brief outing might be allowed if you don't push yourself too hard."

"That's good news," my dad squeezed my shoulder encouragingly.

"Thank you," I told the doctor, "I want to go."

Dr. Harrison's nostrils fluttered. "As I said, don't get your expectations set too high. It's too early to make predictions and things could change in an instant. It's best if you don't plan too far ahead."

He shot a quick look at my mother, turned on his heel, and swept out of the room before any of us could ask any more questions.

"That man," my mother said under her breath. "Still, it's good news. Honey, we should be celebrating. It's too bad Angelika's concert is this weekend. I hate to go away and leave you. We can cancel the trip, or one of us could stay home. Your sister will understand."

Angelika would most definitely *not* understand if our parents missed her big concert on the mainland, especially when she'd gotten them VIP tickets and backstage passes. They'd had to miss so much of her skyrocketing career already because of me.

"You should go. I'm fine and Angelika would be really disappointed if you didn't show up. Besides, it will give me a chance to practice."

"Practice what, Bree?" my dad asked.

"Well, like walking and sitting up and stuff. The horse show isn't very far away and I need to know if I can handle a day out."

They exchanged uneasy looks.

"I can't just lie here all day doing nothing. It's boring."

"Breanna, not too long ago you were being brought back from the brink of death," my mother said flatly. "You have to take it easy. I mean, this horse show thing is a fine goal to look forward to but not if you're going to push yourself too hard. You need to rest and I'm just worried that this is too soon—"

"I know. I get it. I feel the same way. But, the point is that I'm alive right now and I think I should enjoy that in whatever way I can."

My rough voice cracked a little, still unused to speaking so much.

"But *horses*," my mom said in bewilderment, "I just don't understand this sudden ..."

"You know what," my dad said, rising to his feet and drawing my mother up with him, "I think it's time we headed out, Cecilia, we have to catch the first ferry tomorrow morning. There will be plenty of time to talk about all this when we get back."

He leaned down and kissed the top of my head and then they were gone.

Perfect, I thought, *alone at last. Now I can begin to put my plan into action.* I had no intention of letting another single moment of my life be spent *resting*.

Chapter Twelve

✤✤✤

Despite everyone's dire predictions. I continued to improve day by day.

By the time the day of the horse show arrived. I was able to get out of bed and totter around the entire building if I took my time and held on to things. My body was still adapting to the new demands I put on it and I lost my breath if I rushed, and lost my balance if I forgot to concentrate. But still, it was miles different from where I'd been a few weeks ago.

I could also sit on the couch or in a wheelchair for hours at a time, although it wasn't that comfortable, and I had graduated to eating three bland, pureed meals a day while the gastric tube still gave me the rest of my nutrients.

Dr. Harrison had made vague mumbling comments about maybe taking out my feeding tube if this went on much longer. But the worry was that this remission thing was only temporary and that they'd have to do surgery all over again to put it back in if I took a sudden relapse.

I refused to think about any of that. My only goal was to take things one day, one step, one moment at a time.

My first wish was coming true. I was going to a horse show.

I woke up before the sun did, full of anticipation.

Somewhere out there, eager riders and grooms, blurry with sleep, would be stumbling to their respective barns to feed an early breakfast. I had a rough idea, from reading a million online horse articles a day and watching countless videos, what horse show prep would be like. They'd groom the horses until they shone and then braid and put on shipping boots and monogrammed coolers. The trailers would already have been loaded the night before, but there would be a hurried last-minute check to make sure all the right gear had been carefully packed away.

Some people would be excited, some bored, and some would be wracked with nerves, pale-faced and trying to quell their churning stomachs.

I wouldn't be nervous, I thought, *I would just be grateful to have a horse to show at all*. Of course. that was easy to say from the relative safety of my warm bed. I'd watched my sister battle nerves before going on stage so I had an idea of what it felt like.

It seemed like forever before my parents arrived. My IV line had been detached a week ago with only the greenish bruise on my hand to show where the needle had been buried.

My hardest chore that morning had been figuring out what to wear. Somehow white hospital pajamas and a housecoat wasn't the look I was going for. But the few clothes stored in my pint-sized closet hung on me like a hollow scarecrow, now about four sizes too big for my skeletal frame. Finally, I settled on black leggings and a long, flowing shirt that went down past my hips. At least the emerald green of the shirt brought out the colour in my eyes.

My mom had brought me an ornate hand-held mirror back from the mainland when they returned from watching Angelika's concert. She'd found a Lebanese specialty shop downtown where they sold food imports and artwork and things. The mirror had been carved from fragrant cedar and had an intricate design of shells embedded on the back of it.

"I saw it and thought of you right away. You have no idea how nice it is to be able to buy things for you again."

I'd hugged her hard, both for the thought and the expense.

Now, I dug around the bedside drawer to find my scanty supply of make-up. My kit was over a year old so the mascara was a little lumpy and I had to chisel at the eyeshadow to make it powdery again. Still, the effect was all right once I was done, at least my face looked less skeletal.

Now to find the right head-covering. We hadn't bothered trying to get a wig for me since my illness had progressed so rapidly so I was stuck with an assortment of caps or bandannas to cover my baldness. Losing my hair had mortified me at first, but I'd long ago stopped caring too much.

This one will do, I thought, carefully tying on a dark green bandanna over my head. It matched my shirt and gave me an edgy sort of look.

The only thing left to cover up was the oversized white bandage on my neck where the incision from my breathing tube was still healing.

I found a soft, purple silk scarf among my things and draped it carefully around my neck, covering the bandage completely.

"Wow, honey, you look great," my mom said in astonishment.

Both my parents stood in the doorway staring at me with stunned expressions; as if they were seeing a ghost. My mom reached out and squeezed my dad's hand, which was the first time I'd seen them touch each other in a while.

"Um, thanks," I said, feeling a little awkward. "Are we ready to go?"

My parents hovered over me, each of them gripping onto a handle of the wheelchair as they rolled me down the path to the car. I could have easily walked the distance but they insisted that I rest whenever I could.

It felt nice to sit in a car again after so many months. Watching the scenery roll past outside the window was as exciting as watching a blockbuster movie. Houses, trees, people! All the activity on the sleepy street was almost overwhelming for someone who hadn't been outside in months.

The horse show was held at a large public park set right in the middle of the city next to the recreation center.

A few people were milling around the parking lot. And for some reason, I was hit with a sudden bout of shyness. These people were all bustling around their normal lives and here was me, this bald imposter in a bandanna, pretending to have a purpose here, too.

"I could just do this without the wheelchair," I said, my cheeks burning. Maybe if I *walked* in I would be less obvious.

"Um, sorry, that's not an option, kiddo. Doctor's orders." My dad looked up as he pulled the folding wheelchair out of the trunk and set it on the ground.

I groaned inwardly when I saw it had the words *Shady Grove Palliative Care* written in bold letters on the back. Why hadn't I noticed that before?

"I knew this would be too much for her," my mom said, glancing around anxiously, "we should just go back."

"No, no. Never mind. I'm fine." I said, hurriedly settling myself into the chair. My dad draped the blanket over my lap and I fiddled with my scarf to make sure it was covering the dressing on my neck perfectly.

Finally, we were on our way. Dad paid for our tickets, which was something I hadn't thought of ahead of time. They didn't have a lot of extra money, which is why I didn't usually ask them for things.

"It's okay," Mom said, catching my look, "it's our treat today. Next time it's on you."

She shot me a smile and squeezed my shoulder as we went inside.

I'm here, I thought, my shyness dissolving in excited disbelief, *I'm actually here. Surrounded by horses.*

The smells hit me first. That rich pungent odour of animals in the sun, the not completely unpleasant smell of manure, the greasy, sugary food truck smells, the trampled grass, the dirt footing in the ring. All of it hit me at once. I just sat there completely silently, taking it all in.

There's a horse, I thought in delight as I caught sight of a massive grey rump in the distance. My dad pushed me through the gate and then I realized we were surrounded by horses on all sides.

It was nearly eleven o'clock by then and the show had been underway for hours. There were sleek, braided horses *everywhere* and most of them were *huge*. They swaggered past us without a glance, shoulders swaying, hooves clopping, tails swinging, completely confident in their utter *horseness*.

Look at those feet, I thought as a giant black animal strode right past me, hooves as big as dinner plates. The ground shook as his feet clacked on the asphalt. He swung his big head back and forth to the time of his walk, like a colossal elephant in the jungle, agreeably following the tall man holding his reins.

Before coming, I'd had some idea that I'd only see the horses from a distance when they were performing in the ring. It turned out that at this show there wasn't a divide between the barn area and the seating area so we literally were in the thick of things.

Riders, horses, food trucks, dogs, and running children mixed in with the general crowd so it became one fantastic spectacle. The smell of fried food, cotton candy, and horse mingled together into a cloud of deliciousness. Forget watching the actual horses in the ring, I could have just sat there by the hotdog concession and people-watched ... er ... horse-watched, all day.

"Do you want to get some food before finding a seat?" Dad asked my mom, eyeing up the hotdog stand.

When I'd lived at home the meals had been pretty healthy. My parents didn't go in for junk food and we couldn't afford to eat out very often, but the smells coming off that food cart were tempting and I could see my mom wavering.

"Yes please," I said, even though he hadn't meant me, "I'll have a cheese dog with relish and ketchup."

"Uh, no ..." Mom said, "you can't eat food like that."

"Okay, let's split some fries then. They're soft and I'll only eat a few."

"Honey, I don't think ..."

"Hot dogs and fries it is," my dad said quickly, pulling out his wallet. "This is a celebration, after all."

Mom sighed but surprisingly gave in.

There were two rings going at the same time. We found a good place to watch the bigger ring, and I sat entranced as a rider on a tall black horse trotted into the arena. The horse stopped in its tracks as it neared the judge's booth and halted, standing immobile while the rider saluted. Then they were back up into a trot again, powering around the ring.

I watched breathlessly, happily nibbling at my fries, chewing each one to mush before I carefully swallowed it. Never had salt and grease tasted so good.

I'd read quite a few articles about dressage in preparation for this day so I knew a little bit about the movements. Although I had no idea what made a high-scoring ride verses a low-scoring ride; all the horse and rider combinations who took turns parading in front of the judge looked great to me.

My parents' expressions sort of glazed over with boredom about fifteen minutes in and my dad even snuck into his leather satchel and discretely pulled out some papers to grade.

I could have sat there happily for a million years, though. I varied between admiring the horses, wondering which ones were Thoroughbreds like Ripple, admiring the riders, and discretely watching all the other people in the audience.

In all my life I didn't think I'd done anything half as interesting.

Suddenly, an old man across the arena caught my eye. He was wearing a cap on his head and he stood hunched near the in-gate, his arms crossed over his chest like he was protecting himself from a cold wind. He wasn't watching the horses, just staring vacantly off into space. His gaze swivelled suddenly in my direction as if he'd felt me watching.

"Hey, is that Lorne?" I asked but when I went to point him out he was already gone.

My parents perked up a little when the musical free-styles came on.

"Oh, your sister would like this part," Mom said and I had to agree. The horse's legs moved in time with the music, noses and ears bobbing so it looked like they were dancing. I wondered if they actually enjoyed the music or if they were just trained to do that. Either way, it was beautiful.

"All right, honey, we'd better head back," Mom said, getting up from the hard wooden bleacher and stretching, "we told the nurses we'd only be gone an hour or so."

"I'm not tired," I said quickly, then looked at their bored faces and sighed. They'd done what they'd promised and brought me here so I shouldn't complain. Next time though, I'd come with a horse-person and we'd stay from dawn to dusk. "Okay, you're right, we should go. But can we check out the stables first? Just quickly."

"Of course. I think there's another exit at the far end where the barns are. We can go out that way instead."

The ground was rougher in this section of the fairgrounds, and the wheelchair bumped over the gravelled patches and cracked asphalt, jiggling my spine and clacking my teeth together. Dad muttered something under his breath about inaccessible terrain and the lack of maintained sidewalks in a public sporting facility.

"Here, I'll leave you ladies here while I bring the car around to the gate." He was red-faced and a sheen of sweat coated his forehead. "I'll only be a few minutes."

"Sure, Dad, we're fine here."

We couldn't get right down to the stalls from here, you had to cross a swath of uneven grassy lawn for that, but there were horses walking everywhere up and down the road that led to the warm-up ring and the competition arenas. Some were fully tacked up and some swaggered around wearing their cooling-out sheets with farm names monogrammed on the sides.

I couldn't believe how beautiful they all were. Their colours in real life were much more vibrant than they had been in the magazines and online. Greys, Chestnuts, Bays, and Blacks. Even a few that were spotted black and white like milk cows. All polished and sprayed so that their short coats gleamed under the sun.

I just wanted to reach out and touch their glossy coats and see what they were like up close.

I wonder if I could ask to pet one, I thought, but I was too shy even though everyone seemed friendly. A few people smiled as they passed but I couldn't seem to work up the courage to call out to anyone to stop.

"Oh, oh dear, excuse me." My mom's voice rose about eight octaves, a mixture of fear and determination that had become so familiar over our last year in the hospital. "Your horse is ..."

She broke off in a little shriek and I swivelled around to see that she had been removed from her position behind me and replaced by a huge, chestnut face.

"Oh," I said, half-gasping in delight. I fumbled with the chair, trying desperately to turn so I could see him better. But before I could maneuver around he just stuck his nose over my shoulder and put his gigantic head in my lap, lipping at the empty fry-carton I'd forgotten to throw away.

I squeaked in alarm and then froze, too afraid to move lest I scare him and he attacked or something. It was one thing seeing horses from a few feet away but having one land in my lap was something else. The sheer size of him and, well, the *presence* of him, was overwhelming. His eye was right next to mine, huge and

65

searching. The smell of horse filled my nostrils and suddenly I knew for certain that he wasn't going to hurt me. I reached up and tentatively touched the side of his nose, marvelling at how warm and silky his fur was.

He snorted softly, lipping at my blanket.

"Monty, you are SO bad."

He jerked backward, his jaw bone roughly smacking mine in the process, and then he reappeared in front of me, this time with a small, tough-looking teenager holding his lead rope with both hands.

"I'm so sorry," she said, her cheeks flushed with embarrassment. "I just took my eyes off him for *two* seconds so I could check my phone. *Two seconds*. He was grazing peacefully and as soon as I was distracted he pulled the lead out of my hand and took off. He is such a brat. Are you okay? He didn't hurt you, did he?"

"No," I said, ignoring the aching throb in my cheek where his bony jaw had hit me. "He's so beautiful. Is he a Thoroughbred?"

"Umm, I think there's a little on his mom's side. He's registered as a Canadian Sport Horse. Too bad there's no registry just for bad, too-smart-for-their-own-good horses."

She looked up at him affectionately and ran a hand down his neck. "Truthfully, he's a wonderful horse, and he's fun to ride. Do you do dressage?"

My mom made a little irritated sound behind me. She'd recovered from nearly being bowled over by Monty and was now clutching the handles of my wheelchair for dear life. She was in full protective mom-mode now.

The girl widened her eyes and flushed even more. "Sorry, was that a stupid question? I talk without thinking all the time."

"No," I say quickly, "it wasn't stupid at all. I haven't ridden at all yet. But I'd like to. Could I pet him again?"

"Sure, pat his shoulder here. I'm Chloe, by the way."

"I'm Bree. He's so soft. And he smells so good; like flowers."

"Well, he should smell good. I spent all morning bathing and grooming him, and trying to get the manure stains off his legs. He loves to roll in any dirt he finds, just like a piglet."

I ran my hand over his silky shoulder readjusting my ideas about what horses were like. I had thought they'd be like the one in my dream; all-knowing and magical, sort of like unicorns. It turned out that they could be bossy, like getting dirty, and have a sense of humour.

"There's your father," my mom said, her voice full of relief, "we'd better go."

"It was nice to meet you," Chloe said, pulling Monty away, "you should look up our barn if you have a chance. Green Oaks. My coach teaches a few riders from the Para-Equestrian team and we have some great horses. I'd better go get this guy ready, though. He's already ridden his tests but we're doing the *Prix Caprilli* next."

"Goodbye, and thanks," I called as she sauntered away with Monty in tow.

How amazing would it be to just be part of this world? To casually be walking my very own horse around these fantastic show-grounds.

"Oh, my goodness, that was terrifying. Did he hurt you?" Mom leaned down in front of me, reaching out to straighten my bandanna which had slipped over one ear.

"Mom, I'm fine. Stop fussing. Everything's fine."

"You need to get back right away and rest. I knew coming here wasn't a good idea."

It was best to ignore her. I let them shuffle me into the waiting car and watched the scenery pass by while she loudly repeated the whole story about meeting the girl and Monty to my dad.

"You should have seen how big this animal was up close. He could have *killed* us," she said again. "He practically assaulted Bree."

I caught Dad's worried glance in the rearview mirror and smiled dreamily. The blanket around my shoulders still smelled like horses.

"Well, she looks okay to me," he said reassuringly. "And she did get her wish to meet a horse up close and personal."

My wish. Two wishes actually. To go to a horse show and to pet a horse in real life. But those had been this morning's pale, uninspired wishes. Now I wanted so much more. I wanted to ride. I wanted to show. I wanted to not be sick anymore. For the first time, I'd found something I wanted to live for.

Chapter Thirteen

Exactly one week later, Dr. Harrison showed up to tell me that they were kicking me out.

"I have no explanation," he said quickly before my mother could ask any questions. "But I think we can safely say that Breanna is in the early stages of what may be a remission. Either way, she isn't palliative at the moment. As long as things continue to trend this way, I think she can transition back to life at home."

There was a long, shocked silence.

"But what if it's just a temporary remission?" I asked.

"We can't know that for sure. But what I do know is that you don't need to be taking up space in one of the beds here. That's the bottom line."

And that was it.

Before I knew it, I was shuttled back to the hospital to have my feeding tube removed. While I was recovering from that there were more diagnostics and I was visited by multiple specialists.

"They just don't understand what caused your remission," my dad said soothingly when I complained about being stuck with needles so much. "If it was one of the drug trials that worked for you then knowing the answer could help so many other people."

It was hard to complain after that.

While I recovered I had to go to physiotherapy twice a day. I still felt weak and I tired easily doing the most basic things. But, a week later, when I left the hospital, I could walk on my own without holding on to anything, I could eat normal food as long as I took my time and didn't inhale it, and I could start, cautiously, making some plans for the future.

Walking in the front door of my childhood home, a place I hadn't seen in over six months, was surreal.

I stood there, trembling in the entryway, thinking that this must be a dream. I had honestly never thought I'd be home again.

My parents were having a hard time with it, too. My mother chattered nervously, non-stop, fluttering around me like a butterfly as I moved cautiously about the house, reaching out to touch me every few seconds as if I'd disappear if she took her eyes off me.

"Let's give her some space," my dad said, "she probably wants to have a rest and get settled."

I slowly climbed the stairs to my room, stopping to catch my breath when I reached the landing. Stairs weren't something I'd encountered yet and the short climb made me wheeze.

The second floor of our small house was made up of just three bedrooms and a bathroom. The door to Angelika's old room stood open and I went to her doorway and stood outside, looking in.

There was very little left of my sister in there. She'd torn down all her old posters and packed all her stuff when she'd furiously left home to live with my ex-boyfriend, Duncan, in his dorm room. That was the same day my dad had caught her sleeping with Duncan in my parents' bed while I was in the hospital and she'd been full of outraged anger.

Her relationship with Duncan hadn't lasted more than a month before she'd moved on to somewhere, or someone, else, leaving a trail of heartbroken people in her wake as always.

I sighed and pushed open the door to my own room, which had not changed a bit since I was a child. There was my old narrow bed with the same sheets I'd had since I was fourteen. The shelves were stacked with books and puzzles and an old stuffed, threadbare bear named Rolo. The mirror had photos stuck in the corners and a medal I'd won for winning a short-story contest.

This room felt like it belonged to a completely different person, someone I'd known a long time ago but lost touch with. It didn't feel like me at all.

I lay down on the bed, wincing as the springs squeaked in protest.

I was supposed to have moved out of here for good last year, I thought with a sigh.

It was funny how such carefully laid plans could just disappear in an instant.

Chapter Fourteen

I'd come home on a Thursday and my parents had both taken a few days off work so they could get me settled. This meant that they spent all their time anxiously hovering over me, making sure I didn't keel over in front of them or anything.

By the time Monday rolled around I was more than ready for them both to go back to work.

"Your father will check on you at lunchtime," my mother said, her eyes wide with anxiety, "and you make sure to keep that cell phone with you at all times. I will text you every hour and I expect an answer back."

"Okay, okay, Mom," I said, "don't worry so much."

"I have to, it's my job. Please remember to chew your food carefully and make sure—"

"Right, I've got this." I let them hug me one last time and then shut the door firmly behind them, turning the lock with a feeling of relief. Finally, alone at last.

Ironically, I was hit by loneliness about twenty minutes after they left. It was crazy. I should have been thrilled to finally have some space but the truth was that I felt anxious and lost. I had a smoothie for breakfast and then padded from room to room, not able to settle. I turned on the television and then turned it off again. I tried to read but just couldn't relax enough to get lost in a book.

I made a stab at reorganizing my room and had a nap. But all the while in the back of my head was that restless feeling that I was wasting time here, that life was passing me by with every tick of the clock and that I should be doing *something* more important.

Just before lunch, my phone pinged.

Hey, honey, are you doing okay? I'm stuck in an emergency meeting here but I can escape home if you need me. Just say the word.

I stared down at the phone and sighed.

No, it's okay, Dad. I'm totally fine. See you tonight.

The minute I tossed my phone back on the couch there was a loud knock at the door that nearly made me jump out of my skin.

I padded down the hall and threw open the front door. I probably should have been more cautious just in case it was a serial killer or something but honestly, at that point, I would have welcomed any distraction.

The elderly man on our front porch smiled at me tentatively and pulled his cap down more firmly on his head.

"Hello, Breanna."

"Lorne," I said in disbelief, "what are you doing here?"

"Well," he said, coughing to clear his throat. "It's a bit complicated. I probably shouldn't be bothering you when you're busy."

"You're not. I'm doing absolutely nothing. Please come in. We can have tea or cookies or anything you like."

I was so grateful to see him that I practically pulled him inside. He resisted for a moment and then let me drag him to the kitchen and plunk him in a chair by the kitchen table while I hurriedly put the kettle on.

"It's good to see you. How on earth did you find me? How are you doing?"

He looked a little overwhelmed at my barrage of questions.

"Er, I went to Shady Grove to see how you were. Gretta"—he

paused, his lower lip trembling—"she asked me to look out for you before she died and I felt bad that I hadn't done it. I was so sad afterwards ... it took me a long time to get up the courage to go back there."

"Gretta asked you to look out for me? But why?"

"She liked you. And for some reason, she had it in her head that you were going to get better and carry on a sort of pet project of hers."

"Oh," I said slowly. "Was that the October horses thing she talked about? I didn't understand what she meant. I couldn't find anything on the internet except about Romans and chariot racing and things."

"Oh," he laughed, "it was sort of an inside joke we had. The racing season here finishes at the end of September or early October, depending on the weather. That's when the track closes for business. Everyone either hunkers down for the winter or heads south to keep racing. And that's when the horses who won't be racing the next year can be had for cheap, or often free."

"You can get a horse for free?" I was suddenly all ears.

"If you're clever and willing to put in some time and effort." Lorne chuckled. "It's a gamble, you see. Horses stop racing for a few reasons. Maybe they're just too slow, or don't want to race, or maybe they can't handle the pressure of the track. Or maybe their bodies or their minds are breaking down. You don't get to ride them before you buy them. You just have to meet them and go on gut instinct and hope you don't get a lemon. You can get an excellent young horse that needs a little polishing up or you can be saddled with an unsellable terror who does his best to kill you."

"Oh." I didn't like the sound of that. I had never been one to take a gamble. I preferred life to be safe and predictable.

"We bought many racehorses over the years, but usually from trainers that we trusted and who had a good reputation. But once in a while Gretta just liked to take a risk and grab something unknown at the end of the season. She had a great eye for horses and good instincts. She rarely brought home something that she couldn't turn around eventually. She called them her October horses because that's when she usually got the leftover ones that nobody else wanted. She was an expert at finding diamonds in the rough."

"Why did she take a chance on them, though? Why take the risk?"

"Well," Lorne hesitated, "sometimes those free or cheap horses would otherwise end up in some pretty shady situations. Either people took them on and then couldn't handle or afford to feed them, or the animals were misunderstood and passed from home to home until they end up at an auction and sold for dog food. It's the downside to horse racing, unfortunately. We were lucky to know some great trainers who would work hard to place their retired horses in just the right homes. But then some were purely in it for the money and *they* had no qualms in dumping an animal as soon as it wasn't earning its keep."

"That's awful," I said. Horses were so rare and special to me. I'd no idea that not all of them ended up in loving homes.

"It's no different than any other horse sport. Horses get sold and moved around all the time. It's the name of the business. Sometimes they get a soft landing and end up in a forever home, and sometimes they fall on hard times."

I stared down at my tea, feeling a little depressed.

"But, that means there are lots of opportunities for us to do what we can to help these horses out. I think that's the mission Gretta wanted you to carry on with."

"Me?" I said in astonishment. "I don't know anything about—"

"Pshaw," he waved my objections away with a chopping motion of his hand. "You can learn as you go. You ride and you know the basics already. A good teacher should be able to whip you into shape in no time."

Know the basics? Anything I knew about horses had been from the internet. I hardly thought that qualified me for much. *Gretta must have told him that I was a rider.*

"Lorne," I said gently, "I think there's been a misunderstanding—"

"I know, I know, you like *Dressage*." He said the word like it was something distasteful. "That's not a crime, Breanna. I think it's about as exciting as a three-hour nap but at least it teaches you one end of a horse from the other."

"No, that's not what I—"

"And of course you're weak, and out of shape, and you're still healing. You'd have to be eased into it. I know, Gretta told me all that."

"She did?" I looked at him uncertainly.

"You'll think I'm a crazy old man." He rubbed a hand across his face, looking embarrassed. "But I swear sometimes it's like she's in the room with me, giving me guidance and direction. I can practically hear her voice. She told me that you'd be at that horse show if I went and there you were."

"Oh, that *was* you. I thought so."

"I was too depressed to say hello right then. But I saw you there with your family. By the time I'd come to my senses and went back to Shady Grove to find you, you'd already been discharged."

"They kicked me out," I said with a laugh, "apparently, I'm in recovery."

"Yes, well, I had to do a little hard snooping to find your address, but I'm glad to see that you have a little more meat on your bones and some pink in your cheeks."

"I am feeling better. I'm just bored."

I stopped, realizing that I hadn't felt lost or anxious the whole time he'd been there. Somehow, that strange, restless feeling that had gripped me earlier had disappeared.

"So, any idea what you'd like to do next?" He leaned forward expectantly, like it was a test.

"Well … I'm *supposed* to be resting."

"Uh-huh?"

"But what I'd really like to do is see another horse again. Maybe even ride one. When I'm strong enough, I mean."

"Well, what if I could arrange for you to meet another horse?"

"You could? Really?"

"Sure, he's getting a little long in the tooth, but I think you two would enjoy each other's company. We could go this week."

"Yes," I said quickly, "let's do it."

I looked up at the clock. It seemed like Lorne had just gotten there but we'd spent over an hour sitting at the table. My dad would be home fairly soon.

If I'm going to visit a horse, I want to spend quality time with it. Uninterrupted time, without my parents hovering over me.

"Tomorrow morning," I said added, "if that's okay with you. Ten o'clock?"

That way my parents would be long gone and I'd have the whole day to do what I wanted. It wasn't like I needed their permission to go anywhere, but I still didn't want to start an argument. My mom could be so stubborn when she got an idea into her head and I knew she wouldn't approve of me doing anything interesting so soon after being released from the hospital.

"That's fine," Lorne said, "my schedule is wide-open."

He ran out of things to say after that. As soon as he'd gulped down the rest of his tea, he pushed his chair back roughly and stood up. We said our goodbyes at the door and he promised me that he'd be back again the next morning.

As soon as he'd gone, I ran around cleaning up all traces of his visit. I didn't need my parents asking me questions yet. I put our cups in the half-full dishwasher and started its cycle and then I spent a few minutes cleaning the rest of the kitchen, wiping the counter and the table as if my parents were going to search them for fingerprints.

I wasn't sure why I wanted to keep my visit with Lorne a

secret from my family. I fully planned to tell them later, once I'd met the horse, and maybe had had a chance to ride. I just wanted tomorrow to be nobody's business but my own.

As soon as the kitchen was clean I went down to the basement to do a load of laundry. I didn't have that many clothes that fit me and I wanted to find something nice for my outing tomorrow. I paused halfway through the rec room, gazing in awe at dozens of tables my dad had set up for his models.

Amazing, I said to myself. It was hard to believe that my boring old dad had made all those intricate life-like scenes.

In the months I'd been away, his collection had grown to massive proportions. I set the laundry basket down and wandered from table to table, looking at the elaborate miniature worlds. Each table represented important times and places in history. Some of them, like the completed Battle of Kadesh to my right, were labelled with little metal plaques but for the rest of them, you had to guess what was happening.

I leaned down to study an intricate town set up at the base of some incredibly realistic looking mountains. It looked like maybe a western gold mine town. There were horses and pack mules everywhere. And a train was set in the middle, on the banks of a clear blue lake that I knew had been carefully made with a complicated mixture of wood-glue, paint and varnish. Little plastic people bustled everywhere, frozen in the middle of loading the train.

I wonder if I'll ever do something grand enough for some future model-maker to make a scene of it?

I doubted it; I'd settle for just doing something a *little* out of the ordinary like ride a horse.

Finally, I pulled away, reminding myself of all the things I still had to do.

I was humming with energy by the time my parents got home and, instead of lying on the couch like an invalid, I got up to help them make dinner.

"Well, you must be feeling good," Mom said, reaching out impulsively to feel my forehead.

"Yes." I batted her hand away impatiently and then cringed at the crestfallen look on her face.

"Sorry," I said quickly. After all she'd been through, I knew that she can't help hovering and worrying. But her constant anxiety made me feel claustrophobic.

She turned away and made herself busy chopping vegetables, the knife thwacking through the carrots with deadly force. Whack, whack, whack.

"So, what did you get up to today, Bree?" my dad asked. He'd made us an appetizer tray of soft cheeses, hummus, and unbaked pita. All things that were safer for me to eat.

"Nothing much," I said carefully, "just a few chores and watched television."

"You should start writing again. You were always good at that. A boy in one of my classes ended up in a wheelchair after a skiing accident. He has a very popular blog and people from all over the world follow him."

I perked up with interest. I'd used to love writing short stories and journals. I'd even won two hundred dollars in a local short-story contest. I hadn't felt like doing anything but lie there when I was in the hospital but maybe now I could try writing again. I could write about my dream and about Gretta.

"She doesn't need you pushing her to *do* things right now," my mom snapped, "she just needs to rest."

We both stared at her in surprise. Mom had always been feisty but it seemed to me that she'd been extra waspish lately, especially with my dad.

"Well, I'll be down in the basement if you ladies need me," he said, pretending not to be offended. He disappeared down the basement steps to his workroom and I had the sudden urge to follow him.

"I spoke to your sister today," my mom said abruptly, her back stiff and her knife slicing rapidly through the garlic.

Ah, so that was what all the tension was really about. My infamous sister.

"That's nice," I said in my most neutral, pleasant voice. "How is she doing?"

"Oh, you know how she is. Busy, busy, busy."

I sure do, I thought sarcastically. She was a busy one all right.

"The thing is," my mom went on, her shoulders rising even higher until they were right up next to her ears, "she's going to be in town this coming weekend and I thought ... I mean, she could always get a hotel if you're uncomfortable."

"You want her to stay *here*?"

"Breanna, it's her house, too. Well, I mean it's our house but you're both our daughters. She's your sister."

"By blood only," I said stubbornly, already sensing that this was a lost cause. My mom had a blind spot where Angelika was concerned. "She gave up being my sister a long time ago."

"Breanna, don't say that. She made a mistake but I know she loves you."

"No, she made a choice." I'd already been through this with a very outraged counsellor at the hospital so I was pretty confident that I wasn't crazy to not want my lying sister in my life. "She made a choice and she has to accept the consequences. And the consequences are that I don't want to be around her. Ever."

"*Breanna*, that's enough—"

"Look, I can't stop her from staying here. She's your daughter and I get that you want to see her. But I don't want to hang out with her or talk about *feelings* or anything like that. I don't want to pretend that things are normal and that nothing happened. I'll just stay in my room or go out for the day when she's around."

She didn't say anything else but her whole body trembled with repressed emotion.

That was the thing about Mom. No matter how tightly she'd

stuck by my side over the last year, when it came right down to choosing sides, she was always going to pick Angelika. That's the way it had been all our lives. I didn't think it was something she could even control. She always went out of her way to treat us equally, but there was just something special between my sister and her that couldn't be duplicated.

"I'm not hungry tonight," I said finally. "I think I'm going to go to bed early. See you in the morning."

I was up the stairs and in the safety of my room before she could even turn around.

Chapter Fifteen

The next morning I was up before my alarm went off. Since I'd skipped dinner the night before I knew I'd have to make a good show of eating breakfast or my mom would spend the whole day worrying about me and possibly would decide not to go into work at all. I didn't need to give either of them a reason to come home early to check on me.

"Do you have any plans today, pumpkin?" my dad asked as he laboriously constructed a triple-decker sandwich on rye.

"Oh, you know, more of the same. Just resting, I guess. I might try writing a little like you suggested, though."

Mom shot me a sideways look, her mom-radar kicking into gear.

I'd always been a terrible liar but I did my best to keep my expression neutral while I ate my cereal.

"If you decide you like it again, you might want to start thinking about some school programs for next year. It's never too early to start working on your application."

"Oh, Stewart, for heaven's sake, it's too soon to make plans for the future," Mom said in exasperation. I could tell she regretted the words as soon as they'd left her mouth.

What she'd meant was that we didn't know how long a reprieve this was. Would I be home for a few weeks before things went south again? A few months, or a year? Or an entire lifetime? It was like there was a dagger hanging over my head by the thinnest thread and who knew when it might drop?

"Well." Dad cleared his throat a few times. "I'll bring home some brochures tonight for you to look at, Bree. You might find something that interests you."

"Sure, thanks, Dad," I said smoothly, "that would be great."

I had no intention of going back to school. But it was nice of him to at least think that I had *some* sort of future.

It took them ages to finally leave and it was with relief that I shepherded them to the front door.

Mom hugged me hard before leaving; trying to convey her apology and her love and her worry all in one tight squeeze.

"I love you," I said impulsively, "see you tonight."

And then I was thankfully, finally, alone.

I did the dishes and wiped the counters and then flew through the house tidying wherever I saw something out of place. I threw on laundry and cleaned the upstairs bathroom for good measure. I didn't know how long I'd be with Lorne and I wanted the house to look like I'd spent the day at home feebly working on chores.

Deciding what to wear had taken me quite a while the night before. I'd wanted to wear jeans but every pair I owned rubbed the tender spot on my stomach where my feeding tube had been. The skin was healing but it was still sensitive. In the end, I found a decent pair of flared yoga pants and a nice hoodie and I managed to dredge up a pair of low, lace-up boots that looked a little like those short boots that the horse-girls in the magazines wore.

I packed lunch just in case we were gone all day and made sure my phone had a full charge so I could take photos and field incoming texts from my parents.

Then I sat at the kitchen table staring anxiously out the window for the entire next hour.

He's not coming. He's changed his mind. I shouldn't be getting into a car with a stranger.

All these thoughts churned restlessly through my head so when the old, brown BMW finally nosed into our driveway I leapt out of my seat and was out the front door in an instant. I remembered at the last minute that I needed to lock it behind me and then I had to run back inside to frantically find my keys.

Thankfully they were on my dresser and I was back in the driveway before Lorne had even gotten out of the car.

"Thank you for coming," I said breathlessly, sliding into the plush leather passenger seat. For an old car, it sure looked fantastic inside. Our family car was always full of Dad's paperwork and food wrappers, stacks of books, and general dirt. This one looked like it was polished daily and it smelled like leather cleaner.

"Of course, I always keep my promises," he said seriously and I could tell he meant it. There were some people that you could instinctively trust and some people, like Angelika for example, that you knew would sell you out in a heartbeat.

"There's your coffee and your donut," Lorne said, "I didn't know what you wanted so I just guessed."

"Oh, thanks," I said, sniffing at the coffee appreciatively. "So where exactly is this horse we're going to see?"

Lorne slowly backed the car out of our driveway and rolled down the street, and after five blocks I promptly became lost. I'd only had my driver's license for a short time before I got sick and I'd never had my own car so my internal map of places not covered by public transit was a little hazy.

"He only lives about twenty minutes away. He's been mostly retired for a few years but he loves to be fussed over."

"There are retirement homes for horses?"

"Well, yes. This is just a boarding barn that specializes in taking in older horses. There isn't a usable riding ring anymore but there is lots of pasture and a nice network of flat trails nearby. Old horses have some special needs."

It sounded like paradise to me. I had so many more questions but they dropped away as I stared at the changing scenery outside. We'd barely crossed out of the city limits and already the buildings had been replaced by pine trees and occasional plowed fields and pasture. The mountains hovered just within view, their tops already covered with snow.

I hadn't been out of the city for so long. I'd nearly forgotten that all this *wilderness* existed just a short drive from my doorstep. I had never been much of a hiker and I was too afraid of wild animals to go very far into the woods, but I did like to sit in quiet, green spaces and read a book, or just listen to the wind in the trees.

I hadn't known how badly I'd missed that during my year of dying.

Despite the crisp, fall air, I rolled down the window and let the wind blow across my cheeks, inhaling as deeply as I could into my lungs. I did that twice before I broke into a coughing fit.

"Sorry," I choked, powering up the window. "I'm still not used to that."

"You had surgery on your lungs?"

"Yes, last year they took part of the top half of my left lung out. Then I got pneumonia and this massive infection. It's so hard to fight things after the chemo. Dr. Grace said that the breathing thing should get easier and easier now, though. I'll just have to take it easy for a while."

"Should you be out and about then?" Lorne asked, looking worried.

"Sure, as long as I don't try to run any marathons, it should be fine." This part was actually true. The doctor had even said that light exercise was good for me at this stage.

Lorne didn't look convinced but luckily we were already

pulling up a rutted, gravel driveway. There wasn't a sign or any number to mark this place as a horse barn. Half-dead winter pasture flanked the driveway on the left and when we reached the top of a small rise I saw a long, metal-sided brown barn that looked like it had seen better days. Weeds grew up everywhere, giving the place an abandoned look.

"Where are the horses?" I asked doubtfully, staring through the windshield. I hoped it wasn't like one of those movies where I'd allowed a near-stranger to drive me out to the country to kill me.

"Don't worry, they're here. They're probably out in the field. Come on. Grab that bag of carrots for me from the backseat."

I slid out, suddenly unsure that I wanted to be there. It wasn't a clean and fancy place like on the internet or in the magazines. The parking lot, if you could call it that, was rutted and muddy.

The air smelled strongly of manure and, as we approached the barn, I could see why. Sitting right out in the open between the boggy parking area and the barn was a giant brown pile of old straw, hay and manure that steamed in the chilly morning air.

Oh, gross, I thought, wrinkling my nose. My boots skidded a little on the slick ground and I looked down to see that I'd stepped in a water-filled hole and they were now muddy right up past the laces.

Lorne had taken off his shoes at the car and had pulled on a pair of rubber boots from the trunk. They were green and came up nearly to his knees but I could see right away that they were a better choice than my boots had been.

Inside the barn was much better. The concrete aisle had been swept clean and the air smelled of hay, shavings and the delicious, pungent odour of horse. I counted twelve stalls; all of them empty. The five at the far end were bedded deeply with clean straw and had fresh hay and water inside but the seven stalls closest to the front door were just bare concrete and looked like they hadn't been used in a long time.

"You have those carrots?" Lorne asked brusquely and I held up the bag in answer. "All right, let's go find him."

Lorne rolled back a big door at the end of the barn and I stared at the scene ahead of me in awe. The barn was situated at the top of a small hill and, from where I stood, I could see miles of undulating hillside stretching out before us. Beyond the upper part of the pasture that I could see were pine woods and beyond them, jagged mountains rose on the horizon.

I stood stalk-still, feeling like I'd been deposited on a different planet. It was so beautiful and peaceful.

"Hey, Berrrrrrrrlioz," Lorne bellowed suddenly beside me, scaring me half to death. Who knew such an elderly man could be so loud. At least he could have given me some warning. "Berliozzzzz."

For a moment there was silence, and then from far away came the thundering of feet. Not just one set of hooves but a whole herd of them. Galloping, careening and doing little kicks of joy in the air they swept up the hillside at full speed.

Lorne had said that they were all elderly horses but they didn't look it at that moment. They thundered up to us like an avalanche, snorting and blowing and swirling their heads in circles.

"Okay, settle, settle," Lorne said, laughing, "all of you behave yourselves. We have a guest. "

When they'd stopped prancing and had arranged themselves into an orderly row at the fence, I counted five of them altogether. They were all different colours; brown, grey, red, black, and even one with brown and white patches like a cow.

"Which one is ours?" I asked. "I mean, yours?"

"Can you guess?"

I looked at them all carefully and shook my head. "I know he's a boy and a thoroughbred. Other than that I can't really tell them apart. I know nothing about horses."

He frowned and took down a canvas halter hanging on a hook

near the gate. "Hmm, Gretta said that you were a big horse enthusiast. If you want to make a career with them you'll have to get used to trying harder than that."

"What?" I choked. "A career?"

I paused for a second, considering. Could someone actually make money working with horses? I'd never even thought of that. Weren't they just very expensive pets for rich people?

Lorne shrugged. "That's what she said. Come on, we can't keep him waiting."

Lorne opened the gate and went over to buckle the halter on the head of the tall, black fluffy horse with the greying muzzle. It wasn't only his muzzle that was greying. It was the hollows over his eyes and the tips of his ears. He looked like he'd been sprinkled in snow.

"He's beautiful," I said as Lorne led him past me toward the barn, "and he's so fuzzy."

"He gets a pretty thick winter coat now that he's older. Each of those horses can have half a carrot. Just make sure there's enough left for this guy. He'll expect a treat after his grooming session. We'll meet you inside when you're finished."

"Um, okay," I said uncertainly, reaching into the bag of carrots. As soon as the bag rustled, all the attention was on me. The whole herd stood with pricked ears and such eager expressions that I had to laugh.

"Okay, one for you and one for ... ow," I yelped as the brown and white spotted horse nipped the carrot sharply out of my hand. Those teeth *hurt*.

Oh, wait. I'm supposed to hold treats flat on my hand, aren't I? I wouldn't forget that again. The next few went more smoothly and I managed not to lose any fingers. By the time everyone had had a treat, my hand was slick with horse slobber.

Gross, I looked around to wipe it on something but everything within sight was muddy. In the end, I just dried my hand hurriedly on my pant leg. I had a feeling that staying clean would be impossible anyway.

I trudged into the barn to find Lorne standing in the center aisle with the horse attached to two ropes that ran from either side of the wall.

"Bree, this is Berlioz, or Bear for short."

"Hi there," I said softly, holding my hand out as I inched forward.

His soft whiskers tickled across my palm and then he gently reached up to touch my cheek.

"Would you like to brush him?"

"Oh, yes, please. How old is he?"

"He is thirty years old now. Hard to believe. We owned him as a four year old. Somehow we kept him all this time."

"That's amazing. I didn't know horses got that old."

"Horses are a long-term commitment," Lorne said, handing me a hard plastic brush, "but they are a lifetime passion as well. I wouldn't have changed a thing despite all the long hours and back-breaking work, and the financial strain. A life doing what you love is a life well-lived."

I ran the brush gently across the horse's plush, black coat, hoping I was doing it right.

"His fur is so soft," I said, pausing to rest my cheek against the animal's fluffy shoulder. It was like hugging a warm, plush toy.

Lorne took another brush and went to Bear's far side and together we worked in companionable silence. Berlioz was half-asleep the whole time, his eyes closed and his lower lip drooping.

"I think he likes his massage," I said, laughing.

"That he does. He was a bit of a firecracker in his youth but he settled down nicely over time."

"Berlioz was a composer, right? Is that who he's named after?"

Lorne shrugged. "Something like that. That's his registered name and we didn't see any need to change it up. He was Bear to us and Berlioz to the world. He was a very good eventer in his day and a brilliant dressage horse. You should have seen him back in his prime."

"Well, he looks pretty good to me now," I said and was rewarded with Lorne beaming me a rare smile. The truth was that I didn't know enough to tell the difference between a fancy horse and an old, retired horse. I was just glad to be around anything with four legs and a tail. Especially one that was as sweet as Bear.

"Would you like to ride him?" Lorne asked out of the blue.

I stared at him open-mouthed. "Can I? Really? Wouldn't it be too much for him? I don't want to hurt him."

Lorne chuckled low under his breath. "I didn't mean for you to gallop him across country. You look to me like you weigh about thirty pounds soaking wet. I think the old guy can handle a short walk down the trail. It's up to you."

"Yes, please," I said, ignoring the warning voice inside that told me that it was too soon, that I was still healing and weak. "As long as you're positive he won't mind."

"Well, we'll bring the carrots along just in case he needs a break."

I know I shouldn't be doing this, I thought as Lorne reappeared from a little room with a red saddle pad and a brown leather saddle over one arm. *The doctors would say it's too early. My mom would say it's too dangerous. But I'm doing it. I might never have another chance to try. So, I'm doing it anyway. I am.*

"Here, put this on," Lorne said, handing me a dusty, velvet-covered helmet. I looked at it skeptically and brushed the worst of the dust off. I slipped it on and fumbled at the harness under my chin until everything fit securely.

Bear woke up long enough for Lorne to slip a bit into his mouth and adjust the bridle carefully over his head.

"Right, you ready to ride?"

I nodded wordlessly, suddenly struck with a clawing, nervous feeling in my belly. I numbly followed him outside to a low, wooden block.

"Okay, hurry up and climb on. Don't land like a sack of potatoes. Think light and agile, sink like a feather."

Following those vague instructions, I clambered up on the box and reached out tentatively to touch the leather saddle. It was smooth and soft, like a luxurious couch in a specialist's office. It looked expensive, like I could accidentally scratch it with the slightest touch.

"Well, aren't you getting on?"

I can do this, I thought. *It's just like in the videos. I just put my left foot in the metal thing and swing my leg over.*

I put a hand on Bear's neck, stuffed my foot in the stirrup and the next thing I knew I was sitting on my very first horse.

I reached down to pet Bear's mane, overwhelmed with my accomplishment.

"Er, so how long has it been since you've ridden?" Lorne asked, staring up at me in confusion.

"Um, well, about that ..."

But before I could say anything else, Bear tossed his nose impatiently and took off in an active shuffle down the driveway.

"Oooh," I cried, half-scared and half-delighted that we were actually moving.

Lorne appeared beside me again, a little out of breath, and quickly clipped a lead rope to bit-ring.

"You just let the reins sit on his neck," he said, puffing a little, "I'll do the steering this time."

The warm autumn sun shone down on us and I tilted my head back, eyes closed and soaked in the warmth.

"Okay, just an easy walk down to the bridge and back. I think you can both handle that."

Bear's gait was gentle and comfortable, like being on a swaying couch. You could almost fall asleep up there.

"It helps if you sit up straight," Lorne said dryly and I opened my eyes to see him watching me with an amused look on his face.

"What do you mean?"

"You're hunched over like a hobbit. A rider sits up straight like a soldier but with the grace of a ballerina. Shoulders straight, chin up, legs stretched down. See, much better."

I wasn't so sure that it was an improvement. Instead of relaxing into Bear's motion, I felt stiff and awkward.

"You like music, right?"

"No." I shook my head. "My sister does, though. She sings professionally and plays a bunch of instruments."

"Right, well, riding is like a duet, or maybe like a dance. Do you know how to tango? Or Salsa?"

"Definitely not, but I think I understand what—"

"It's in the hips, in the shoulders, in the rhythm, in the perfect connection, the perfect understanding between two dance partners. Cha-cha-cha. Yes?"

"Right," I said to be agreeable. *Nope*, I didn't have a clue.

"You hold your body like a dancer and then you give in to the music."

I thought about that. Gradually my stiff posture relaxed and I found myself swaying again with the horse's movement. Bear's hooves made a steady thudding sound on the dirt path, the leather saddle creaked and all around me birds chattered excitedly from tree to tree.

It almost made me forget that I'd ever been sick at all.

"This is amazing," I said under my breath. I hadn't meant for Lorne to hear but he looked over his shoulder and gave me a brief smile.

When we reached a small, wooden bridge over a small stream, Lorne said it was time for us to turn around.

"You two are both out of shape," he said, poking Bear gently in the neck, "you need to build up slowly. We'll get you out and about in no time."

"You mean we can do this again?" I asked in delight. I had been sure that Lorne had figured out by now that I wasn't a real rider and would never let me near his horse again. "Really?"

"Well, I haven't got too much else to do with my time and I'm guessing you don't, either. And Bear here likes the company and the gentle exercise. Before she got so sick, Gretta used to take him out two or three times a week just to stretch his muscles and keep him from getting bored. He's been a bit neglected lately without her."

"I'd love to. As long as you're sure it won't hurt him."

"What's that old saying? Movement is medicine. Use it or lose it. Something like that. Even old horses need a bit of exercise. Just like me, I guess." He patted his stomach ruefully. "Too many snacks and not enough walking doesn't do anyone any good."

When we got back to the barn, Lorne watched me skeptically, and without helping, while I figured out how to slither out of the saddle and clamber down on the ground.

Ow, I thought ruefully, rubbing my jaw from where the leather had scraped my skin. The scar on my stomach throbbed and I resisted the urge to pull up my shirt and make sure it was still okay.

The riders in the videos I'd watched always made everything seem so elegant.

"Are you all right?" Lorne asked when I stood there clutching the stirrup leather and trying to catch my breath.

"Yeah," I wheezed, "I'm fine. I just need a minute."

"Right, well then let's untack him, brush him, and put him back out with the others. Then we can discuss exactly what sort of horse experience you have under your belt."

"I didn't lie to Gretta on purpose," I said, hobbling after him and Bear. "It just seemed so important to her that I be a rider. I didn't want to disappoint her by telling the truth."

I broke off, watching while Lorne silently pulled off Bear's tack. He gave the animal a pat and then handed me a soft, round curry comb and motioned toward where the horse was standing. I began to work the brush over his coat in circles and suddenly found my voice again.

"I *do* like horses. Now. But that didn't start until right before I met you and Gretta. When I had that dream. Since then all I've wanted to do is have the chance to be around horses and to ride. I'm sorry that I'm not the person who can help you with your October horse thing. Gretta was wrong about me."

"Maybe she was," was all he said.

He didn't look angry. He whistled under his breath as he ran his brush briskly over Bear's coat and didn't say a word as he led the big gelding out to the pasture.

I trailed behind, wondering if this would be the last time I'd see this farm after all. It had looked so rundown when I first arrived but somehow, in the last hour, I'd grown to love it.

By the time we were back in the car the excitement of the day had caught up with me and I was yawning and a little unsteady on my feet.

"Is it too much for you?" Lorne asked bluntly, looking at me with concern.

"No, I'm fine. I just need to build my strength up. The doctor's said it would take a while."

"Hmph," he said, "you think you'd be able to come here regularly to brush Bear and maybe keep him exercised?"

"Really?" I nearly squealed with excitement and had to struggle to compose myself. "You mean, you don't mind that I don't know anything?"

"Well, I figure that everyone has to start somewhere. You might as well give Bear some attention and learn something at the same time."

"Yes, thank you; that would be amazing."

I wanted to reach out and hug him in gratitude but he shot me a warning look that kept me in my seat. On second thought, he didn't seem like much of a hugger.

"I have an appointment in town tomorrow but how about we do this again the day after that?" Lorne asked. "Same time, ten o'clock?"

"Definitely, thanks again. You have no idea how much this means to me."

I stood outside on my driveway and waved after the car until it disappeared. It was only once I was alone that I realized how weary every bone in my body was. I hoped I hadn't pushed myself too far.

It was worth it, I told myself firmly. That was my third wish done. I'd ridden a real horse. But now that had opened up the door for so many more wishes.

I want to learn how to use the reins properly and dismount without falling. I still have to have my first trot and canter and go over a jump and ride in a show. And maybe have a horse of my own.

I had this crazy feeling that if I just keep adding wishes, things I wanted to do in life, that I could keep living forever.

I looked down at my filthy, hairy clothes, and the mud coating my messy boots, and groaned. My mom would smell horse the second she walked in the door if I didn't take care of this right away. I had laundry to do and boots to scrub before I could even think about having the nap I so desperately wanted.

Chapter Sixteen

"Breanna, have you seen that bag of apples I had sitting on the counter?"

"Um, what bag?" I asked innocently, which was better than outright lying. Luckily she was distracted and not paying close attention to me. That *might* have been the same bag of apples I'd brought to the barn yesterday morning to share with Bear and his friends.

I'd learned that there were five of them altogether. Besides Bear, there was the paint horse, Nipper, who could bite if you weren't watching him. There was a huge, kind white mare named Slate and her best friend, a bony brown mare named Flicker. And there was a little red gelding with a blaze named Cooper.

"Darn it, I was sure I bought some. I wanted to make a pie tonight. Apple pie is Angelika's favourite."

"Huh, that's too bad." I manage to keep the sarcasm out of my voice. I was not looking forward to tonight's dinner.

"I'll be upstairs if you need anything," I said, retreating to my room. Going up the stairs, I winced a little at the dull ache in my back and thighs. Today had been my third day out at the farm. Even at the walk, riding Bear across uneven terrain caused my unused muscles to protest for hours afterward. But I loved it more than I'd ever loved anything.

Despite the constant pain in my body, I was pretty sure that I was improving. At least I could get on and off with embarrassing myself.

"That's better, more like a ballerina less like a lumberjack," Lorne had told me that morning, which had made me choke with laughter. I had briefly taken dance class as a kid and I was pretty sure the instructor had told my parents not to waste their money.

I could now groom Bear from head to toe, using the proper brushes, although it took me a while to pick out his feet. Crouching over like that compressed my lungs and made it hard to breathe, but if I moved slowly and took breaks between each foot I was able to get it done.

"Will I see you tomorrow?" Lorne had asked.

I had been sorely tempted but the next day was Saturday and I wasn't ready to explain things to my parents quite yet. Especially with Angelika being home for the weekend. She'd be sure to twist things around to try and ruin it for me. Right then, horses were my thing alone and I wanted to keep it that way, at least for another week.

"Sorry, I have a family thing this weekend. Would Monday be okay?"

"Sure, sure. That's fine. You're doing good, kid."

That was high praise coming from Lorne, and I went into the house singing happily under my breath. I had found a pair of old rubber rain boots in the basement that fit me reasonably well. They were blue with yellow sunflowers on them but I didn't think Bear minded what I wore. It was better than me having to scrub my leather boots in the kitchen sink every afternoon. I was always paranoid that I'd left some traces of mud or fur around for my parents to find.

I had taken to hosing down my rubber boots at the barn and stuffing them in a plastic bag that I hid in the very back of the utility room in our basement. Nobody ever went in there if they could help it.

I'd gotten home and cleaned up just in time that afternoon. Both my parents arrived home a little ahead of time. Mom was already anxious about Angelika's visit. She flitted around the house in paroxysms of worry, prepping for dinner and dusting and moving the furniture around until I wanted to scream at her to stop.

"Why don't we go downstairs and get out of your mom's way?" Dad said and I was only too happy to agree.

"How's Attila the Hun coming along?" I asked, bending down to peer at the table where the Battle of the Catalaunian Plains was unfolding.

"Oh, good, good. The landscape is just about done. Now I'm starting with the horses."

My dad not only exhaustively researched these battles to make sure the scenery and buildings were historically accurate, but he also built thousands of little people, horses, and other objects out of wire and clay. He then painted them so that they were perfect tiny replicas. I honestly didn't know how he had the patience to do one figurine let alone thousands. Each scene took him months to finish.

"He was quite the horseman, that Attila," my dad said, picking up a tiny, clay horse that hadn't yet been painted. "The Huns were brought up riding practically from birth."

"Lucky," I said and looked up to find him staring at me curiously.

"Are you still interested in horses?"

"Yes," I said cautiously, wondering where this was going. Did he know about Lorne and Bear somehow?

"Well, don't forget your birthday is coming up at the end of the month. We could look into maybe visiting a stable or something if you're feeling up to it. I can ask one of my students if we could take a tour and maybe we could arrange a few lessons."

"Really? That would be great, thanks, Dad."

"As long as you don't overdo it. How's the writing going?"

"Oh, fine, fine." This was half-true. I hadn't written any stories but I'd started a journal where I wrote down everything I'd learned from Lorne and Bear each day. It helped to note anything that I'd improved on or things that had frustrated me. It also reminded me to look up anything I hadn't understood at the time.

"Let me know if you want any help setting up your blog. I'm always here to help."

"Right," I said. I hadn't thought that far ahead yet. I didn't think anyone would want to read anything that I had to say. I wasn't an expert on anything.

"Oh, and let's not mention the horse thing to your mother just yet. Not until we've worked out the details."

"Agreed," I said, glad that we were on the same page.

Chapter Seventeen

I was watching from the upstairs window when Angelika came home. Her little black Porsche, a lease not a purchase, sped down the quiet street at about five times the legal speed limit and made an abrupt turn into our driveway.

Same old Angelika. Always such a show-off.

I sighed and turned back to my wardrobe. I was torn between dressing up to look good in front of her or dressing down to show how little her presence bothered me. It was a hard decision.

I finally decided to wear a nice black, flowy top that I hadn't worn in a while, a silk scarf to cover the scar on my neck and some soft blue leggings.

I tied my bandanna carefully and applied a little make-up. I studied myself in the mirror. The hollows under my cheekbones had filled in a little and the autumn sun had pinked my pale skin just the tiniest bit. I was a little fatter too, which for me was a good thing.

You'll have to do, I told my reflection and headed downstairs.

The table was set, candles flickering already from the center and the good china laid out as if it were Christmas. Mom was going all out.

"Hey," I said casually, strolling into the living room where the three of them were seated awkwardly on the sofa.

To her credit, Angelika looked extremely uncomfortable to be there. She already had a glass of red wine clutched between her hands and from her dilated pupils I'd say she had something else on board as well. As soon as she saw me she took a huge gulp of wine.

Her blonde hair was ice-white and had been cut on a sharp angle just behind her ear on one side down to her shoulder on the other side. She wore a short black dress and thin, strappy black shoes with five-inch heels. Her nails were manicured into sharp red points that she tapped nervously against her wine glass.

She would have looked perfect on a runway. Edgy, artistic, untouchable. But, sitting across from me on my parent's well-worn couch that hadn't changed since I was ten years old, she looked like an alien dropped into our midst.

"You look good," she said abruptly, staring at me with a glassy expression, "you look ..." she waved a hand in my direction as if searching for the right word.

"Alive?" I said flatly.

She froze and I could see Mom tense up from the corner of my eye. Dad sighed heavily and I had a feeling that this was going to be the longest weekend in the history of long weekends.

"I was going to say, *happy*, you look happy."

"Thanks, so do you." She didn't, though. She looked beautiful, successful, and almost rich, but there were dark circles under her eyes and faint worry-lines across her forehead. "How's the music?"

"The music is good, as always, but the rest of it is stressful. We go on tour next week and I'm not sure that our new manager has it organized properly. It's his first time coordinating everything and well ... I just hope we have a place to sleep every night and that we get paid. Those sorts of things. How about you? How's your ... er, stuff going?"

She paused, frowning, and I could see her searching for something specific to ask me about. If I wasn't in school anymore and I wasn't actively dying then what was I doing with my life?

A small part of me longed to tell her about the horses, to have something fantastic and exciting to talk about but I bit my tongue. I knew from experience that if you gave Angelika something important to latch onto, she would find a way to take it from you. That was just the way she was made.

"Everything is good," I said calmly, "Mom, dinner smells nice. Can I help you get anything ready?"

Mom leapt up like she'd been stung and made a bee-line for the kitchen. I followed, leaving my poor dad to entertain Angelika. I knew that he hadn't quite been able to forgive and forget that he'd walked in to find her naked, in my parents' bed of all places, with Duncan. It had taken months for him to start speaking to her again. They were still on shaky ground.

I helped load the food into the fancy serving bowls Mom had dusted off for the occasion and ferried everything to the dining room table.

"This is going well," my mom said in an unnaturally high-pitched voice. By that time she was practically thrumming with tension and her shoulders were somewhere up around her ears. I didn't know why she got herself so worked up over pushing us together to be some sort of happy family.

"Mom, it's fine. Don't worry," I reassured her, "dinner will be great."

And I was right. Angelika's pattern was to eat first, drink a lot, then drop some bombshell after dinner. So while we were actually eating she was on her best behaviour. I'd already planned to escape to my room directly after dessert and leave my parents to deal with her drama. If I was really lucky, she'd cause a fight and storm out and I wouldn't have to see her again all weekend.

Unfortunately, she was a little ahead of schedule that night.

"So, I saw Duncan the other day in Vancouver," she said casually just as I was taking the first bite of my lemon meringue pie.

I froze, thrown completely off guard. With difficulty, I schooled my face into what I hoped was indifference, took a deep breath, and reached for my water glass.

This is not a drill. This is an emergency situation. My brain was screaming but I shut it down and made myself go to that numb, disengaged place where I'd learned to disappear to during my time at the hospital when the pain was too much to bear.

My parents both froze in place wearing identical horrified expressions.

Angelika's eyes went wide and her cheeks flushed, but she was like a train-wreck that just couldn't stop even though she knew she was about to go off the tracks and tumble down a mountain.

"We went out for coffee to catch up on old times," she said, her voice pitching upward. "He asked about you, Bree. I should have given him your number. He's still really hot. You really should forgive him and give him another chance. I know I would."

Her words fell into a bottomless cavern of disappointment. My parents, not mine, because I had zero expectations for my sister.

"Well," I said finally, "I guess that's my cue to go upstairs. Thanks for dinner, Mom, it was great. Goodnight."

I scooped up my dessert plate, because there was no way I was missing out on pie because of this, and I was halfway to the stairs when my dad loudly pushed back his chair and stood up. "Angelika, you will apologize to your sister and then you will leave this house."

"Stewart," my mom protested, "I don't think—"

"I said, you will apologize and then you will leave."

"Okay, jeesh, sorry, I don't know what all the fuss is about. It's not like he was that great of a catch anyway, was he? I mean, it didn't take much to—"

I picked my pace up on stairs, firmly blocking out whatever she was about to say.

Once I was safe in my room, though, I couldn't resist tiptoeing over to the vent on the floor. It was an old childhood trick I'd learned. If you sat cross-legged on the floor next to the vent and listened carefully you could hear everything that was said downstairs. I slowly ate my pie and listened to the fight unfold.

"Angelika you need to leave. I think you've done enough damage for one night."

"Stewart, she's been drinking all night, she can't drive," my mom said angrily. "She's supposed to spend the night with us here."

"Well, she can take a taxi to a hotel then. I'll even pay for it. She can cool down and think about what she's said. And, if she apologizes to her sister, then she can spend the rest of the weekend here."

"This is bull," my sister said, her voice loud and slightly slurred. "I'm not going to put up with this."

"I'll call you a taxi," my dad said calmly, in his disappointed-teacher voice. That voice used to drive us crazy when we were kids, it was worse than being yelled at.

"No, I'm going to drive and you can't stop me," Angelika yelled, sounding about six years old.

My mother said something in protest, but it was drowned out by the front door slamming. The big engine outside revved to life and my sister's car peeled away up the street with a squeal of tires.

Then there was just silence.

I got dressed for bed and turned out the light, wondering why it had always been this way with Angelika. As kids, our relationship had been volatile at best. She'd been born a year after me and it was like she'd gone out of her way to outshine me in *everything* right from the beginning.

When we were toddlers, if I built a block house, she would build one three times higher and with a balcony or something. When I fumbled my way through beginner classes in things like ballet, gymnastics, or music, she would insist on joining too, even though she was younger, and she would be just so damn good at everything. There was nothing she could do that wasn't instantly perfect. And it didn't help that everyone always went on and on about how adorable she was and how talented.

And the worst thing was that every time I got sick of being terrible at my lessons and quit, she'd insist on quitting too and we'd be on to something else. It was an endless cycle and finally, I just stopped trying out for anything at all. It was easier to just quietly read in my room.

The only thing Angelika had stuck with was music and that was probably only because she'd become sort of famous with it early-on. Right from the beginning, she had this angelic voice and she could teach herself to play pretty much any instrument. When she was twelve, she'd locked herself in our upstairs bathroom and recorded herself singing and playing the guitar. She'd slapped it on YouTube and become an overnight sensation for about two weeks. She'd gotten some small sponsorships and a huge internet following and, after that, there had been no stopping her.

So far the only thing I'd beaten her at was getting sick and nearly dying. I knew she'd been genuinely upset when I'd been hospitalized, but I also knew that it had driven her half-crazy that my parents had to spend a year and a half focused on *me* rather than her skyrocketing career.

I guessed that was partly why she'd slept with Duncan and then promptly abandoned him.

When I'd woken up from surgery, she'd already flown halfway around the world to sing at some music festival and poor Duncan was left alone crying and stammering apologies at my bedside until I'd had him escorted out of my room, out of the hospital, and out of my life.

Chapter Eighteen

We didn't hear from Angelika again that weekend. She didn't apologize and she didn't show up to spend quality family time with us.

My dad shut himself in his office and busied himself with going over his lesson plans for the next week. My mom went on an angry house-cleaning spree that involved a lot of scrubbing and banging things around. And I spent the weekend researching barns where I could take a few riding lessons.

I wasn't in any way breaking my promise to Lorne to spend time with Bear, but it wouldn't hurt for me to take a few proper lessons so that I could progress a little more quickly.

By the time my birthday rolled around, I would be so much stronger and have more stamina. Researching possible barns gave me something to focus on. That way I could almost forget the triumphant expression that had spread across my sister's face when she'd watched me struggling not to let her words hurt me.

The great thing was that there was no shortage of stables to choose from. I filled two sheets of paper with names, numbers, and locations in no time. I could jump, do dressage, ride western, herd cows, or just trail ride if I wanted to.

I didn't realize the downside of the situation until I started calling them for pricing.

"*Seventy* dollars an hour," I said in astonishment to the first bored-sounding instructor.

"Our lessons are forty-five minutes and that price is pretty standard," she said impatiently, "you might be able to find cheaper lessons *somewhere*. But remember that you get what you pay for. And if you want to compete then you'll have to commit to at least two lessons a week. More, if you want to do the bigger shows."

"Oh," I said, gulping hard. A hundred and forty dollars a week, minimum. Yikes. There was no way we could afford that. "And is there a chance for someone to work off lessons by, um, cleaning stalls and things?"

"Not at this time," she said crisply, "we are fully staffed. But you could call around."

"Okay, thanks," I said in a small voice but she'd already hung up.

After that conversation, I felt a little depressed; it took me a while to get my courage up to start calling around again.

It became easier each time and the outlook was a bit brighter once I'd talked to a few more people. Lessons in my area ranged from fifty dollars and up to ride a school horse. Or slightly less if I had my own horse to use.

But if I had my own horse then I'd be paying to feed and board him. And he'd need shoes and probably all sorts of other things I don't know about.

A few of the people I spoke to very kindly let me know that while they did allow *some* students to work off their lessons, they preferred that I have more experience handling all sorts of horses before working there.

"It's nothing personal, dear," a sweet-sounding older lady said, "but some of our boarders aren't very well-behaved. You should take some lessons first and get used to the routine. Maybe next year there'd be a space for you to work off lessons.

I should just be content riding Bear for now, I thought, *it's a great opportunity that I'm lucky to have. I shouldn't be impatient for more.*

As much as I loved my short, ambling, rides down to the bridge and back, I was ready to try something more challenging. I was happy grooming Bear and had graduated to being able to tack him up properly by myself, but the woods were calling and I wanted to spend hours in them exploring. Last time we were out, Lorne had even let me use the reins on my own, which had been pretty easy since we were only going in a straight line.

"Thumbs on top and no pulling," were the only instructions he'd given me but that seemed simple enough and Bear had just plodded along like usual.

It was a very quiet weekend. My parents barely spoke to each other and my dad took his meals in his office or hid downstairs working on his models.

I mostly stayed safely in my room, out of the way of my mother's anxious cleaning.

I couldn't wait for Monday to come.

Chapter Nineteen

It was almost worth having to wait the whole crappy weekend because, when we arrived at the barn, Lorne had a surprise for me.

"Julie asked if we could take Nipper out with us on our walk today," he said, "he's bored and has been chewing the boards in the pasture. She thinks he needs something new to focus on. We can go a little further today if you like."

"Oh," I said, delighted, "that would be great."

Nipper was the big brown and white Paint horse, and I knew he belonged to the woman who lived up in the big house on the hill, overlooking the barn. It was Julie who took care of the horses when we weren't around. She fed them, turned them out and cleaned their stalls. But she didn't ride, not even on the trails.

"She had a bad accident," Lorne had told me, "so she doesn't ride and she doesn't like to socialize with new people because of the scarring. Although I think she looks just fine. She has a son about your age, but he doesn't live at home anymore."

Because all the horses were retired seniors, their owners didn't come up very often. So it was the perfect place for someone who preferred to be around horses rather than people.

Most of the boarders were happy to drop their senior horses off and maybe visit once a month, if that, and I'd never seen anyone else around when Lorne and I visited Bear.

Nipper was Julie's own retired horse. He didn't look quite as old as Bear, although he was fat and out of shape, and, true to his name, he was a bit of a nipper. You had to watch him when you were handing out treats or you were likely to lose a finger. And he would playfully grab your jacket or arm when you led him if you weren't careful, too.

"I don't have to ride him, do I?" I asked anxiously as Lorne slid the saddle onto Nipper's plump back. The horse was excited by all the attention and kept lifting his head in the air, eyes wide and nostrils flaring. Whenever Lorne wasn't paying attention to him he'd reach out one front hoof to paw the barn floor.

"No, no, you stick with Bear. I'll ride this beast. Quit that, Nipper."

I was worried about Lorne for a second when we led the horses to the mounting block. He was old after all, and Nipper just didn't want to stand still. But there was a tiny second where the horse paused in his prancing and Lorne sprang into the saddle like someone much younger. Nipper hunched his back for a second, ducked his nose, and let out a small, excited buck.

"Stop that," Lorne said mildly, not looking overly concerned. He circled Nipper in a big loop around us while I nervously slid onto the back of the ever-steady, half-asleep, Bear and then we were off.

I'm really riding, I thought, torn between anxiously watching Nipper's antics and congratulating myself on having my first real ride without Lorne walking beside us at Bear's head.

Gradually, I relaxed. The sun was out, the birds were singing busily, and Bear swayed steadily underneath me in a dependable sort of way.

Up ahead Nipper had hit the end of his energy reserves and

had dropped from a prance to a walk, and we were gradually able to catch up.

"This is great," I called to Lorne and he smiled back at me in agreement.

We went over the wooden bridge and down through the woods, past a little rushing stream that I hadn't seen before. The fall air was clear and crisp, and I inhaled deeply, surprised to feel my left lung responding almost as well as the right.

I'm getting stronger, I thought, feeling a thrill run down my spine, *maybe I really am getting better this time.*

I reached down to run my fingers through Bear's silky mane.

The loop through the woods took us just under an hour. It was the longest I'd ever ridden and all I could think about was that I wanted to be back out there more than anything.

I slid to the ground and noticed that Bear had a little bit of sweat on his neck and chest, and that his breathing was a little heavier than normal.

"Is he okay?" I asked Lorne worriedly.

"Yep, he's just old and out of shape. We have to build him up very slowly. But he's enjoying himself more than he has in years. Don't worry, he'll tell us if he's had enough."

Lorne groaned under his breath as he stiffly slid down from Nipper. When he reached the ground he held onto the stirrup leather and slowly stretched himself upright. As he straightened there were a series of cracking and popping sounds from his back and joints.

"Are *you* all right?" I asked anxiously, looking at the pinched expression on his face. I'd seen that look many times in the hospital when people were trying to push through pain.

"Fine, fine," he said and took a deep breath. "My hips just aren't what they used to be. I'll be all right in a minute."

I let Bear stretch his nose down to nibble on the winter grass, wishing there was a way I could help Lorne feel better.

"There," he said finally, taking a deep breath, "now let's get these ponies groomed and back out on pasture."

I kept half an eye on Lorne while I groomed Bear's thick, winter coat but, besides moving a bit more slowly, he seemed pretty much back to his old self.

"Foot, please," I said to Bear and he slowly, obediently lifted each large foot in turn, letting me pick them out.

It was amazing to me how familiar the routine had become after only a week. It was like I'd been handling giant horse hooves all my life. Bear's back legs were stiff so he could only lift his feet a few inches off the ground. I took a deep breath to fill my lungs and then bent over them carefully, cleaning every last bit of dirt away so he didn't get any of the foot funguses or diseases Lorne had warned me about.

"Would you mind checking Nipper's feet for me, too?" Lorne asked a little bashfully. "I'm not sure if my back is up to it right now."

"Of course," I said, though honestly, I wasn't too eager to get close to Nipper at all. He always seemed to have a mischievous glint in his eye; like he might try something naughty as soon as I let my guard down.

"I'll be in the tack room if you need me," Lorne said, hobbling away.

I frowned as I watched him limp past me and then turned to Nipper reluctantly.

"Foot?" It came out like a nervous question. Unlike Bear, he didn't budge as I ran my fingers tentatively down the inside of his fluffy foreleg and tugged at his hoof. "Come on, Nipper, I just want to check them."

Finally, after much pulling on my part and much sighing and ignoring on his part, he finally lifted his first foot a few inches off the ground. It was perfectly clean, but I grimly moved from foot to foot, struggling with him each time. By the time I finished, I was sweating and out of breath.

Nipper gave me a satisfied look and bobbed his nose up and down a few times, hoping to look cute enough to beg a treat from me.

"I don't think so," I said, wheezing a little in an effort to get the words out, "you were not that helpful."

Lorne still hadn't come back so I put their plaid blankets back on and led them, one by one, back out to the pasture.

They didn't run off right away, they both stood by the gate, staring at me expectantly until I produced the carrot they both felt they deserved.

"You two are pretty spoiled, you know," I told them, giving them each a small piece. Nipper and Bear both crunched their treats happily, dribbling blobs of carroty saliva into the mud, and then ambled off side-by-side to find the other horses.

"Lorne," I said gratefully, as he hobbled out of the barn, "thank you so much. That was my first real trail ride. Are you sure you're okay, though?"

"Just a little tired, that's all," he said, waving away my concern, "we might have to take it easier on my old bones tomorrow."

I'd completely lost track of time. We'd been out for the whole afternoon so, by the time Lorne, pulled into my driveway, I only had an hour to tidy the house and wash my horsey laundry.

I finished just as my dad's car rolled up the driveway. Then I remembered my boots by the front door. Grabbing them, I ran downstairs as fast as I could and stuffed them in the basement utility room then dashed back upstairs so that I was lying on the couch with a blanket, innocently watching television, by the time he came inside.

"Well, you look like you've had a restful day," he said, smiling tiredly as he dropped his keys into the ceramic bowl on the entryway table.

"Yeah, I just took it easy," I said, stifling a yawn.

As soon as he was upstairs and I could hear the shower running, I bolted to the basement and washed the boots thoroughly in the utility room sink before stashing them away again. My mom could smell dirt and mess a mile away. I would have to be more careful next time.

I ran back up to the couch and snuggled under the covers. I hadn't realized how tired I was because the next thing I knew I was fast asleep.

Chapter Twenty

I had worried that Lorne might not show up the next day. That he might be too stiff and sore after his ride. But he arrived at the same time as always.

"I have a present for you," he said, tossing a plastic bag into my lap as soon as I got into the car.

I opened it eagerly and found three pairs of honest to goodness proper breeches. There was a cream coloured pair, a blue one, and a dark brown. I ran my fingers over the thick, stretchy fabric, hardly able to contain my excitement. There was a small hole in one knee, so I knew they were used but still, they were clean and the fabric looked older but high-quality. They were so much better than the thin, yoga pants I'd been wearing.

"Oh, thank you so much," I said, barely restraining myself from leaning over and hugging him.

"They were Gretta's from when she was younger. That woman never threw anything away. You might need a belt until you put some meat on your bones but I think they'll do."

"They're perfect," I said, vowing that I'd make them fit no matter what.

"She had big feet or I would have grabbed her old boots for you, too."

"Aren't these okay?" I said, looking down at my blue, flowered rubber boots. I'd grown quite attached to them by that time.

"Er, well, they're fine for now. You'll need something more serviceable eventually. Maybe your parents would get you some for Christmas."

"Ah, maybe," I said, thinking of how expensive the boots were that I'd looked up online. My parents had nearly had to remortgage the house when I got sick. I wasn't going to ask them for anything extra. Ever. But maybe I could ask for boots instead of lessons for my birthday.

"Most tack stores have a used section, you know," Lorne said, looking at me sideways, "you can find some good deals there sometimes."

"Really?" I perked up. That sounded more like it. "Okay, maybe I'll have a look. I have a doctor's appointment next week so I can see if my dad will take me after that."

"Can't you drive on your own?" he asked bluntly.

"Well, yes, I can. But we only have one car between all three of us and I didn't have my license very long. And I know that at least one of my parents will want to talk to the doctor, too."

"I see. You're still doing okay though, right?" He didn't look at me when he asked, just focused straight ahead at the road.

"Well ..." I hesitated since this is such a loaded question. "I *feel* good, anyway. Really good. Spending time at the farm with the horses has made me so much stronger. It's just that sometimes the bloodwork tells a different story. They don't actually have an explanation as to why I'm doing better. It could have been the drug trials or maybe my body responded to something else."

"Hmm," he said, frowning. "That must be hard, not knowing."

"It's the worst. I don't know how to plan for a future I don't know will exist."

"Well, really everyone's in that same boat, though. Gretta threw herself into her riding as if going to the Olympics was a sure thing. Anything could have happened to stop her in her tracks; an accident, a family tragedy, a financial crash. But she plowed ahead just as if those potential disasters didn't exist. I think that's the only way someone can live a full life."

We were silent for a few minutes while I pondered that. What a leap of faith to just go ahead as if everything was fine when there was a good chance it wasn't. On the other hand, what was my other option? Sit around on the couch all day wishing I was doing something amazing? What if I *did* live until I was ninety and I'd sat around all that time worrying that death was going to find me again?

"You're right," I said slowly. "Did Gretta get to ride at the Olympics?"

"Actually she didn't, but she came close quite a few times. She got to ride in international competitions all over the world and many of her students became world-renowned competitors. Two of *them* went to the Olympics and one came home with Silver. And you know, you'd think she'd be furious that she didn't meet that ultimate goal, but she wasn't. She pushed herself and her horses to the very limit of their ability and in the end it was enough, and she was happy."

We pulled up to the barn and I forgot about everything but the horses waiting for me.

"I'm going to run and change," I said, and hurried into the minuscule bathroom to try on the breeches one by one. They were a bit baggy on me but I was pretty sure that once I'd gained more fat and muscle that I'd fill them out nicely. I was just glad to have anything at all to wear. Especially something that had been Gretta's. I felt braver in them, like she was there watching me and infusing me with courage.

I didn't have a belt but there was a heap of orange binder-twine in one corner of the tack room and I quickly twisted a few strands together to create a makeshift belt. With my coat pulled down over it, nobody would even notice.

"You'll fill them out soon enough," Lorne said, limping down the aisle and for the first time I realized how slowly he was moving. His ride had taken a lot out of him yesterday.

Bear had already heard the car and was patiently waiting at the gate, and to my surprise, Nipper was standing close behind him.

"They want their carrots," I said, laughing but Lorne shook his head.

"That's part of it, for sure. But those horses both worked hard their whole lives. Being retired and put out to pasture to lounge around all day is not everyone's cup of tea. Some of us, I mean some horses, need a purpose to keep going. A reason to get up in the morning."

"Yeah, I get that," I said, looking sideways at Lorne. He didn't look like the type who'd be content lounging around, either.

We put Bear and Nipper in the cross-ties and I took my time grooming, making sure that Bear's thick coat was dirt-free, and that his mane lay silky and smooth against his neck.

"You finish with Nipper for me, would you?" Lorne asks. "I'll get Bear tacked up."

"Okay," I said, sighing heavily. I did not enjoy spending time with Nipper like I did with Bear. The big horse had way too much personality for my taste. I never knew what he was going to do next.

"Right, let's get you all tidy," I said, moving toward him tentatively with a brush in my hand. But he wasn't having any of it. He snaked his head out and grabbed the brush neatly from between my fingers, waving it up and down in the air right in front of my face.

"Hey," I cried out in surprise, "that was rude." But as soon as I reached for it he flung his head in the air and sent the brush sailing to the far end of the barn when it landed with a clatter.

"Nipper," I said in astonishment, just staring at him.

He arched his neck as if he were incredibly proud of himself and pricked his ears as if expecting a treat. His eyes were bright with fun and he wiggled his upper lip in the air a few times, making me laugh despite myself.

"You're awful," I told him. "You completely did that on purpose."

He bobbed his head eagerly up and down as if agreeing with me.

"Right, let's try that again." I retrieved the brush and this time I moved more carefully around him, avoiding his teeth. He seemed to be done playing, though. He stood perfectly still, only rolling one eye backward to watch what I was doing and wiggling his top lip ever so slightly. He even picked up his feet without too much of a struggle.

Lorne had already tacked up Bear and now he appeared with Nipper's tack over one arm. He moved slowly, he was paler than usual, and his breathing seemed a bit funny too.

"Are you sure that you feel well enough to go on a trail ride today? I could just put Nipper back out in the pasture and we could play with Bear instead."

"No," Lorne said, "we've already gotten him out, he'll be disappointed if we put him away now."

I very much doubted that.

"Here," I said, "I'll tack him up then and you rest for a bit."

He gave in without an argument, which was a little worrisome on its own, and I carefully saddled and bridled Nipper, trying hard to do everything properly.

He stood surprisingly still while I adjusted everything and didn't even bite when I practically stuck my entire hand in his mouth to hold the bit inside. It was surprisingly difficult to coordinate sliding the top of the bridle over his ears while also getting the bit between his teeth. Horse people on the internet made everything look so easy.

"Don't forget to tighten his girth a few more holes when we get out there," Lorne reminded me, "he holds his breath a little and the saddle will slip if it's too loose."

I put on my borrowed helmet and hurried to catch up with Lorne who'd already hobbled beside Bear outside.

"Aren't you going the wrong way?" I asked as he headed away from the mounting block and up an overgrown path to a small paddock.

"Oh," I said when I finally reached him. It wasn't a paddock at all. It had probably been a riding ring at some point. Now the half-rotted wooden fence sagged on all sides and grass grew up through the sand in clumps. There was an old mounting block, green with age, in one corner and Lorne led us through the rickety gate and waved me over to it.

"Tighten your girth," he reminded me as he handed me Bear's reins and took Nipper's from me.

I scratched Bear's neck and then carefully tightened the girth a few holes, looking over at Lorne to see if it was enough. When he nodded I put the reins over Bear's head and positioned him beside the mounting block so I could get on.

"Great," he said, moving over to sit on the block that I'd vacated, "now walk on."

The ring was too overgrown to do anything else *but* walk. Even at this slow pace, Bear tripped over the larger clumps of grass and stopped to try and eat every time he caught sight of anything especially delicious.

"Drop your feet out of the stirrups and just let your legs hang," Lorne said and I did, enjoying the feeling of my body swaying in time with Bear's steps. "Now switch direction. Then circle down at the end. Do you know what a twenty-meter circle is?"

I shook my head and Lorne's sigh was audible even from across the ring.

"Well, you're going to have to start doing some homework. I never did enjoy teaching beginners much. It might surprise you to learn that I'm not a patient man."

I raised my eyebrows but said nothing. I was just happy that he was letting me ride at all.

"Whenever I tell you a term you don't recognize, you're going to go home and look it up. Right?"

"Right," I said. "I can do that."

Lorne grunted but seemed satisfied with that answer. We circled a few times and I was just starting to think that I was a pretty good rider in my fancy new breeches when Lorne waved me back over.

"That's enough for Bear for one day. We don't want him to overdo it. I'll hold him while you get on Nipper."

Oh, no, I thought, a sinking feeling in the pit of my stomach. Why hadn't I seen that coming? I didn't want to argue though, and I didn't want to admit that my palms were instantly slick with sweat and my heart was suddenly going a million miles an hour. All I could see in my head was all the leaping and bucking Nipper had done the day before.

My hands trembled on the reins as I led Nipper slowly to the mounting block.

Control your breathing, I reminded myself, *you are not going to pass out here. You are a rider now, you have real breeches, Gretta's breeches, you can do this.*

Instead of easing lightly into the saddle, I sort of scrambled aboard, slamming my feet into the stirrups and gripping the reins tightly, waiting for him to leap sideways or bolt or something.

Nipper tossed his nose abruptly in the air, dragging the reins through my fingers, and then started to move slowly backwards, reversing steadily away from the mounting block.

"What is he doing?" I squealed, using my other hand to clutch the front of the saddle.

"He's trying to figure out why you have a death-grip on his reins," Lorne said dryly. He hobbled to my side and tugged the reins through my fingers until Nipper dropped his nose with a sigh of relief. "You were cueing him to back up. He was just doing what you asked."

"Oh," I said, flushing with embarrassment. "I thought he was going to buck."

"I wouldn't have put you on him if I thought he'd buck," Lorne said seriously. He reached down and adjusted my foot in the stirrup and patted my leg. "Yesterday he was excited because he hadn't been out in a long time. He just needed to blow off steam. Now he's ready to get down to work. He's a good horse, kiddo. You can trust him. Now just pretend you're riding Bear. Do some circles down at this end."

"Okay," I said, trying to force myself to relax. I made sure not to pull his mouth again, but I still squeaked every time he tripped or dipped his head down. Finally, after he'd circled a few times without doing anything scary, I let out a deep breath and tried to find a more comfortable position.

The saddle Lorne had put on Nipper was old and obviously hadn't been oiled in a long time. The leather was rough against my legs and my seat-bones poked into the rough hide uncomfortably.

"Good, now turn him the other direction."

I obeyed and found that his faster reactions and quicker step were actually a little more fun than Bear's languid stride. He felt full of life as he bobbed along, his ears pricked and his hips swinging.

"You look good. If this ring was in better shape, I'd say we could do some trotting, but as it is, I think we'd better wait. How about some easy leg-yields?"

I had no idea what he was talking about but he had me turn

when we were partway down the short side of the ring and head back toward the gate. And then he asked me to look toward the outside rail and just gently step into my outside stirrup. To my surprise, Nipper drifted automatically back to the rail.

"He moved sideways," I cried excitedly, "like a dressage horse. I did dressage." Nipper's ears flicked backward toward me.

"Er," Lorne raised his eyebrows and crossed his arms over his chest, and I could see him struggling to come up with the right thing to say. "Well, you are making steady progress," he finally said diplomatically. "Now, let's try the other direction."

I really could have ridden Nipper forever that day but after about a half an hour, Lorne made us come in.

"We don't want these boys to do too much too soon," he said, "or you, either."

"Oh, it wasn't too much for me," I said quickly, sliding somewhat competently to the ground, but I knew my face was flushed and my breathing was a little shallow. It wasn't because of overexertion, though. It was because what I'd learned was suddenly so new and exciting. A little window had opened up to show me a tiny glimpse of what might be possible if I kept on with my riding. It was probably silly that moving sideways at a walk should fill me with so much inspiration, but sometimes it was the little things in life that made a difference.

"Do you think that we would be able to do some trot work if I cleaned up the ring?" I asked, eyeing the greenery. "Would Julie mind?"

"No, she wouldn't mind," Lorne said thoughtfully, "but it might be too much for you. Weeding is a lot of work."

"I'm not afraid of work," I said quickly, "and I wouldn't have to do it all at once. I could pull a few at a time whenever we came out."

I reached down to tug experimentally at a clump and was rewarded by it pulling easily from the loose sand. Nipper's ears popped forward in excitement and he grabbed it instantly out of my hand, shaking it up and down in the air triumphantly, showering us both with sand.

"See, it wouldn't be too hard. I could tackle a corner every day."

"Suit yourself," Lorne said, shrugging. But a smile tugged at the corner of his mouth.

Chapter Twenty-One

The next day was very similar to the last. We brushed and tacked up both horses and walked around the ring again with Lorne shouting instructions at me now and then.

He had given me a list of terms to memorize and I now knew, at least in theory, what twenty-meter and ten-meter circles looked like, what a leg-yield looked like from the ground, and that crossing the diagonal meant switching directions from corner to corner across the ring.

In practice though, it wasn't so easy.

"That is an egg, not a circle," Lorne barked as I tried to guide Bear's shuffling steps into an elegant circle. I hated to say it but now that I'd experienced Nipper's more active walk, Bear seemed painfully slow. It felt disloyal to even think that, though.

"Does he look okay to you?" I asked Lorne worriedly when the old horse tripped on an especially large clump of grass.

"Well, he might be having an off day. These last two weeks have been more excitement for him than he's had in a long while. Maybe let's give him a break."

Bear looked the same as he always did when I jumped off and

gave him his carrot. He seemed content and didn't look at all unhappy. Maybe I was just imagining it.

The circles went a little better once I was up on Nipper, and we even practiced stopping and backing up a few steps, this time quietly and properly rather than me pulling on his mouth like I had the day before.

"Thank you, boy," I said to him when he was untacked, groomed, and heading back out to pasture. "You have no idea how much this means to me."

Maybe he did though, because after he'd eaten his carrot, he leaned his head on my shoulder for a moment and closed his eyes, sighing deeply.

Wow, this is so sweet, I thought, my heart fluttering. *We're bonding.* Then he lifted his head, nipped me soundly on the arm and took off at a canter, flinging his hind legs out so that mud from his hooves spattered my face.

Nope, not sweet. So bad and so gross. I wiped the mud off my face and trudged grimly out to start weeding the ring.

It turned out that there were many types of weeds in the ring but they all fit into one of two categories; easy pullers and immovable earth-bound devil-weeds.

The easy-pullers slid effortlessly from the sandy ground, and all I had to do was lightly shake their roots free of earth and toss them in the wheelbarrow. It took me about four seconds to pull each one.

The earth-bound weeds, however, left me pulling, kicking, digging, weeping, and pleading to pry them from the soil, and it took me nearly twenty minutes to wedge them free.

After an hour of that, I was more exhausted than I'd been in my life, and my hands were raw and actual white blisters were forming at the base of my fingers.

So this is what manual labour is like, I thought as I wheezed and gasped over yet another clump. *I can't think of why people like gardening and landscaping.*

When I stood up to check my progress, the tiny area I'd weeded looked pitifully small. It would take me years to clean all this up. We didn't even have one ten-meter circle free of weeds yet.

"Almost ready to head out?" Lorne asked, coming over to survey my work.

"Er, I suppose so. I'm not as far along as I thought I'd be."

"No? Well, the part you've uncovered looks good. I bet this will be a nice, usable ring once you've spruced it up."

"Really?" I said doubtfully. I looked at it again and shrugged. The clear patch of sand did have a sort of fresh, ring-like quality to it. And not all the weeds were the awful type. If I kept at it steadily, a little bit every day, it would be finished eventually.

When I got home, I rooted around in the utility room until I'd found an old pair of gardening gloves that had belonged to my mom and a few rusty hand-tools that were meant for pulling out weeds. Mom had loved gardening when I was little, but she'd given it up years ago when she'd had to go back to work full-time. Both our front and our back yards were just lumpy, uninspiring lawn that my dad forgot to mow on a regular basis.

I put the tools next to my boots and hurried upstairs to shower.

By the end of the next day, I'd cleared an entire twenty-meter circle and Lorne rewarded me by saying that on my next riding day we could try a few steps of trot.

"I have the doctor tomorrow," I reminded him, "but I'll be ready the day afterward. And I'll try and see if I can go to that tack store you told me about."

My research into riding lesson prices had pretty much convinced me that my parents, no matter how well-meaning, were not going to be able to afford more than one or two lessons for my birthday. And honestly, I felt guilty even accepting a present like that. But they might be able to get me a pair of decent riding boots and some gloves.

There was only one way to find out.

Chapter Twenty-Two

Doctor Grace was my oncologist and she'd been with me since I'd first been diagnosed. There was a whole team of people who came and departed from my treatment, depending on what was happening, but she'd been on the whole bumpy ride right until I'd been deposited in palliative care.

Her face lit up as soon as she saw me, and she came forward and wrapped me in a big hug.

"You look amazing," were the first words out of her mouth. "You have no idea how happy I am to be able to say that. How are you feeling?"

"Great," I said and filled her in on how much better I was doing. She examined the healing scars on my neck and stomach from my last surgeries, marvelled over how my hair was slowly growing back, and then gave me another tight hug.

"Well, your test results are fantastic right now so we're keeping our fingers crossed. I think we'll requisition more blood-work today just in case, but as long as it looks clear, I'd say you can stay away from this place for a couple of months at least. We can widen out the time between appointments and tests the longer you're clear. How does that sound?"

"Great," I said again and then stiffened when she suddenly reached down and picked up my hand, turning it over and examining my blistered palms.

"Wow, what happened to you? Have you been rock climbing or something?"

"Er, gardening?" I said, half-telling the truth.

"Oh, well, good for you. Having an active hobby is a great idea. Just take it slow and don't overdo it. Give your body a chance to rebuild itself. And maybe get some gloves."

"I've got some now," I said quickly, "but, it's okay if I keep doing it? It won't hurt me?"

Dr. Grace tilted her head to one side, studying me carefully.

"I mean," I said, "sometimes it's hard work and there's a bit of er, digging and lifting. That won't slow down my healing, right?"

"No, I think as long as you go slow then you'll be okay. Listen to your body, don't work to the point of exhaustion, and make sure you make good food choices and stay hydrated. Beyond that, just go out and have some fun. Honestly, after all you've been through you deserve it."

I left the office glowing with happiness, allowing myself to feel the first sparks of hope I had in a long time.

If my mom had been there, she would have started grilling me the second I walked out of the exam room; actually, she would have insisted on being glued to my side during the whole appointment, but my dad's style was, thankfully, more laid-back. He sat in the waiting room, with his chin resting in one hand and an open book in his lap.

"Good news, Mr. Connor," Dr. Grace said, gliding out of the room behind me and moving behind the small reception desk. "Besides doing a little too much gardening, Breanna is looking pretty darn good."

My dad looked up with a smile and shut his book, rising to his feet.

The printer whirred and a couple of sheets of paper spat out, and Dr. Grace went over to grab them.

"Here," she said, handing the papers to me. "Take these to any lab. I'll call you as soon as all the results have come in. Hopefully, we only have to see each other for social visits and not these pesky medical appointments."

We all laughed and my dad draped his arm over my shoulder as we headed back to the car.

"Congratulations," he said, his voice thick with emotion. "I'm so happy for you. For all of us. But, what was that she said about gardening?"

"You heard that, hey?"

"Yes, and I saw the state of your hands. I'm surprised your mother hasn't interrogated you about that yet. You're lucky she's been distracted."

"Yeah, Angelika's been good for something. Um, I've just been doing some weeding." Not a complete lie.

"I see. But not at our place?"

"No, not at our place. Okay, fine, I'll tell you, Dad. But this is just between you and me, okay?"

"I don't know, Bree, I don't like hiding things from your mother."

"Right, well, how about you just don't bring it up unless she asks? You don't have to keep it a secret forever. I just want it to be *my* thing right now, without anyone interfering or worrying."

"Okay, I get that. So, tell me about it."

While we drove, I started at the very beginning. I told him about that first, life-altering, dream in the hospital, about meeting Gretta and Lorne, and my growing interest in horses.

I told him about Lorne tracking me down, and about going to meet Bear, and about starting riding, and about Nipper's funny personality.

Mostly, I tried to convey how magical it was being around the horses and how the hard work didn't bother me because it made me happy.

"Well, that's all that matters, Bree. You deserve to be happy, that's all we want for you."

"So you won't tell Mom?"

"I'm not exactly sure why you'd want to keep it a secret, but I guess I understand you wanting to do your own thing."

Perfect.

I'd done my research and had discovered that the tack store Lorne had told me about happened to have an old-fashioned diner right next to it. The half-plan that I'd formulated the night before was to eat and then just oh-so-casually suggest that we check out that horse store next door. Just for fun. Now, I didn't have to be subtle, so I pointed it out on our way into lunch.

"Since lessons are so expensive, I thought maybe my birthday present could be a pair of riding boots or gloves instead."

"Well, I might be able to donate to the cause," my dad said, "if it's what you want."

We spent the rest of lunch talking about other things. Since Dr. Grace had reminded me how important eating healthy was to keep my body strong, I virtuously ordered my grilled cheese with a salad on the side instead of fries and skipped dessert.

Finally, it was time to do some shopping.

"You go ahead," my dad said, handing me a wad of twenty-dollar bills. "I'll wait in the car while you do your thing. I promised your mother I'd call and tell her how the appointment went anyway."

"Thank you," I said, hugging him tightly. Turning on my heel, I pulled open the door to the shop.

The first thing that hit me was the most delicious smell. A potent mixture of leather, polish and cleaner, and sweet molasses horse treats. The second thing that hit me was a small, lean Border Collie puppy, all claws and fur and lolling tongue. It hit me square in the chest with all four paws out.

I staggered backward, barely stopping myself from falling.

"Oh, my gosh, down, Indie, down. I'm so sorry."

The little dog dropped to the floor, crouching and wriggling, its eyes fixed on my face as if it wanted nothing more than to leap up and lick me again.

"I'm so, so sorry," the girl said again, coming out to grab the dog by the collar and half-drag her behind the counter. "She's only five months old, I usually keep her contained back here but it's been a slow afternoon so I let her out. Are you okay?"

"I ... I think so," I said, adjusting my bandanna self-consciously on my head to cover my partial baldness. I resisted the urge to check the scar on my stomach. It was throbbing but I didn't see how she could have done any real damage through my clothes. I could still feel the spots on my arm and chest where her claws had raked me, though. And there was a stinging sensation on my neck and cheek.

"This is so embarrassing. I know just how it feels when she does that. She's all claws. Sometimes she gets so excited she'll nip your nose, too. You're lucky you missed out on that."

"Really, it's okay."

"Well, you let me know if you need any help finding anything."

I nodded, shrugged off any lingering pain, and stared around the vast store in amazement. How could riding horses require this much *stuff*?

There was an entire wall devoted to just bridles in every shade of brown imaginable and a row of black ones as well. Beside the bridles was a whole bunch of leather gear and accessories that I didn't even recognize.

There was a huge section of beautifully coloured saddle pads, some with braided trim or sparkles or with fluffy sheep-skin attached.

I have so much to learn, I thought, feeling a little overwhelmed. *I have no idea what half of this stuff is for.*

"Is there anything in particular you're looking for?" the woman asked, as she passed by with some leather halters over one arm.

"Well, I need boots," I said slowly.

"Sure, we have those. Field boots, dress boots, paddock boots, muck boots?"

"Um, I was sort of thinking of the tall ones that go up near the knee and that are made out of rubber," I said slowly. I couldn't for the life of me think of what they were called. "I have a pair of short boots, but it's really muddy where I ride. And I have a pair of rubber gardening boots, but my, er, instructor says they are not that great for riding."

"Ah, I see," she said carefully, surveying me quickly from head to toe. Clearly, she saw that I knew nothing. "Well, I'll show you what we have."

She led me to a wall full of various sizes of boots, and I could see right away that their prices ranged between somewhat affordable to very, as in more than one of my mom's paychecks, expensive. "You *could* go with the basic high rubber boots. They're the cheapest. They'll be waterproof and look the part from a *distance,* but they'll be cold in winter and they're not very flexible. And you won't be able to show in them."

She stopped and looked at me, and I bit my lip. The wad of bills my dad had handed me had seemed like a lot a few minutes ago, but now I saw that they wouldn't go very far.

"There are also these other rubber boots here that are lined and *might* be a little better for winter. And there are some budget-conscious options for paddock boots, those are the short ones here, and for synthetic tall boots. They still look stylish but are made of a sort of faux leather. And then, of course, we have lots of leather options."

"Right," I said, studying all the boots carefully and pretending not to linger on the prices. My gaze was drawn back time and again to a pair of buttery soft, brown leather boots with elegant, curved lines that flared around the calves. I could just imagine how I'd look in them with my breeches. Too bad they were over eight hundred dollars.

"Oh wait," she said suddenly, "we have a used section, too.

There are always some boots in there, but I'm not sure what sizes we have in. If you can't find something that fits, I can always take your name and number; if something comes in that's in your size then I'd be happy to give you a call."

The used section was in a little alcove and was stacked full of all sorts of things jumbled together. There were even saddles, some looking nearly new and others ancient, battered things that looked like they'd been left out in the rain.

There *were* quite a few boots, most of them leather boots that looked like their owners had dropped them off after a hard ride without bothering to clean them first.

These might polish up nicely, I thought, picking up a pair of, what I now knew to be, field boots. The laces had rotted out and the inside calves had been worn to a high-varnish. *But that still leaves the problem of all the mud at the barn.*

As beautiful as leather boots in general were, they just weren't going to be practical for a whole muddy, snowy winter at Lorne's. I needed something I could hose off daily.

Right, that solves it then. I reached into my pocket and carefully pulled out my money to count it. I wasn't sure what they would come to with the taxes but I might just have enough to buy the new, cheaper, rubber boots off the shelf.

Suddenly, two rolls of leather stuffed into a back corner on a lower shelf caught my eye.

"Oooh, belts," I said out loud as I unrolled them one by one. They were both made of buttery soft, tooled leather, and I looked at them enviously. They were extra small which would fit me perfectly right then until I gained weight. They would be much better than using twine. But, it wouldn't be happening today. I didn't have enough for even *one* of them and the boots.

"How are we doing here?" The woman was back but her smile dropped away as she looked closely at my face. "Oh, darn it, you *do* have a few scratches on your cheek from that crazy dog. I am so sorry about that."

"Honestly, it's okay," I started to say but she waved me off.

"Tell you what, today we're having a fifty percent off sale on boots. Was there something that caught your eye?"

"Oh, wow, really? You don't have to do that, I'm fine."

I followed her back across the store, still holding the belts, and stared at the wall of boots with new eyes. The cheaper leather ones were now *almost* within my reach.

"Please, it would be my pleasure," she said, "it's the least I can do. And I'm always happy to help out a new rider."

"I'd like to try those ones on, please," I said, pointing to the tall rubber boots that came with the warm, winter lining. It was the right choice. As soon as I pulled them on I could feel that they fit very well, and they'd be waterproof and hold up for years to come. If I survived long enough to enter a show then I'd see about saving up for the fancier ones. Right now I needed the basic necessities.

In the end, she not only let me have half price off the boots but insisted that I should get a belt for half price, too. Which meant that I was able to get a very cheap pair of cotton gloves and was even able to buy a small bag of horse treats for Bear and Nipper.

I thanked her about a dozen times and then, just as I was about to push my way back out the door, a stack of yellow flyers caught my eye. They were piled on a plastic mounting block and it was the silhouette of a running horse that made me hesitate.

"Help yourself," the woman urged, "the seller is a local customer of ours and he's going to be very motivated to unload those horses."

"Are they racehorses?" I asked, picking up a flyer.

"Yep, well most of them will be pretty fresh off the track. He's taking a bit of a risk bringing them all over here from the mainland to sell. But he seemed pretty confident that they were good animals that would have no trouble finding new homes."

"Huh, do you mind if I take one of these?"

"Of course not. The sale is only one day, October fifteenth, tell your friends."

"Bye, and thanks again." I pushed my way outside and headed back to the car with my purchases tucked under one arm.

"Hey," my dad said, looking up from his book with a smile. "Wow, you found quite a few things."

"There was a sale," I said, leaving out the part about being attacked by an overenthusiastic dog. "Thank you so much for the early birthday present. Boots, a belt, and gloves are exactly what I needed."

"I expect you'll appreciate that more than the silver bracelet your mother was about to pick out."

"Oh, please no. No jewelry."

"That's what I thought," he said, laughing. My parents had never really known what to get me for Christmas and birthdays. Since I'd hit my teens, they'd settled on just giving me books and gift cards. I was sure he was thrilled to have finally found a useful present for me.

When we reached home, he pulled into the driveway but left the car running.

"I'll head back out and pick your mom up from work," he told me. "I'll be back in half an hour. You might want to keep your horse things somewhere ... inconspicuous, if you don't want her asking any questions."

"Thanks, Dad," I said, reaching over and giving him a one-armed hug. "You're the best."

"I hope so," he said. "And you'll take it easy with those horses and not do anything dangerous or crazy, right?"

"Yes, very easy. I will follow the doctor's orders one hundred percent."

"Right, well, I guess that's all I need to know then. You're in charge of your own life."

Almost, I thought, *at least it's starting to head in the right direction, anyway.*

Chapter Twenty-Three

✦✦✦

W hen I eagerly, but a little anxiously, presented my new purchases to Lorne the next day, he nodded approvingly and offered me a rare smile.

"You're getting pretty fancy, kid," he said, "maybe we should clean out those lockers in the tack room and find a spot for your things."

It turned out that the door at the back of the cluttered tack room led to another narrow room that was full of dusty lockers.

"Wow, there's room for so many people here."

"This barn had its share of boarders back in its day," Lorne said brusquely, "it was a bustling place. I guess it's gotten a little run down over time."

"Huh." I tried to imagine it but couldn't really see beyond the three inches of dust coating everything.

"You get this area cleaned up and you'll have a nice place to keep your stuff."

We decided to give Bear a break from exercise that day since he'd seemed a little slow last time he was out. But we brought him in with Nipper and brushed him carefully in the cross-ties, and then Lorne put him in one of the empty box stalls with a flake of soft, green hay while we went to the ring with Nipper.

I did my usual circles and serpentines and changing directions across the grassy ring, and then added in some sideways leg-yields all the while waiting for that moment when Lorne would say that it was finally time to trot.

"Okay, come on over," Lorne said. He'd moved to the center of my freshly weeded twenty-meter circle and was standing there with a long, cotton line in his hand. He clipped it onto the near ring of Nipper's bit and gave the horse a bit of carrot from his pocket.

"What's that for?" I asked, looking skeptically at the line.

"Just a bit of added control," Lorne said, which sounded a little ominous to me. What was he thinking was going to happen here?

He had me walk Nipper in a big circle around him but I kept waiting for something to go wrong so I wasn't as relaxed as usual.

"Right, well, you'd better get on with it. Give him a bit of a squeeze with both legs."

That was a bit vague but I gave Nipper a bit of a bump with both heels and was rewarded by him giving a little grunt and lurching forward into a choppy trot with his head in the air.

I was instantly thrown off balance, bouncing all over and clutching at mane, saddle, reins, whatever I could reach to make the painful jiggling stop.

"Whoa," Lorne said and brought Nipper to an awkward halt.

"That was awful," I said, wheezing as I struggled to catch my breath. There was already a stitch in my side and my lungs burned.

"Terrible," Lorne agreed, patting my leg. "You know, now is probably the time I should confess that I never had any luck teaching beginners. By the time they came to me, they were already seasoned competitors looking for some polish and expert advice. I preferred working with the horses rather than the people. Gretta had much more patience than me. Even our daughters refused to take lessons from me."

"Okay," I said slowly, "well, what would *Gretta* have told me if she was here? What did I do wrong? I'm not ready to give up yet."

Lorne looked at me thoughtfully and then moved back into the center of the circle. "She'd say that you were off-balance. Next time sink your weight right down through your legs to the balls of your feet so that you're equally weighted in each stirrup. And sit up straight. When you started trotting, you tilted forward over his neck and your legs curled up, and then you hung off the reins. You need to stretch your lower half down and your upper half up."

"Right, I can do that." I took a deep breath and sat up straighter. I felt my previously-unused ab muscles protest as I stretched upward; it wasn't like they'd had much work to do over my short life-span. But, with my posture straight and relaxed, and the rest of my weight sunk into the stirrups, I already felt more secure in the saddle. "Okay, what's next?"

"This time when you ask him to move forward, you want to be more subtle. No kicking, just a gentle squeeze. Don't worry about the reins, he's not going anywhere."

Nipper was still tense from our earlier fiasco so it didn't take more than the gentlest squeeze for him to shoot forward into a trundling trot. This time I was ready for him though, and I was able to sit his jarring trot much better than I had the first time. At least I didn't pull on his mouth.

"Now, instead of sitting, rise and fall to his rhythm, find the tempo and flow with it."

Posting, I remembered from my late-night reading. There was something about diagonals that I was supposed to know too, but right then I just did my best to raise and lower myself in sync with Nipper's trot to avoid getting bumped around.

"Am I doing it right?" I asked breathlessly.

"Are you bouncing all over the place?"

"No?"

"Then you must be doing okay. Now take a walk break and we can try the opposite direction."

It took a while for my lungs and heart to slow to their normal speed.

"What about the diagonals?" I asked once I'd stopped gasping for air. "Aren't I supposed to pay attention to his shoulder or something?"

"Let's not worry about that today. We don't want to muddy the water with too much theory. Are you ready for the other direction?"

"Yes," I said, but I was still thrown off balance when Nipper lurched into another trot.

Remember to control your breathing, the thought appeared out of nowhere and I automatically sucked in a ragged breath. My lungs expanded greedily and I naturally fell into that breathing ritual I'd had in the hospital. Inhale. Hold. Exhale. Hold.

To my surprise, Nipper's ears flicked back toward me and he slowed down, dropping his head and letting out a huge sigh of his own.

"Good," Lorne called. "Whatever you're doing, keep it up."

But, I'm only breathing, I thought. I didn't dare stop or change the rhythm though; that jarring trot from earlier was not something I wanted to repeat.

By the time I'd trotted two more times in both directions, Nipper was puffing and I was ready to nap for about a hundred years.

"Good job," Lorne said, "tomorrow we'll go on another trail ride. We don't want to do too much ring work or you'll get stale."

I didn't think there'd ever be a danger of that. I loved every single thing I was learning even when it was confusing and painful. I was going to need to soak for hours in the tub to give my poor muscles a break.

I was tempted to skip the weeding after my ride but I forced myself to do it anyway.

Just one small section, I told myself. Nipper's hooves had done a good job churning up the sandy ground and the weeds came out more willingly than usual. By the time I was done, I'd managed to clear away all the edges of my twenty-meter circle and now had a large professional looking square.

"Well, would you look at that," Lorne said, "it's starting to feel pretty fancy in here. Soon you'll be wanting to fix and paint the fence and put up some dressage letters."

I looked around the falling-down ring trying to imagine what it must have been like back when it was cared for. How hard would it be to have it looking nice again?

I was so tired that I drifted off on the way home and nearly forgot to give Lorne the flyer that I'd snagged from the tack store the day before.

"Eh, what's this?" he said, squinting down at the paper as if he couldn't make out the words even though they were printed in gigantic letters.

"It's a horse sale," I explained, fighting back a yawn. "The lady at the tack store said they were all horses fresh off the track. He's shipping them to a barn here to sell. October 15th, one day only."

"Hmph," Lorne grunted and, when he didn't say anything more, I climbed out and left him staring down at the flyer.

"See you tomorrow," I called as I headed to the house but he only waved a hand vaguely in response.

Chapter Twenty-Four

❦

"You do have your driver's license, right?" Lorne asked, rolling down his window as soon he pulled into the driveway the next morning.

"Er, yes, technically I do. I haven't driven in a long time, though. Not since before I got sick."

"Perfect, hop in then."

"What?" I stared at him in astonishment as he clambered out of the driver's side and ushered me in behind the wheel. "No, I can't. I don't even remember how."

"Bah, it's not rocket science. It's just like riding a bicycle. I'll be right here if you get in trouble."

"Lorne." I crossed my arms over my chest and stared him down. "I'm not driving your car. What if I crash it? I can't pay to fix it, you know."

"Yeah, yeah, I'll worry about that if it happens. The truth is that all this driving is murder on my back and hip. I have to cut back on either riding or driving. Too bad because I thought we'd try a new trail today."

He sent me a hopeful smile.

"Okay, okay," I said, giving in. "Fine, but if we get pulled over by the police, you're taking all the blame."

Luckily, I lived on a very quiet street because it took me a few minutes to remember where everything in the car was. Like the gas, brakes, and turn signals, and a few important things like that. A few blocks down was a small plaza with a big parking lot and Lorne made me pull in there and practice some circling, stopping, and backing up just like when I was starting out riding Nipper. After twenty minutes of that, I wasn't doing quite so much lurching and we pulled out onto the road again.

Mid-morning traffic was pretty-low key but still, I stayed hunched forward, peering defensively out the windshield, gripping the wheel with both white-knuckled hands and saying fervent prayers in my head.

Once we'd reached the country roads I was able to relax a little and by the time we pulled into the barn driveway I was limp with exhaustion but a little triumphant too.

"Good job," Lorne said which was completely underwhelming considering that I'd actually gotten us there in one piece. He really had no idea how much danger he'd been in.

Nipper and Bear were already at the gate and I led them in one by one, put them in the cross-ties and gave them their carrots.

"Are you boys ready for your trail ride?" I asked them and they both pricked their ears and bobbed their heads, which I took as a yes.

I'd assumed that I'd be riding Bear on the trail, but Lorne said no, I should tack up Nipper.

Despite all the good work Nipper and I had been doing together in the ring, I was still nervous. I couldn't quite shake that image of him bucking and prancing that first day Lorne had ridden him.

You're going to have to get over that, I told myself firmly. *Nipper has been nothing but good lately.*

Still, I had to do my breathing exercises to stay calm as I slid onto his back from the mounting block. He didn't prance at all, just turned around once to bump my boot with his nose, and then headed toward the trail of his own accord.

"Wait for Bear," I said nervously, circling back to where Lorne was still adjusting his stirrups. Bear blinked a little in the morning sunshine, his lower lip drooping as he settled in for a quick nap.

And then we were off with me and Nipper leading the way. His head bobbed excitedly with every step, his ears were pricked and he appeared to be enjoying himself much more than in the ring. I could feel the soft vibration of him mouthing the bit through the reins.

The sun was warm on my face and Nipper's footfalls thudded rhythmically on the hard ground.

"Okay, you can trot back to us," Lorne called, and I swiveled around in surprise to see that we'd now left them very far behind.

I felt a shiver of excitement. My first trot on my own.

"Come on, Nipper," I said, "just like in the ring." Only it wasn't, it was so much better. Nipper floated across the ground back toward Lorne and Bear, his neck arched and his powerful hindquarters propelling us along. It was like flying. We got there in about a minute, and I was a little clumsy getting Nipper to walk, his head shot up and his ears went back.

"Sorry," I told him, running a hand down his neck.

"Nice forward trot," Lorne said approvingly, "you moved with him very well. Next time less hand when you stop. Think about slowing him down gradually from much further back, like a snowflake drifting to the ground."

"Okay, I can do that." Despite accidentally pulling on Nipper's mouth, I thought my first solo trot had been pretty successful.

It didn't take us long to get far enough ahead to turn around and try it again. This time, though I still lost myself in the amazing feeling of going forward, I also stuck to the plan of gently asking him to slow down without pulling. We were walking by the time we'd reached Lorne and Nipper seemed much happier about the whole thing.

"That was acceptable; so much is about pre-planning with horses. You want to set yourself, and them, up for success. You'll figure it out eventually. Now, I think Bear and I are going to stop here to do some grazing. You two go on ahead as far as you like and turn around when you're ready. Meet me back here in twenty minutes."

"Yes, sir," I said laughing, because he sounded like an old army sergeant or something.

Nipper was only too eager to keep going and when we reached the woods, he picked up the pace a little, flickering his ears back at me a few times as if waiting to see what I'd do.

"You want to go faster, don't you?" I said. "Well, I guess a little bit of trot in this direction won't hurt."

I tentatively brushed my calves against his furry sides and that was all the signal he needed to spring forward into that rollicking trot again. It was a mixture of terrifying and fantastic all rolled into one, a little bit too fast, a little bit of out of control but also exhilarating and I never wanted it to stop.

Nipper must have felt the same way because he kept rolling steadily along, snorting softly under his breath as we thudded up the trail.

"Okay, Nipper, we'd better walk, I need a break," I said, leaning forward a little to catch my breath. My lungs were working overtime. But apparently leaning forward was some sort of signal to him because his swaying trot changed to something else; a smooth rocking-horse canter.

Wow, I am totally cantering, I thought with a mixture of pride and fear, *and I don't have a clue how to stop him.*

He seemed like he'd just keep on cantering forever if I didn't do something, so I tentatively took a light feel of the reins and sat up, sinking my weight down.

Drift like a snowflake to a walk, peacefully and slowly, I thought and, after a moment's hesitation, and probably because he was just out of shape and tired, he actually did what I'd asked.

"Oh, good boy, Nipper," I said gratefully, leaning down to hug him around his neck, "you are such a good boy."

I let myself stay draped over his neck for a few minutes, gasping and waiting for my poor body to recover. Finally, I sat up.

"We'd better get back, Nipper, we've been gone for ages." This time we walked the rest of the way back, both of us needing the extra time to cool down and catch our breaths.

"How was it?" Lorne asked, taking in my flushed face and the dried sweat on Nipper's chest. He was still perched on Bear who'd fallen fast asleep with a big clump of half-dead grass hanging out of his mouth.

"Good," I said, not ready to tell him what had happened. I needed some time to process it on my own. "Nipper took care of me out there."

I threw my heart into weeding that afternoon and managed to get the entire upper half of the ring cleared.

Half down, half to go, I thought proudly. I hoped I could get it done before winter set in. The last two weeks we'd been lucky. There hadn't been any rain and the brisk fall air had been crisp but with no promise of snow. I would love to try cantering Nipper in the ring.

That night, when I was curled up in bed, I wrote a list of all the things that I had questions about. *How do I know if I'm posting on the right diagonal? Does it hurt the horse when I'm on the wrong one? How do I ask for a canter? How do I ask for the canter to stop?* I had so many questions and Lorne wasn't really big on explaining things.

"You just need to learn by doing," he'd told me when I started to pour out all my questions to him the other day. But that was easier said than done. Making a mistake often meant accidentally hurting Nipper. There must be a way for me to improve more quickly than this.

I pulled my laptop into bed with me and fired it up. The first step was to do some homework.

Chapter Twenty-Five

The next day, Lorne made me drive the car to the barn again and then we had another trail ride.

Luckily Nipper was tired from all the excitement from the day before and was happy just to walk and trot. This time, when I posted, I leaned far forward over the saddle and looked down to see which of his shoulders was coming back when I rose out of the saddle and which front leg was stretching forward.

So if I pretend that his right side is the outside rein then I should be rising when he stretches that front leg forward. I sat for two beats and then rose again. Then switched for two beats and matched my posting to the other side. Did it matter which one I rode on when I was out on the trail? Nipper didn't seem to care one way or the other.

"I have a surprise for you," Lorne said, once we'd cooled the horses down and put them away. "Well, I have a surprise and a proposal."

"Er, what?" I said, looking at him in horror. In my head, I had the sudden image of him pulling at out a ring and creakily dropping to one knee.

"A *business* proposal," he corrected quickly, "good grief, don't look at me like that. I'm old enough to be your grandfather. Just come out to the ring. Your surprise is there."

I grabbed my weeding tools and hurried out to the riding arena, stopping dead in my tracks when I was halfway there.

Not only had the rest of the weeds been pulled from the ring, but the broken boards had been replaced with new ones and the posts had been straightened so the long side didn't sag anymore. Then the ring had been raked flat. It actually looked pretty respectable.

"Wow, my weeds are gone," I said, joy mixed with a little disappointment. It had been *my* project and it was a little annoying to have it taken away so suddenly, just when I was making real progress.

"Julie's son was home and she asked him to run the rototiller through here and fix the worst of the boards. Then she pulled out the old chain harrow for the ring. We'll have to drag it every few weeks now if we're going to use the ring steadily."

"It looks amazing," I said honestly.

"Yep, Julie was hoping you might be able to get the fence painted before winter comes. She left some cans of paint and some brushes in the tack room."

That fixed my mood instantly. A new project to start on was exactly what I needed.

"I can start that right now," I said happily and turned toward the barn, ready to check out my supplies.

"Slow down, you still need to hear about my proposal ... er, I mean project," Lorne said, falling into step beside me.

"What project?" I asked, slowing down so he could keep up.

"Well, you know I made some promises to Gretta before she passed. I think she talked to you about her October horses project."

"Right, the end-of-season racehorses. I remember."

"Well, I thought that maybe you'd help me with one last venture, in memory of Gretta. I'm not getting any younger, but I bet that I have one more horse in me if you're able to help. It would be a project horse to sell, of course. There's no guarantee of much money in it, but we could share the profits if there are any."

"Oh, that sounds amazing," I said, taken with the idea right away, "but I could only help with time. I don't have any money to help buy a horse."

"Oh, you leave that part to me. I'll worry about the money."

"I'm in," I said and we laughingly shook hands to seal the deal.

"Great, I'll pick you up tomorrow morning at six-thirty. We need to be at the sale barn early."

"Wait, what? We're going tomorrow?"

"That's when the sale is. No time like the present, I say. Now get to work on that ring."

The day was unseasonably warm, just like the entire autumn had been; it was like the whole season had done its best to stay warm and beautiful just for me. It was the loveliest fall I'd remembered seeing in my life.

The paint cans were in the tack room, along with brushes, a stir-stick, and some plastic bags to try and keep things clean. A few years ago I'd spent weeks helping my dad to paint the entire basement when he'd set up his model room so I knew a little about painting. I found an old hoof-pick so I could loosen the lid on one of the paint cans and carried everything back to the ring.

When I reached the gate, I paused to admire the smooth surface and the repaired boards once again. It really did look amazing.

"Do you like it?"

I whirled around to see a boy, not much older than me, coming down the hill from the house. He had black hair and dark eyes, and his skin was deeply tanned as if he'd just come from somewhere tropical.

He must be Julie's son, I thought, studying him as he came toward me.

I realized I was staring and that I hadn't answered his question.

"Yes, I love it," I said quickly, feeling my cheeks flush. "How did you do it so fast? The weeding was taking me forever."

"Mom rented a tiller and we dug up all the weeds, and I then I found the chain-harrow stuffed in a shed under about a ton of dirt, and I dragged the ring flat once it was weeded. It looks good, doesn't it?"

"It looks wonderful," I said honestly.

"My mom wanted to surprise you," he said, "she saw how hard you were working on it and she wanted to thank you for spending time with Nipper."

"Oh, that was so nice of her. But I should be the one thanking *her*," I protested. "She's so nice to let me ride Nipper. I would have told her myself but Lorne said ..."

"Yeah, she prefers not to socialize."

There was an awkward pause.

"I'm Breanna," I said finally.

"Yeah, I know. I'm in one of your dad's classes actually, he's a great guy. I'm Nicholas."

"Nice to meet you. Is it a History or English class? He teaches so many I can hardly keep up."

"Civilization Collapse in a Modern Context."

"That sounds cheery. How did you know I was his daughter?"

"He was talking to one of the horsey girls and asking her about places his daughter could take lessons. Then he mentioned that you were helping out with some senior horses with Lorne and I put two and two together."

"Oh, he wanted to get me lessons for my birthday. I mean, extra lessons besides all the ones Lorne's been giving me. I was never going to stop riding Nipper and Bear."

"Don't worry, I get it. Did you find a place?"

"No, they're really expensive. Besides, I'm learning lots here."

"My mom used to teach lessons, you know. She was really good."

"Really? Why did she stop teaching?"

He paused and looked down at the ground, digging the toe of his boot into the sand.

"Did Lorne tell you anything about the accident?"

"Not really. He said that your mom had been hurt and that afterward she didn't want to be around people anymore. She preferred horses."

Nicholas laughed. "She probably always preferred being around horses. But, yeah, we were all in a car accident when I was just a kid. My mom was hurt badly and my dad, well, he didn't make it out of the hospital."

"Oh my gosh. I'm so sorry about your dad. I didn't know. Were you hurt?"

"Not really. I mean, I broke my arm and some ribs, but that was nothing compared to losing my dad and having my mom so wrecked."

He took a deep breath and shrugged.

"Sorry, I don't know why I said all that. I rarely talk about it."

"No, that's okay, I don't mind. I've spent a lot of time in the hospital. I get it."

"Yeah," his eyes flicked up toward the teal bandanna I'd tied around my head that morning. My hair was actually starting to grow in, but I wore the things out of habit and because it was way too cold out to be even partially bald. "I remember your dad mentioning you were sick last year."

"He did?" I felt a flicker of irritation. I'd never enjoyed being talked about.

"He didn't give details or anything. I think he had to miss a bunch of classes when you were ... er ... not doing so well."

"Yeah," I sighed. "They both had to miss so much work. I feel awful about that. They nearly had to remortgage the house."

I broke off suddenly and looked away. Now it was my turn to

be embarrassed about saying too much. There must have been something in the air.

"Come on," Nicholas said, "I'll show you where the harrow lives and how to use it. You should rake the ring at least once a week to keep the footing conditioned."

"Okay, thanks. How do you know all this stuff?"

"I grew up in the horse world. I know things." He sent me a grin.

We walked up past the ring toward a little cluster of small buildings on the right.

"Did you ever ride?" I asked.

"A little, when I was a kid. My parents bought me a pony before I was even born so there were some pretty heavy expectations that I'd be a rider, too."

"Lucky. What happened?"

"There weren't any traumatic events or anything, I just preferred to do other things."

"Like what?"

"Oh, reading, science experiments, doing homework."

"A bit of a nerd, hey?" I said teasingly

"More than a bit, I'd say."

"Did my dad tell you about his models? The ones he builds in the basement."

"Of course, everyone knows about those. He's famous."

"Right," I shook my head, amazed again at what weird things people could be famous for.

"What degree were you working toward when you were in school?" he asked.

"Um, well, English. It was sort of just one of those things I enrolled in because I didn't know what else to do with my life. I liked to read a lot so it seemed like my least boring option. In hindsight, I should have just worked or travelled until I knew what I wanted to do. How about you?"

"I'm going to teach, like your dad. I've always wanted to do that."

"I'm always amazed when people are born knowing what they want to do with life. My sister is like that."

"You have a sister?"

"Yes," I said incredulously. "My dad didn't talk about her? She's a legitimately famous musician ... or starting to be, at least. She's on her first tour right now."

"Oh," he said, looking impressed, "no, he didn't mention it. Only you."

Hmm, that gave me pause. When had life become so polarized in our house? For as long as I could remember, Dad had been on my side and Mom on Angelika's. Was it because my dad and I both preferred to quietly read books and talk about ideas while my mom and sister were naturally more outgoing? Or was it because my mom had spent so much time ferrying Angelika around to all her classes that they had just naturally gravitated together?

I hadn't realized how much it had been like two families living side by side in the same house instead of all four of us being a big family unit. Had it been that way even when we were small?

Nicholas threw open the shed door and I blinked in the dim light.

"There she is," he said, pointing to an old green lawn mower that had seen better days. "Can you drive one of these?"

"I'm sure I can learn," I said, looking at it doubtfully.

"It's easy, here, I'll show you."

He quickly went over how to start the ancient thing and showed me where the key hung on a nail just inside the door. I was pretty sure I could figure it out when I needed to.

"The harrow is already hooked up to it so you just have to drive it out, drag the ring, and put it away. And in the summer you can mow the lawn afterward."

"Ha, ha," I said and was rewarded by a stellar smile that lit up his whole face.

He had to leave after that, which was unfortunate because I had enjoyed being around someone my own age for the first time in forever. Especially someone so easy to look at.

"I'll make sure to drop in and check out your progress on the fence," he said, giving me a salute with one hand as he walked back up the hill.

I have a new friend, I thought happily as I opened the first paint can and got to work on the arena fence. My days just kept getting better.

Chapter Twenty-Six

I'd taken my breeches and boots home with me the night before so I could be all dressed and ready to sneak out first thing in the morning, as soon as the alarm went off. I hadn't dared to make coffee or eat breakfast at the risk of making too much noise, but I had stashed apples and granola bars in my pockets for breakfast, and I'd packed a lunch so that at least I wouldn't starve.

The air was much chillier before dawn and I slipped on a heavy coat, a hat, and gloves so I could wait outside.

I'd told Lorne to park down the street so that the rumbling car didn't wake up my parents on their day off but I wasn't sure if he entirely bought it.

I'm spending a day with a friend, read the note I'd left on the counter, *I'll be back this afternoon.*

It wasn't a total lie. But it would be enough to keep my mom from panicking for at least a few hours.

As soon as I saw the headlights, I trotted down the driveway and met him a few doors down from ours.

The car smelled fragrant with coffee when I slipped inside.

"I didn't know what you wanted so I got you a double-double, a box of muffins and some donut holes," he said, grinning at me from under his cap.

"Perfect, thank you," I said, practically inhaling the first sip. "I owe you, big time."

"Just pick us out a good horse today and you don't owe me anything."

"Me?" I said, nearly choking on my coffee. "I hope you're not relying on me to pick out a winner. I literally know nothing about horses."

"You know more than you think," he said, looking amused. "But don't worry, I'll be there to help you."

Slightly reassured, I filled myself with coffee and muffins for the rest of the trip and wondered what sort of morning we were in for.

Our destination was about an hour away and, being toasty warm and full of food, I was nearly half-asleep when we made the sudden left-hand turn up a long, manicured driveway. The sun was just up but I could make out immaculate white-board fencing running for miles on both sides of us. Up ahead was a hulking building lit up from within, light spilling out two huge doors into the parking lot. Another truck pulled in behind us and I could see a few people milling around.

"Hopefully we won't have to get in a bidding war with anyone," Lorne said, frowning through the windshield. "Remember, we're not looking for anything fancy. Those will go quick enough. We're searching for an overlooked diamond in the rough here. Some of these horses look like nothing until they mature and it takes a practiced eye to sort out what's a young horse that needs more time to grow and what's just a badly conformed horse that will stay that way forever."

"Okay," I said, licking my lips nervously. I already felt like I would be way out of my league here.

"Don't worry, if we don't see anything we like today, then we'll try somewhere else. The only reason there's so much interest in this lot is that they're all here in one place to look at. People like it when they don't have to go searching. Now, come on."

The cold air hit me as soon as the door was open and I shivered, despite my winter coat.

An overly-large, unsmiling man with slicked-back black hair appeared in front of us, blocking our way. He looked like he could have been a bouncer or a hitman at some mafia bar, and I shrank back a little when his gaze settled over me. Lorne, however, had a completely different reaction.

"Riley Hennington," he said happily, and the man's face lit up with a smile, transforming him into a lovable teddy-bear of a man.

"Lorne, you old dog," he said, slapping Lorne on the shoulder, "there must be some good horses here if you crawled out of the woodwork. What do you have your eye on?"

"Oh, just looking, just looking," Lorne said. "This young lady here was hoping for a bit of dressage prospect."

I am? I thought incredulously and stood up straighter, hoping to look the part.

"I didn't know you were still teaching. Good on you. I was so sorry to hear about Gretta; you know how much she meant to the community."

"Thank you," Lorne said, the smile slipping from his face. He cleared his throat a few times.

"Well, they've just set up the coffee," Riley said quickly, "so go in and have a look around. The horses only came in last night, you understand, so some of them are a bit unsettled. There's ten here and Brandon says he has some leads on a few more on the mainland if you don't like what you see. You're early enough that nobody's bought anything yet, though Tansy's eyeing up the big grey so I wouldn't get in her way. Give us a shout if you need anything."

"Will do," Lorne said, steering me toward what I now realized was a big indoor arena.

This is my very first time at an indoor, I thought, *I'm just ticking off the milestones this month.*

They'd set up the inside of the ring with a group of ten portable, metal stalls that were just made of fencing panels linked together. Each small stall had been set up with a hay net and a water bucket and inside each stood what was potentially our new horse.

I stood there trying to look calm and professional when all I wanted to do was start jumping up and down like a little kid squealing. Instantly, I wanted to take them all home.

Even from this distance, I could tell that every one of them was beautiful. Their coats shone under the artificial lights and their huge eyes surveyed us with a variety of expressions ranging from bored to terrified. Some of the horses were eating quietly while others paced up and down, and one angry one at the far end banged it's hoof against the bars repeatedly with a terrible, clattering sound until somebody bellowed at it to stop.

A few of the horses were being led around the outside of the ring, including a giant grey horse that I guessed was the one Riley had been talking about earlier. A blonde woman stood off to one side watching it walk up and down with a smooth, measured stride. Her gaze lingered on it hungrily.

"She should buy it," Lorne said, giving the big animal a passing glance, "but that's out of our league. I'm going to go say hello to a few friends, you check those horses out and see if anything catches your eye."

I watched him walk away, the weight of responsibility pressing down my shoulders. What did I know about choosing horses? What if I bought a lemon?

Well, I could pick out which ones look friendly, I thought, *that's a start.*

Slowly, starting on the left and working my way to the right, I moved from stall to stall, studying the horses carefully from about ten feet away. I could rule the big grey out right away since Lorne said he wasn't for us, and the chestnut that flattened her ears and snapped her teeth at me was off the list, too. The bay at the end who kept pacing and pawing the bars could be scratched off the list, so that made seven left.

I went back to the first stall and worked my way through them again. The two that were nervously pacing I could probably eliminate, although who knew if they were just unsettled in their new surroundings or if that was their true personalities? That left five that seemed calm.

What about this one? I thought, stepping forward to where a smaller bay with a white star on his head was watching me quietly while he ate his hay.

Aces are High, a sign on his door read. *Four starts, zero wins. Retired sound.*

"Hey, boy," I said softly, leaning on the bars, "Do they call you Ace? Are you friendly?"

He pricked his ears and whickered softly, reaching his nose out and then hobbling a few steps toward me.

Oh, he's lame, I thought, my heart sinking. I looked him over carefully until I thought I saw the problem. His one back leg was puffy and he was reluctant to put any weight on it when he came over to lip gently at my sleeve.

"That's too bad you're hurt, buddy," I told him, reaching out to scratch him gently behind his ear. "You look like a nice boy."

He was a little on the smaller side and he wasn't quite as shiny as the other horses. He had a fluffier coat and looked younger and less well-muscled than his companions. He reminded me a little of Bear, actually; a steady character who would be a good friend. His dark, kind eyes seemed to look right into my soul.

"Sorry, Ace," I said, pulling myself away reluctantly. "I don't think Lorne would want me to pick a lame horse, no matter how nice you are. We have to be practical."

I forced myself to move down the row of stalls again and not look back. Surely, there would be a sound horse here that spoke to my heart as much as the little bay did.

Where did this one come from? I thought, stopping in front of a light chestnut with a huge, white blaze down the center of its face. He blinked at me calmly and took a bite of hay.

Oh, right, he'd been one of the frantic pacers that I'd scratched off my list a few minutes ago. Now he looked like a completely different horse. A woman stood in front of his stall, looking him over carefully, a gleam in her eye.

I skirted around them and went on to the next horse. This one was a bored-looking grey who didn't look up from his hay.

"How's the horse hunting going?" Lorne asked, coming up behind me, beaming. He looked completely in his element here; there was a definite spring in his step.

"It's very hard," I said in frustration. "I'm terrible at this."

"Nothing caught your fancy?"

"Well, yes, but his back leg is swollen and he's limping. The sign said he retired sound, though."

"Hmm." Lorne shrugged. "These guys literally just came off the track so you're going to get some bumps and swelling some-times that pops up. Let's take a look."

I led him back to the little bay, feeling a surge of hope. Maybe this horse really would be the one.

"Hey there, son," Lorne said, slipping inside the metal gate and shutting it carefully behind him. "Let's see what you have going on."

He took a moment to pet the bay, running his hands over his neck, shoulders and back, probing for any sign of tenderness. Then he ran his hand carefully down the swollen hind leg, frowning as he felt the area just above the hoof.

"Well, is he okay?" I asked anxiously.

"Hmm." He frowned and shook his head. "Hard to tell until the swelling goes down. Or without an X-ray. Something is going on in there. Maybe just soft-tissue damage, maybe not. Maybe he even got a knock on the trailer ride over."

"Is an X-ray expensive? What will happen to him if we don't buy him?"

"Now, now, don't let your heart lead your wallet too much. We don't want to buy trouble when there are plenty of sound horses out there. He's undersized and he doesn't seem to have much of a spark to him, even if he is decent-looking. Let's look at these other horses first."

I groaned inwardly and followed him down the line. I was glad that he moved past the chestnut ear-pinner quickly, at least we agreed on avoiding *that* one.

"Well now, you're interesting," he said, looking at the bright bay mare at the end. She lifted her head and stared at him boldly, her nostrils flaring slightly.

"Oh no, you should have seen her before," I said, trying to guide him back to the other horses, "she was banging on the bars like a crazy thing until somebody yelled at her. She looked scary."

"Well, let's see what she's like up close." Lorne was running his gaze over her with a particular glint in his eye that made me think that this might be a done deal.

Please let there be something wrong with her, I thought uncharitably and then instantly felt guilty. A true horse person should love all horses, shouldn't they? But the little dark bay seemed so much nicer than this bossy-looking mare.

The horse stood still and didn't make a fuss while Lorne stepped in and ran his hands carefully over her.

She stood stalk-still, every muscle in her body tense but unmoving, as he examined her legs and feet.

Even though she was well-behaved, I didn't like the look in her eye at all. She wasn't relaxed like Ace was, she gave the impression that she was a predator, just waiting for her moment to attack.

She didn't hurt Lorne though, she waited until he'd stepped

back through the gate before she flattened her ears and then suddenly, without warning, launched herself at the unsuspecting horse stabled beside her.

There was the sound of groaning metal as the fence panel between the two horses shuddered under the impact of her hitting it full-force.

The poor horse beside her, one of the nervous pacers from earlier, sprang away from her outstretched jaws just in time and pressed himself up against the far wall of his stall, trembling and whinnying anxiously.

"Hey, stop that," someone yelled at her, but she'd already turned away and went back to her hay like nothing had happened. She looked pretty pleased with herself, actually.

"Oh, she's got loads of personality," Lorne said, smiling. He took a look at the tag on the door and laughed. "Enter the Dragon. That seems appropriate somehow. She's brave and she knows who she is. I like her. Let's find out what they're asking for her."

Oh, no, I thought, my heart sinking. I really didn't like this horse. I couldn't see myself enjoying brushing her or ever riding her. She would never be a friendly horse like Bear ... or like Ace.

"Hey, Brandon," he said loudly, to a tall, thin man who was hovering at the edge of the crowd, "we'd like to see this one move out and also the little lame bay down at the other end."

The man hurried forward quickly. "Lorne, none of these guys are lame. They all checked out, sound."

"Sure, sure, the limping one with the puffy ankle then. Let's see this Dragon trot out first."

Brandon looked at her and grimaced. "She's a bit of a handful," he admitted, "she's still jacked up from the track. Here, I'll get a groom to trot her out for you."

"Just bring her out and trot her around a few times," he said casually, catching the eye of a startled, young groom who looked like he'd rather enter a real dragon's den than touch that horse. I didn't blame him. Poor guy.

I stood as far back as possible as he gingerly led Dragon out of her stall and began to pilot her around the outside of the ring. She wasn't exactly mean to him. She didn't bite or kick him, but she charged forward boldly, half dragging him through the soft, arena footing, and it took all his strength to get her moving in the other direction. She flung her front legs out as she trotted, her head held high in the air. Suddenly, she let out a piercing, bugling neigh that rang out loudly across the arena, stopping everyone in their tracks.

Everyone turned to stare at her and I didn't blame them. She was magnificent in that terrifying, deadly way that a wild animal might be when it's lunging toward you. She surged forward with a burst of energy. And then the groom stumbled and went down.

To her credit, she *did* jump over him before she went tearing around the ring like a mad thing, plowing straight through the crowd at a full gallop. The poor groom held on to the lead for about thirty seconds too long before he hit the refreshment stand and sent the fancy table, the hot coffee pot, and all the cups toppling to the ground.

Half the people ran to help him to his feet and the other half concentrated on corralling the Dragon back into her cage before she could terrorize anyone else. I'd retreated out of the way to the safety of Ace's stall. Some of the other horses had gone wild with excitement over all the drama but not Ace. He just stood there, eating his hay, watching it all go down with a mildly perplexed expression on his face.

It took a while for order to be restored and for the poor groom to be whisked away to the emergency clinic to have his coffee burns, and the bleeding gash on his head, treated.

And while all the dust was settling and the arena was still in chaos, Lorne turned to me with a glint in his eye and said, "Well, I think it's time for you and I to do some horse-trading."

Not more than half an hour later we were headed down the road, following our rented horse trailer back to the farm with our precious cargo in tow.

"What an excellent morning," Lorne said to me in delight, "they practically paid us to take her away."

"Yeah," I said dryly, "I can't imagine why that would be."

Still, it had been worth it, because when Ace had lurched out of his stall, dead-lame, Brandon had made us a package deal that neither one of us could refuse. Not that I'd want to; with just one glance of those big soulful eyes, Ace had already found a permanent place in my heart.

"She's not going to hurt him, is she?" I asked anxiously, twisting my fingers together in my lap. Next to Dragon, Ace had seemed minuscule and very fragile when he'd been loaded into the trailer beside her. She took up her entire stall, a great hulking menace who'd started banging her front foot angrily on the floor of the trailer the second she'd been squashed inside.

Ace had looked very uncertain when they'd loaded him next to her and he'd shrunk as close against the far wall as possible to get away from the angry mare.

"Don't worry," I'd called to him, "it's a short ride."

Not short enough, his expression seemed to say.

The banging had slowed once the trailer started moving but, with the window rolled down, I could still hear Dragon's angry neighs every few minutes and the occasional *thunk* as she kicked the walls.

I'd breathed a huge sigh of relief when we'd finally pulled into the farm driveway.

The other horses had already been turned out for the day. We'd had one stall set up already for our new horse, but as soon as the car stopped, I ran in to get a second one prepared for Ace with bedding, fresh hay, and a water bucket.

"All right, where do you want them?" the driver said impatiently, leaning out his open window. He was a burly, bearded man named Angus who'd been nice enough to transport them for us at the last minute.

"Oh, here is fine," Lorne said, waving a hand around the muddy yard, "we'll put them in the barn for now until they settle down."

As soon as the back ramp was dropped, Dragon let both hind legs fly, snapping the chain that held the safety bar across her butt and narrowly missing Angus's face.

"Oh, really?" Angus said, his expression darkening.

Dragon shifted from side to side as if she were winding herself up for another explosion, and beside her Ace whinnied anxiously.

"It's okay, boy," I called to him, hoping that it was the truth.

"I'll unload the mare first, I guess," Angus said grimly. He went around to the little escape door in the side, fiddling with the rope. Suddenly, Dragon flew backward with a clatter of hooves, flared nostrils, and wild, rolling eyes. She truly looked like a dragon at that moment, utterly wild and very dangerous.

Angus had looped a thick chain over her nose and then back through her mouth like it was a bit. When she turned to bolt, he planted his feet and gave the lead rope one swift yank that made the chain make a loud, popping sound. Her nose flew up in the air and she shook her head once, then stood stalk-still, staring around the property as if calculating her next move.

"This one is a real pistol," Angus said, eyeing the mare distrustfully. "She needs a firm hand." He glanced sideways at the both of us and frowned. "It's not just the two of you handling the horses, is it?"

"Oh, no, we have a good team here," Lorne said, and I turned to look at him with raised eyebrows. He didn't quite meet my eye.

"Okay, because this here is a *lot* of horse. If you want my advice—"

"She can go in the barn there," Lorne said, cutting him off.

"... if you want my advice," Angus said again, leading the snorting Dragon inside, "she'd be better off just going for hamburgers before anyone"—and here he looked pointedly at me —"gets hurt. There are plenty of good horses out there. This is not a child's horse."

And I'm not a child, I thought angrily, resenting the fact that I looked about twelve years old for the millionth time.

"I won't be handling her," I said quickly, before he could carry on giving advice, "Ace, the gelding, is my project."

But suddenly, I wondered exactly who *would* be handling Dragon every day. Was Lorne going to get dragged around the property on the end of her lead rope like the groom had been? Did he even know what he was doing?

"Well, that other horse might be all right ... if you can get him sound, that is. If you'd like my advice—"

I hurried after him to the trailer to retrieve Ace.

Angus backed the little gelding carefully off the trailer and handed me the lead-rope. From the barn we could hear the sound of Dragon already pawing the side of her stall angrily, her rumbling neigh echoing across the landscape. Angus shook his head.

"Some horses just don't deserve a second chance," he said ominously, "this world is full of good horses out there looking for homes. No need to waste time on ... well, a mare like *that*. Best of luck, though. Give us a call if you need anything."

And with that, he hopped back in his truck and lurched the rig down the driveway without a backward glance.

"All right, Ace," I said, stroking his thin neck gently. His eyes were wide and his mouth was pinched shut. He trembled a little as he stared around the property, looking like a lost little kid who had been deposited in a new school all on his own.

He pressed close to me as I led him to the barn, blinking a little when he walked inside.

Dragon was at the nearest edge of her stall, her ears flicking nervously in all directions. She grabbed a mouthful of hay and paced to the far side, staring out the back door to the lower pasture where she could just see all the senior horses gathered at the gate, excited to get a glimpse of the new intruders.

She held her head high and let out a piercing whinny that nearly made me jump out of my skin. Ace jumped too, one of his feet landing solidly on mine.

"Ow, ow, ow," I said, pushing him off me and leading him into his stall.

"Welcome to your new home, Ace," I said, slipping off his halter and stepping back to let him explore.

He circled the stall once, checked out his water bucket with a mildly suspicious snort, and then dove into his hay. I stared at him with pride; a horse of my own. Or at least a *horse-project* of my own. It all seemed like a wonderful dream and I couldn't believe how much my life had turned around in just a few short months. How could this be me?

"Well, I think I'm going to lie down for a short nap before your ride," Lorne said, yawning. "This morning has been just a little too much excitement."

I felt the same way. When Lorne hobbled into the tack room to stretch out on the couch, I shook out some extra hay at the front of Ace's stall and sat down in it, leaning my back up against the wall.

Dragon settled down a little once Lorne was gone. Her pacing slowed and I heard her splashing in her water bucket while she took a drink. Then there was just the steady sound of hay being munched between her big teeth.

"You're so handsome, Ace," I said, pulling out my phone and taking a few artistic shots from different angles.

Back in the hospital, when I'd reached my lowest point and was so sick all the time, I'd deleted all my social media accounts in a fit of depression. I'd cut myself off from the few friends I'd had left even though my counsellor had urged me not to isolate myself. It just seemed like too much effort to stay connected and I could never think of anything good to say. I hadn't felt pretty enough for selfies in a long time. And I'd assumed that people didn't want to hear from me when I was sad or sick.

But now with Ace here ... well, that was a different story.

"Everyone would want to see pictures of how handsome you are," I told him, flicking through the list of filters to see which one showed him in the best light. "In fact, maybe I'll just make you your own Instagram page so your fans can follow your progress."

In the past, I would have definitely made fun of people who made media pages just for their pets. I would have mocked them. A lot. And now here I was, living the dream. I couldn't even imagine what Angelika was going to think.

"Well, we just won't let her know we're back online, will we?" I told Ace who was now contentedly eating his hay like he'd lived here all his life. "Hopefully, she'll stay on tour for the next year and I'll have found my own place to live my life then. Somewhere far away from her. With any luck, I'll never have to cross paths with her again."

That was probably just wishful thinking. I sighed happily anyway, wondering what the next year would bring. I had told myself to just take it day by day, appointment by appointment, but with Ace here I couldn't help but plan for the future, even just a little bit.

We would heal his sore leg, and then I'd start riding him, and he'd be perfect. And we'd jump and event and do dressage and herd cows and trail ride and have all sorts of adventures.

I suddenly wished I'd brought a pen and paper because now I had the overwhelming urge to start writing again. What if I started a blog about retraining Ace? People would definitely want to read that. Or about an out-of-shape beginner learning to ride. Or about someone who was supposed to have died beating the odds, even for a short time.

Hmm, I thought, sorting through the apps on my phone. *I was pretty sure ...*

Yes, there it was. At one point in my past, when I'd been in University, I'd downloaded a writing app so that I could jot down my ideas and impressions when I was on the move. I must have forgotten to delete it.

I opened it, pausing to glance at all the old, long-forgotten, story fragments still sitting in there and then opened a new, fresh page.

Without hesitating, I began to write.

Chapter Twenty-Seven

When Lorne had bought the horses at the sale, Brandon had been very vague about their history. He'd known the few facts that were written on their cards and that was it. He didn't know what the horses were used to eating or how they liked to be handled, or if they'd ever been turned out on pasture before. He didn't know if they allergies or phobias or any likes or dislikes. We were basically starting with blank slates.

"Best to just leave them inside with hay and water today," Lorne said, once he'd woken up from his nap. "We'll figure out a feeding program for them and pasture-turnout tomorrow."

It was looking quite possible that Ace might need stall-rest or at least limited turn-out for a while. We planned to just give them some time to decompress and then reassess early the next morning.

"You don't want to go out into the cold without a blanket," I crooned to Ace, brushing his black mane for the millionth time while he calmly ate his hay. "You're already too skinny as it is."

It was hard to believe that Ace and Dragon were nearly the same age. There was only a year between them but they looked like they came from different planets.

Ace was narrow-chested with long, gangly legs and every rib showing through his rough coat. Beside him, Dragon was all strapping muscle, her wide-barrel chest and rippling haunches glistening under the dim barn lights. She looked fit and dangerous while Ace still looked like a fuzzy baby horse.

"Different trainers, different body types," Lorne said, shrugging, when I'd asked.

"But don't you think Ace is awfully thin?"

"Yep, like a greyhound dog is thin. Some horses are just like that when they're in full training. Believe me, those trainers don't skimp on food. He's probably hitting another growth spurt, too. Don't be surprised if he looks like a completely different horse next year."

I hoped so. I couldn't wait to see him once he'd fattened up and wasn't lame anymore.

That afternoon we'd brought Nipper and Bear in for their grooming session and then we'd taken Nipper to the ring for a short ride, but it was hard for either of us to concentrate.

I couldn't stop thinking about my potential future with Ace, and Nipper couldn't focus on anything but the hysterical neighing coming from the barn. The second we'd left, Dragon had thrown the mother of all tantrums.

"Will she break the barn down?" I asked worriedly as I tried to concentrate on rising and sitting to Nipper's erratic trot. He kept his head high in the air and his nose turned toward the commotion happening down below.

"Probably not," Lorne said doubtfully, "but I should check on her. I guess we'll have to cut your ride short today."

The sun went down earlier every day and it was dipping close to the horizon by the time we were ready to leave. We'd already brought in the rest of the senior horses for Julie and given them their hay.

The older horses were all very excited over the new arrivals. They arched their necks and did a bit of prancing as they had to pass Dragon while she plunged around her stall and shook her head menacingly at everyone.

But by the time we left, she was grumpily standing with her ears pinned taking out her anger on her hay net.

I hoped she wouldn't give Julie too much trouble when it was time for the late-night feeding.

My stomach growled with hunger, the lunch I'd packed was just a distant memory, and suddenly I remembered the vague note I'd left on the counter at home and the fact that I'd left my ringer off all day and had avoided looking at my messages.

I had a feeling that my secret riding habit wasn't going to be a secret much longer.

My mom was waiting outside when we pulled into the driveway, her dark silhouette backlit by the porch light. With the light behind her and her curly hair flaring in all directions, she looked like an avenging angel. By the expression on her face, I guessed that I was in for a massive lecture.

"Do you have any idea how worried I was?" she started yelling before I'd even gotten out of the car.

Oh no. She'd already worked herself up into one of her famous tempers, which usually happened when one of us had scared her. She didn't lose control very often but when she did, it was like an explosion. When she got like that there was nothing to do but let her vent. She always handed out embarrassed apologies afterwards, once she'd calmed down.

"Sorry, I know. I didn't think we were going to be this late."

"We? Who is this *we*? Where have you been? Why are you dressed like that? Why do you smell like farm animals?"

She was in full mom-meltdown, and I knew from experience

that you just had to let it run its course until she was coherent again.

"Bye, Lorne," I said, slamming my door and coming around to his window, "see you tomorrow morning. Seven o'clock."

"Are you sure?" he asked, looking doubtfully at my mom, who was busy shooting daggers at him with her eyes.

"Completely positive. I'll see you then. And thanks again. For everything."

He reached out unexpectedly and squeezed my hand and then I herded my mom toward the house and did my best to explain everything. About Lorne and Gretta in the hospital, about starting to ride, and finally, about bringing home Ace. I glossed over the part about Dragon. The less my mom knew about how dangerous horses could be the better.

It took her about an hour and a couple of glasses of wine to calm down but by the time my dad came home, she had actually started to see the humour in it.

"That poor man must think I'm crazy," she said, recalling Lorne's horrified expression. "I thought you'd run off with some boy."

"No, Mom, you seemed completely normal," I lied. "I'm sorry I didn't tell you about the horses. I just wanted it to be my own thing, you know."

"I do. You've had a hard year, you deserve some happiness. As long as you're sure it's safe."

"Oh, definitely," I said, pushing away the memory of Dragon throwing that poor groom into the snack table. "The horses are very gentle."

"That one at the horse show was very pushy," she said, shuddering a little. "I thought he was about to attack you."

"No," I laughed, "he was just being overly friendly. You should meet Bear and Nipper, though. They're both the sweetest of souls. You could even ride Bear if you wanted to."

"No, no thank you," she said quickly. "But maybe I could come to meet them one day."

"Sure, maybe next weekend once they've settled in." Hopefully, by then Dragon would look a little less ... dragonish.

Chapter Twenty-Eight

I was up well before dawn, already dressed, breakfasted, and waiting at the door when Lorne's car pulled into the driveway. It had been so nice to just make coffee and breakfast without worrying about sneaking around.

"I thought you'd never get here," I said impatiently then stopped when I saw how drawn and white his face was. "Are you okay?"

"You'd better drive today," he said weakly, "my hip is acting up a bit and I'm not feeling quite as perky as usual."

"Okay," I said slowly, trying not to show how concerned I felt. He looked awful. "Are you sure you want to go today?"

"Yes, yes," he said impatiently. "I'm not quite in my grave yet. Just drive."

He seemed a little brighter by the time we pulled into the barnyard and I stopped worrying that I would need to call the ambulance any second.

The senior horses were already outside, and Ace and Dragon were in their stalls eating their breakfast hay.

Careful, she bites, read the note stuck to Dragon's door. Presumably, Julie had found that out the hard way.

Lorne frowned and pulled the note down, crumpling it into his pocket.

"Well, lead him out and see how he feels this morning," Lorne grumbled, "then we'll figure out what to do with her highness there."

I slipped into Ace's stall and buckled on the ratty old red halter he'd arrived with.

I wonder how much a nice, used leather halter would be at the tack store? I thought as I led him out. Ace was definitely the type of horse who deserved nice things.

He followed me obediently enough, but he walked with a halting, lurching stride that was painful to watch. His leg was swollen right up to his hock now.

"Hmm," Lorne said, shaking his head, "that's not good. Tell you what, run some cold water from the hose over that leg for twenty minutes and we'll see if any of that swelling goes down."

He didn't sound that optimistic and my heart sank. I didn't have any money for a vet if Ace was really hurt. What if he needed surgery or something? Or expensive medication?

Ace grazed peacefully while I turned the hose on and carefully sprayed his leg, working my way from hock to hoof over and over again until his leg must have been numb with cold. He didn't protest though, he just swished his tail occasionally and sighed heavily from time to time while I let him graze the short, browned grass near the barn.

In the meantime, Lorne had picked out Ace's stall and was busy rooting around in the tack room. I didn't know what he was doing but there was a lot of thudding and swearing, and every once in a while, he appeared covered in dust so at least I knew he was all right.

"Okay, that's enough cold-hosing. Put him away to finish his breakfast while you ride, then we'll come up with some sort of plan."

Lorne had decided that he was too sore to ride Bear that day so, after a quick grooming session and a carrot, he put the old gelding back out in the pasture and walked slowly with me and Nipper to the ring.

Nipper was up on his toes, still excited about the new house-guests, and he shifted from side to side as I climbed on and settled myself in the saddle. Instead of walking off sedately like usual, he propelled us forward with short, prancing steps.

"He's feisty today," Lorne said with satisfaction. "No sense holding him back when he's feeling the wind up his tail. Let him move out."

"What?" I looked up from where I'd been struggling to turn Nipper in ever-decreasing circles to get him to slow down without pulling on his mouth. It was a trick I'd read in one of my horse magazines and it was sort of working.

"Move out," Lorne said, almost in a shout, "trot, canter, whatever. Just let him go forward."

"But," I said, biting my lip. The memory of my nearly out of control canter from last week was still a little fresh in my mind. I hadn't liked the feeling of being just a passenger.

"He's in a ring," Lorne snapped grumpily. "Where's he going to go?"

Nipper made up my mind for me by suddenly dragging at the reins and pulling me into a hundred-mile-an-hour trot down the long side. His nose shot up and he snorted in excitement and plunged a little to one side.

"Did he just buck?" I asked in astonishment but Lorne just laughed.

"He's playing," he said, waving a hand dismissively, "you're fine."

I didn't feel very fine. My stomach clenched, my feet were braced in the stirrups, and Nipper was rooting uncomfortably at the reins.

"Don't hold him in," Lorne barked, "give him rein and let him go."

Finally, in exasperation and mostly to prove to him that he was full of it, I loosened my death grip on Nipper's mouth and let him go. He let out one buck and then plunged forward into a canter. The first few strides were terrifying.

I'm still up here, I thought, *I haven't fallen off.* I shifted my feet in the stirrups for better balance and leaned forward, crouching down over his withers.

Nipper's ears were pricked and his joyful gallop slowed to a rocking horse canter as he powered around the ring. I realized all of a sudden that he wasn't going to hurt me, he was just enjoying himself. He wasn't bolting or rushing away from me. He was happily cantering around without a care in the world. I inched my fingers up the reins ever so gently so that I had a light contact with his mouth.

Tactfully, trying to not ruin his natural balance, I asked him to switch directions and to my surprise, he looped around and headed the other way almost as soon as I thought up the request. When we crossed the middle of the ring, he gave a little hop.

"Did he buck again?" I asked.

"Lead change." A smile tugged at his lips. "He was a well-trained fellow back in his day."

"How do you know?" I asked, gasping a little for breath. "Did you know him when he was young?"

"You sure ask a lot of questions. How about you just concentrate on your riding."

In the end, it was the greatest, and also most terrifying, ride I'd ever had on Nipper. The speed had been exhilarating but being barely in control was scary as heck. Every muscle in my body ached from clenching to stay on board and there was a stabbing pain in my side from my lungs working overtime.

I also felt like I'd been flopping all over and just guessing what to do. I wished that Lorne would give me a little more direction when I was up there. The instructors that I watched online seemed to shout instructions all the time and give helpful tips. Lorne just sort of let me fumble through on my own.

I knew he was all about the 'learning through doing' philosophy but it'd be helpful to have a *little* input now and then.

"Now it's Dragon's turn," he said gleefully as soon as we were back at the barn. And I felt my heart sink.

I took as long as I could cooling Nipper out, grooming him carefully, putting his blanket on, and turning him back out on the pasture; anything to put off handling that awful mare as long as possible.

"So," Lorne said once I'd dragged myself back to the barn. "I think that our plan is to lead her out to the ring and let her tear around in there for a while to blow off some steam. I don't trust her out with the other horses yet and the fences in the upper pasture are pretty low. She might try and jump them."

"Huh, how do you plan to get her there?"

"Well." He rubbed a hand across his stubbly chin. "I was thinking that I'd put her halter on and then attach two lead ropes, one on either side, then we can lead her together to the ring. How does that sound?"

Like we're both going to get dragged across the ground and be trampled together, I thought grimly. "Fine, I suppose we could try it. But the second she tries to attack me I'm letting go."

Lorne shot me a look and slid into Dragon's stall, crooning softly under his breath.

As soon as he was inside, she flew to the back of her stall and wheeled around to face him, moving her front feet in that weird swaying motion I'd seen her do earlier.

"There's a girl," Lorne said, not moving any closer. Gradually, her head lowered and she stopped her frantic weaving back and forth. And then she blew out a loud snort and shook herself like a dog coming in from the rain, her black mane flying around her like a halo. Then she marched forward and stuck her nose right into the halter.

What on earth was all that about? I wondered as Lorne carefully buckled her halter and clipped a lead rope on each side. He'd run a short chain over her nose and clipped it to his lead rope.

"Here," he said, handing me one of the ropes, "stay as calm as you can and don't get kicked if she bolts. She's not malicious, but she is unpredictable."

Great, I thought, grimacing as I reluctantly took the lead rope. I looked over at Ace who was calmly eating and wished that we'd just brought *him* home from the sale. He was my idea of a perfect horse. Dragon was ...

My thoughts broke off as she bolted through her open stall door, careening down the aisle with both Lorne and I bouncing along behind her. She didn't stop until she'd reached the end of the barn. As soon as her hooves hit the dirt outside, she slammed on the brakes and stood there, looking around with wild, rolling eyes, her head held impossibly high.

Her neigh was deafening and it shook her whole body from head to tail. She towered over us and I wanted nothing more than to unclip her and let her gallop away into the sunset.

"That's a girl," Lorne said, reaching up to pat her already sweat-soaked neck. He was breathing hard and I saw him wince when he took a step forward.

"Lorne, are you sure—"

"Let's just get her to the ring before she blows up."

With those far-from-reassuring words, we did our best to steer the plunging, pulling horse toward the arena. She barely noticed we were there beside her. All her muscles were coiled so hard that it was like brushing against a rock when I accidentally touched her. Sweat dripped from her face, running down her nose like water. She snorted hard with nearly every step.

"What's wrong with her?" I cried as she finally flung herself into the ring, her whole body shaking.

"Stand back," Lorne said. He reached up to unclip my lead and then, moving very swiftly for such an elderly man, he loosened the chain over her nose and set her free.

The second he stepped away from her she exploded. I had never seen anything so terrifyingly powerful. She reared straight up and then launched herself in a series of mighty bucks so high she nearly flipped herself over. Then she spun around, sliding so fast that she twisted and half-fell, her haunches scrabbling through the dirt as she flailed.

Then she was up and running so fast she was just a blur. She was across the ring in two seconds and she barely hesitated before she launched in the air and sailed over the fence like it wasn't even there. In another second she was gone, not even the thudding of hooves to prove that she hadn't been just some awful dream.

"Well," Lorne said, rubbing a shaking hand across his head. "That went worse than I'd expected."

"She's crazy," I said flatly and was rewarded with a glare.

"Gretta would *never* say they were crazy," he said firmly, "she didn't believe in that. She said they were just misunderstood and you had to learn to speak their language. That horse will come around if we are patient and if we work hard."

"Fine," I said in resignation, "but maybe you should go lie down for a little bit, Lorne. That was pretty exhausting. I'll go look for her if you like."

"Good, good." He pressed a lead rope, the one without the chain attached, into my hand and limped back in the direction of the barn, his shoulders hunched.

I sighed as I watched him go. Any more episodes like that with Dragon and he'd be laid up in bed for good. He was much too old to be handling a horse like that.

And I'm much too inexperienced, I thought glumly, climbing through the newly painted rails of the ring and trudging off in the direction the mare had gone. The trailer driver was right; somebody would get hurt if we went on like this. On the other hand, I knew Lorne had made a promise to Gretta and he was going to do his best to keep it. He'd done so much for me that I sort of owed it to him to help out.

I studied the ground as I walked but there was no sign of her, not even hoof-prints. It was like she *had* become airborne and spirited herself away.

The grassy slope beyond the ring looked gradual, but once I was on it I found that it led steeply upward and I was puffing by the time I reached the furthest edge where a clump of scraggly pine trees stood. They had been shaped by the wind over time, their trunks growing on steep angles over the valley below.

I carefully made my way through them to the edge; it would be a good vantage point to scour the lower pastures below.

I didn't see the woman until I'd nearly stepped on her.

"Oh, I'm so sorry," I said.

She was seated cross-legged right at the base of a half-dead pine, her long brown hair tied off in a braid over one shoulder.

She glanced up before looking quickly back down again. But not before I'd caught sight of the mottled scar that ran the whole length and width of her right cheek. It looked rough and pink, like an old burn mark.

Julie, I thought in astonishment. *She exists.*

She half-rose as if to leave and then sank down again with a sigh, resting her chin on her knees.

"The mare is down there," she said, gesturing toward the field below. She tucked her hand away quickly but not before I saw that it too was mottled with old burn marks.

"Great," I said unenthusiastically. From up here, we were looking down at the very back of the senior horse pasture. I hadn't realized how big it was. The herd was by the far corner and there beside them, on our side of the fence, was Dragon.

She looked much different from my safe vantage point; less scary and more like a normal, pretty horse grazing peacefully with all the rest of them.

But the illusion was shattered the second she sensed somehow

184

that we were watching her. Her head shot up, eyes wide and nostrils flaring, and she blew out a crackling snort that sounded like a car backfiring. She did it again, and somehow her wild energy infected the whole herd, and they threw their heads up too and took off like a flock of birds exploding out of a tree-top. Dragon was ahead of them all, running so fast that it almost hurt to watch her.

About a mile up, the fence jogged to the left, making a panhandle shape around the spot where the rocky slope suddenly shot upward into the small cliff we were standing on. Dragon didn't slow down, if anything she increased her speed and without even faltering she leapt the fence and charged off with the herd.

"Oh, she'll hurt them," I cried out, thinking of poor Nipper and Bear about to be mown down by that whirlwind, but Julie shook her head.

"No, I don't think she will. I was watching her graze beside them before you came. She wasn't aggressive at all; she was happy to see them. I think she is just very lonely and very unhappy."

I nodded and pulled my foot out of my rubber boot, examining the spot where my sock had slipped and my heel had been rubbed raw. These boots definitely were not made for walking; I was going to have quite the blister when I got home.

"I've seen you working with Nipper," Julie said out of the blue.

"Oh, thank you so much for letting me ride him," I said, suddenly remembering that Nipper was *her* horse and that I owed her a lot. "He's wonderful."

She smiled and it lit up her face. "I'm glad you're enjoying him. I've been watching you and he looks happy. How are your lessons with Lorne going?"

"Good," I said quickly. Maybe a little too quickly. "I'm really lucky he bothers with me. I wouldn't have done any of this on my own. I love riding here."

"Yes, he's a great man. He was never much for ring work, though; I don't think he saw much point in it. His expertise was always on the cross-country course. Gretta was the one who loved dressage."

"Oh, I didn't know that." It fit what I knew about Lorne, though. He definitely preferred to be out on the trail. "I sometimes wish that he'd give me more direction ..." I paused, not wanting to be disloyal to Lorne when he'd been so kind to me. "I feel like there are things I'm missing or don't have the answers to."

"Oh, what things?" She turned to me and I dropped my gaze to the ground so I wouldn't stare at her burn marks. They didn't even look that bad but my brief glance had shown me that the skin was mottled all down the right side of her face and neck. Her hairline was pushed back a little and the skin was shiny on her forehead. Her eyelid had an odd, stretched look, too.

"Well, um," I said, struggling to concentrate, "okay, well, I'm not really sure of the proper aids to canter. I mean Nipper just wants to go forward so all I have to do is let him go but then I read these articles that say I'm supposed to be putting one leg back and using my seat-bone and squeezing, but I'm not sure how much pressure or where to squeeze. And Nipper was doing these lead change things yesterday all on his own and it was fun and all, but I felt like, well, I felt like a passenger. I'm not sure which diagonal I'm supposed to be trotting on, and I always feel a little out of control. Like things happen and I just sort of have to go along with it. And I trust Bear and Nipper, but it would be nice if I didn't feel like they were just *babysitting* me all the time."

I paused for breath and was surprised to see that Julie was laughing.

"No wonder my son Nicholas said he liked you," she said, "you're pretty funny."

"He told you he liked me?" I said in surprise, and then instantly wished I could take the question back. "I mean, as a friend," I added, feeling my cheeks flame. Boy, I was out of practice of talking with people without sounding like an idiot.

"Yes, he gave me quite the lecture. He said you were good people, and that I should stop being rude and hiding away like some sort of hermit and come down and meet you."

"Oh, I didn't think you were being rude," I said quickly, "Lorne told me you didn't like being around people since ... well, you know."

"Still, it's no excuse. Especially when you weeded the ring and made such a good start at painting the fence, and you're being a good friend to Nipper and sweet, old Bear."

"I love spending time with them," I said honestly, "this has been the best season of my entire life."

A bugling neigh echoed across the fields and I suddenly remembered what I was supposed to be doing.

"I guess I'd better get down there and figure out a way to catch Dragon," I said glumly, trying to imagine a scenario where the mare didn't end up killing me.

"Oh, just leave her. I'll bring her in tonight with the rest of them."

"She's dangerous, though ..."

"Don't worry about it. I've handled my share of lunatic horses. I'll be fine."

I still didn't like it but it wasn't my place to argue. I'd tell Lorne when I got back to the barn and let him make the decision.

"Okay, thanks. I'll go finish painting the ring, then."

To my surprise, Julie climbed to her feet, dusted herself off, and then fell into step beside me. We walked in silence for a few minutes.

"I could help you with your flat work, if you like," she said out of the blue. "And then Lorne can take over again when you're ready to jump."

"You would do that?" I asked in astonishment.

"Of course. Maybe you could help me with some of the work around here in exchange for lessons. There are lots of projects that I've fallen behind on and I'm starting to feel pretty guilty about it."

"Sure, thanks. I mean, if it's okay with Lorne."

"Oh, I'm sure he won't mind," she said dryly. "He's just trying to push you past the beginner stage quickly so you can get to the good stuff. It never really works that way, though. Gaps in a rider's education always pop up in the end."

"I don't mind being a beginner," I said, "I love learning and I want to know everything. I try to read articles and watch videos all the time, but I feel like I'm *just* beginning to make sense of things."

"Back in the old days, that's pretty much how most people learned. You just got on and fumbled around, making mistakes that got you bucked off, throwing yourselves over jumps and learning as you went. Only later did you refine things if you wanted to. Both Lorne and Gretta were pretty much self-taught in the beginning."

"Huh," I said, "when my sister was younger she used to bring home random musical instruments and teach herself how to play them in just a few hours. It always amazed me that she could do that."

It had driven me crazy. She was pretty much a genius at anything she touched. Her teachers never shut up about how naturally brilliant she was.

"Some people learn best that way, they like to figure stuff out on their own. But a horse is not quite the same as a musical instrument. It *hurts* when their backs get thumped or their mouths get mistakenly yanked. Most of them are just too polite to say anything."

"I accidentally pulled on Nipper's mouth yesterday," I confessed, wincing. Julie had probably been watching from the house window and seen everything.

"Sure, it happens. You'll do better next time. But if we make sure that your seat is secure from the very beginning, then you won't bounce around on him. And when you can control the horse's speed and direction without needing to rely on the reins, then you'll be on your way to being a real rider; one who can ride gently and tactfully. Those riders are a joy for horses to carry."

"That's what I want," I said, "more than anything."

"And is your goal Eventing?"

"I want to try everything," I said. "I never thought I'd be well enough to do something like this. I want to do as much as I can before I run out of ... well, just in case I'm not able to ride for as long as I'd like."

I could sense Julie turning to look at me but I concentrated on the ground at my feet.

"Right," she said, "well, let's start at the beginning then."

She was right about one thing. Lorne could hardly contain his excitement when he woke up from his nap and found out that Julie had taken both of his immediate problems off his hands: teaching me and catching Dragon.

"I never could stand the up-down lessons," he said gleefully, "no offence, Bree, you're doing just fine."

"None taken," I said dryly.

"It's just that our barn catered to more experienced riders who were already in a program. They didn't come to us until they were already showing at a fairly high level. Gretta was the one who enjoyed pottering around in the dressage ring, and even she didn't like beginner lessons."

"Let's see this other project of yours," Julie interrupted, walking over to Ace's stall. "At least one of you had the sense to pick out a nice-tempered horse."

I haltered Ace and then carefully led him out of his stall so Julie could watch him hobble down the aisle. The cold-hosing hadn't seemed to make much of a difference so far.

"I was going to give him a few more days to rest," Lorne said.

"I gave him a dose of Bute last night but it didn't take the swelling down much."

"He needs a vet," Julie said bluntly. "We might need to do X-rays."

"I think it's a little soon for that—" Lorne began but broke off when Julie fixed him with a piercing look.

"Fine, fine, I'll give him a call. I don't believe in coddling these horses, though. We can't call the vet out for every little ache and pain."

"Uh-huh, well, what would Gretta say to do in this case?"

Lorne glowered at her and then suddenly his expression softened. "She'd say to call the vet. That girl could never stand to see any animal in pain. She had a good heart."

"The best," Julie said, laying a hand on his arm. "The very best."

They stood there for a moment, not saying a word while I busied myself straightening Ace's black forelock.

"Don't worry," I whispered to him, "we're going to get you all fixed up."

He closed his eyes and pressed his forehead against my arm.

That afternoon I busied myself with slapping paint on as many of the ring fence boards as I could. Winter would be upon us soon and I would have to stop my project once the temperature dropped too much. I worked hard and, to my amazement, I put the final stroke of paint on just as the sun began to head toward the horizon.

I stood back, proudly admiring my work and dreaming of the day when it would be Ace and I in there, cantering around together in circles.

Chapter Twenty-Nine

The next day Lorne had difficulty struggling out of the car when he came to pick me up. He limped to the passenger door and groaned as he climbed back inside.

"You seem to be getting worse," I told him. "Is it the sitting up that bothers you?"

"No, it's the actual driving," he said, "holding my foot up on the gas pedal like that does a number on my hip."

"It's too bad my family doesn't have a second car. They had to sell Mom's car when I got sick. Otherwise, I could pick you up."

He shot a quick glance at me and frowned.

"Well, then I'll just leave my car at your house and you can pick me up in the mornings."

"Oh, no, I couldn't take your car."

He was silent and when I looked over I could see that his cheeks were flushed and his eyes shiny. Was he having a stroke?

"The truth is," he said finally, "that you would be doing me a great favour if you could take on the responsibility of driving. It would be a big relief if I knew you could get out to the horses if there's ever a day where I can't."

"Oh," I said, feeling a sliver of ice lodge in my stomach.

"And, well, there are some days when I'm not feeling well enough to go to town and I still need medications and groceries. If I knew that there was somebody who could help with that from time to time ... somebody that I trusted ..."

He broke off suddenly.

"Of course," I said quickly, "of course I could do that. I'd be happy to help. I was just scared that I'd crash your car or something if you left it with me."

"Bree, you're much too cautious to crash a car. Gretta, on the other hand, was a perfect hellion behind the wheel. She'd slam her foot on the gas and she wouldn't let up until we reached our destination. I can't tell you how many speeding tickets she gathered over the years." He laughed and shook his head fondly. "There wasn't a single thing that woman was afraid of. There wasn't a horse she wouldn't get on or a jump she wouldn't try."

"I'm not very brave," I said, thinking of how uncomfortable I'd been just letting Nipper canter around the ring.

"Well now, there are different types of brave. In the short time I've known you, I've watched you face down your own death and a great deal of pain without a single complaint; I'd say that's plenty brave, if you ask me. Gretta wasn't so much brave as she was fearless. She rarely had to push through moments of doubt and terror that the rest of us mere mortals have to face. She was just built differently."

I thought about that all the way to the barn. Actually, it made me think about Angelika because, as naturally talented as she was, she hated performing in front of live audiences. It was fine at school because she was already popular and well-loved, but as soon as she started performing for people who were mostly strangers, and maybe people who were her competitors who perhaps wished that she'd fail, she'd have to spend about an hour before the performance pacing up and down and running to the bathroom to throw up.

She always pulled herself together in the few seconds before she walked out on stage, but I knew that it was something she *managed*, not something that ever went away.

Julie was already in the barn when we got there. Most of the horses, including Dragon, had already been turned out and Julie was halfway down the aisle with the wheelbarrow cleaning stalls.

"Morning," I called out and handed her the coffee we'd picked up from the drive-thru.

"Oh, thank you, this is nice. It's worth having to put up with socializing with *humans* when they bring you snacks."

She grinned at me and we both started laughing.

"That's exactly what I told her," Lorne said, "I said, Julie can always be bribed with coffee and breakfast."

"Sad, but true. Dragon was reasonably less homicidal when I turned her out, but your little gelding is not doing so well. I've already called the vet."

We slid the door back to his stall and I could see right away that Ace was much worse. The swelling in his leg had now reached his hock and he was in obvious discomfort.

He lurched outside slowly when I coaxed him into the aisle. He didn't object to the cold-hosing session but it didn't do much to bring down the swelling this time. He didn't graze; he just stood there with his head hung low. When I put him back in his stall he barely glanced at his breakfast.

"The vet will be here soon," Julie said reassuringly, "let him rest while we have our lesson."

Julie had left Nipper and Bear inside to keep Ace company so I carefully groomed Nipper and went to get his tack.

"Here," Julie said, "let's use my old saddle today, I brought it down from the house for you to use."

"Oh, that's a dressage saddle," I said, admiring the buttery soft black leather. It had been kept under a special cover so, unlike anything else in the dirty tack room, it looked immaculate and dust-free.

"That's right. We're going to work on your position so we

might as well make it a bit easier on you. This saddle has a deeper seat and the thigh-rolls will help keep you in position."

She handed me a velvety blue saddle pad with gold braid lining the edges and waved me back toward Nipper's stall. She watched carefully as I tacked him up and followed behind as I led him to the ring.

He looked much fancier in his sparkling clean tack, almost like a different horse. He seemed excited, too. There was an extra spring in his step and he practically pulled me toward the ring.

"I'm happy he's being ridden," Julie said, trailing behind us. "He really missed this."

"You don't ride anymore at all?" I asked, then instantly wished I hadn't. The light drained out of her face and she sighed heavily.

"No, not anymore. The whole right side of my body was burnt quite badly. It took a long time and a lot of surgeries just so I could move around properly again. Riding was out of the question for a long time because the skin was so fragile and I was in so much pain. I had enough trouble just feeding myself and raising a son on my own let alone ride."

She set her jaw determinedly, like she was expecting me to argue with her.

"I get it," I said quickly, "I understand. At least you got to keep him."

"Yes," she blew out a deep breath, "I think he kept me sane sometimes. I would just come out here and watch him graze, and later on brush him and take him for walks, and it sort of made me feel peaceful again."

"Yeah, that's how I felt coming out to the farm, too. It's so quiet and happy here."

"All right, that's enough talk. Get up on that beast and we'll start with your position."

The first thing I realized was that the dressage saddle was a million times more comfortable than the old, brittle saddle I'd been riding in. It wasn't just that it was a deeper seat; the leather itself was like settling myself into a well-stuffed sofa that cradled me in exactly the right position.

"This is so nice," I said, beaming at her.

"Yeah, that old saddle Lorne had you using was awful. One of the boarders left it here years ago and I should have just thrown the thing out. Nothing like trying to achieve a light seat and refined aids while you're riding on a slippery, uncomfortable brick. Now, drop your feet out of the stirrups and let's see how you're sitting."

I dropped my legs down so they draped over Nipper's fat sides and held my breath while Julie circled us, studying us from all angles.

"Okay, walk on."

I tentatively nudged Nipper and he strode forward obediently.

"Wow, it is amazing," I said because riding in this saddle was a whole new experience. I could feel *everything*; Nipper's hind legs propelling us along, his back rising underneath me and the swaying of his body. All the new sensations were a bit over-whelming actually, but I felt safe and secure and Nipper seemed to be enjoying himself.

That whole lesson was a revelation and, much like my trans-formational dream in the hospital, from the outside it probably looked like nothing was happening at all. We just walked and did a little bit of trot, but I felt like I'd learned more in that hour than I had in all my lessons with Lorne. Which wasn't a fair comparison actually because Lorne had also been teaching me about horse-manship, trail riding, and stable management, too. Julie was focused purely on my position.

"You need to have a light but consistent contact with his mouth. Pretend like you have a soft, silk thread running between your fingers and his mouth. If you pull too hard, you'll break the thread, but if you have zero contact then the thread will fall out of his mouth and you will have no communication."

"But," I said hesitantly, "online I saw these riders going totally bridleless and the horses seemed to understand everything. Do I even need reins?"

"Good question. Once your seat is refined enough then you can experiment with dropping the reins completely because you'll be connected through your core. But for now, you seek a gentle rein-contact. Got it?"

"Yes," I said, nodding. I let her adjust my fingers on the reins, sliding the supple leather closer toward me. The reins were much shorter than I'd been riding with but I wasn't pulling on Nipper at all. I could just barely feel him gently mouthing the bit.

"Good, now this time when you ask him to move forward, you're going to use your inner calves instead of your heels. Just lightly brush his sides and think forward thoughts. Better."

Once she'd adjusted my position about a dozen times, she let me try a sitting trot, and I floated around with a huge smile on my face. As an experiment, I asked Nipper to move from the quarter line to the rail in a leg-yield. He drifted sideways beautifully, and I grinned, feeling like a superstar.

"Did Lorne tell you what the leg-yield exercise is for?" Julie asked.

"Er, for going sideways?"

She snorted a little with laughter and shook her head.

"No, well, okay I guess yes, that too, but what I mean is that do you know what you're asking Nipper to do when you move him sideways?"

"No, I guess not." I dropped down to a walk and reached out to pet Nipper's neck, wondering if I'd been hurting him in some way.

"What you're doing is beginning to free up his body. You're asking his hind legs to cross and move under his body in order to propel him sideways. It's not as easy as it looks for them, even though it's a pretty basic move. When done properly, he will be utilizing his whole body to stretch and balance. Now, how did you ask him to do that?"

"Um, I looked a little to the outside and I stretched into my outside stirrup."

"Okay, fair enough. I think Nipper likes you so he's anticipating what you want and going through the motions without the benefits of stretching and suppling his body. There's no harm in that of course, it won't hurt him, but if you're going to be serious about schooling horses then you'll need to know the difference.

"I don't think we'll worry about that any more today. Let's just get your position stabilized and then we'll work on the more complicated stuff later."

"Right," I said, sighing a little. Riding with Lorne did have its benefits. He wasn't nearly so fussy and fiddly, and he let me do the fun stuff. I could see how both teaching styles had their good points.

"Now," Julie called, "we have your feet and legs sorted, so let's talk about your upper body position."

By the time my lesson was done, I was exhausted, both mentally and physically. Even though I'd barely broken into a trot, I had discovered dozens of muscles that I'd never used before and every single one of them was now awake and incredibly cranky.

"You did great," Julie said, beaming at me, "you're a good student."

"Thanks," I said, smiling a little shyly. "I really like riding Nipper."

"Well, he's a great horse. Once he's in shape again, you'll get a taste of how powerful he can be."

"In shape again? Isn't he old?"

"He's not *that* old," Julie said, laughing a little. "He was ten when I had my accident so he's only nineteen and he'd had leasers off and on over the years to keep him going. Plenty of years left in his engine. Bear is nearly thirty and he's still tottering around."

Oh, that gave me something to think about. I had thought that my days of riding Nipper were numbered and that I had to be careful not to ask too much of him. This put things in a new perspective.

But before I could dwell too much, I was distracted by a green truck pulling slowly up the driveway.

The vet was already in the stall with Ace by the time Julie and I brought Nipper back to the barn. I wanted to drop everything and rush in there, but Nipper still needed to be untacked, groomed, and put away.

"Here you go, and thank you," I whispered as soon as I'd slid his blanket back on and thrown him a flake of hay. I tossed a carrot into his bucket and then made my way over to where the vet had Ace out in the aisle.

"I can X-ray to rule out any skeletal changes," the vet said in a gravelly voice. He was short and round with a black scruffy beard and an abrupt manner. But his blue eyes were kind and he looked up at me with a smile when my shadow fell over where he knelt by Ace's hind leg. He wore a green pair of overalls and tall rubber boots, and he had a headlamp attached with an elastic tape around his head. "There is a lot of heat and inflammation going on in here for some reason. It's almost like there's an infection. No obvious wounds, though."

"No, nothing," Lorne said, "we've been cold hosing him for a few days and there weren't any cuts. His hoofs are in good condition, no thrush or white line that I could see."

"All right, let's take a look at that hoof then."

The vet carefully lifted Ace's leg and peered down at the underside of the hoof with the headlamp. He pulled a hoof knife out of his pocket and gently scraped away at the sole and grooves. Then he pulled out what looked like a metal sort of clamp and used it to push down gently on Ace's hoof. Instantly, Ace's head shot up and he pulled his foot back with a snort. The vet carefully tried it a few more times in different areas on the hoof but with the same result.

"Something is definitely hurting him in there, but I can't

pinpoint a specific area. I don't think it's just an abscess. The whole hoof capsule seems to be painful. I think that we should go ahead and take some pictures."

Pictures apparently meant X-rays, and when Lorne sighed and nodded, the vet went back out to his truck and appeared a minute later carrying a heavy-looking hard-sided suitcase type of thing and a smaller white box.

"Not like in the old days," he said, noticing Lorne and Julie's raised eyebrows. "Now it's all digital and wireless."

"Hmm," Lorne said skeptically.

As worried as I was about Ace, I couldn't help but find the X-ray part very interesting.

The vet crouched down near Ace's hind leg and set the suitcase down on a hay bale that Julie had brought into the aisle. He flipped the clasps on the lid with a sharp click and lifted it up, revealing what looked like a laptop inside.

He pulled a large, flat plastic piece out of the case and then fired up the laptop.

We waited in silence while he whistled under his breath, hitting buttons now and then until some graphics popped up showing the outline of a hoof.

"Great, we'll start at the bottom and work our way up."

He set the box on one side of Ace and then held the plate against the little gelding's leg. Then he hit the button.

In less than thirty seconds an image began to load on the laptop screen.

"Whoa," I said, because even with my uneducated eye I could see something that didn't belong there.

"Whoa, indeed," the vet agreed, "now, how did that get missed?"

Lorne and Julie leaned forward and Julie hissed under her breath.

"You poor horse," she said, reaching out to scratch Ace's rump.

The picture of Ace's hoof was bisected nearly in half by a long, thin line with a pointy tip. It didn't take a horse person to see that it was a long, sharp nail that had been driven right into his hoof.

The vet set his equipment off to one side and then picked up Ace's hoof again, pulling his hoof knife out of his pocket and poking gently into the left groove that ran beside Ace's squashy frog.

"Sorry, fellow," the vet said, when Ace snorted loudly in protest. He sighed and set the hoof back down gently. "Well, folks, we have a couple of choices. He clearly has something in there that doesn't belong. We can try giving him some sedation and I can attempt to pull it out here or we can book a time to trailer him to the equine hospital, put him right out, and try and resolve the issue surgically. There are pros and cons for both."

"He wouldn't be able to stand well in the trailer," Julie said worriedly, "he can barely put weight on that foot."

"Pull it out here if you can," Lorne said firmly.

"Right, well, I'll give it a try anyway. The hospital would be a more sanitary environment though, of course. You'll have to keep it very clean and soak it every day. Are you up for that?"

He looked at me as he said this and I nodded quickly, eager to show him that Ace was in good hands.

"Okay, let's get this boy sleepy then." He rooted around inside his case, pulled out a needle-topped syringe, and drew up a honey-coloured liquid from one of the many vials in the case.

Ace didn't even flinch when the needle went into his neck. He just heaved a huge sigh and closed his eyes, looking like he was trying to be stoic and not complain about anything.

"This is a good horse," the vet said. "If you can get him fixed up then I'll say you got yourself a nice all-rounder. He's a good citizen."

"Yeah," I said, smiling faintly, crossing my fingers that he'd meant *when* we got him fixed up, not *if*.

We waited for a few minutes for Ace's head to droop. His

lower lip twitched a few times, and then he sagged a little, like he was hoping to lie down.

"Keep him up," Julie said, moving over to stand beside him. She unclipped him from the cross-ties and held on to his halter with just a lead rope.

I stepped aside and went over to see what the vet was doing. He'd arranged a little line of tools on a towel just off to one side and was now cupping Ace's hoof with one hand and very gently paring away at the middle of the groove on the left side of Ace's frog with a hoof knife. He worked slowly and carefully, making one stroke with the knife, pausing, and then blowing the little bits of hoof shavings away. Suddenly there was the faintest rasping noise under the knife.

"Ah ha," the vet said triumphantly. "See, it's buried right at the bottom of the groove."

He dug a little bit more and then I saw the faintest metallic glint in the light from his headlamp. He put the hoof knife back in the little tool belt he was wearing and then pulled out what looked like a streamlined cross between scissors and a pair of pliers.

He carefully fished around in the hoof and then gently began to pull backward. Suddenly, he was triumphantly holding up a long, twisted nail covered in slimy yellow goo.

"Gross." I gagged and looked away.

"Yay," Julie said at the same time.

The vet dropped the nail in a waiting bowl of water and then asked me to hand him the syringe filled with dark, pungent liquid.

"We'll flush it out and give him some antibiotics. We'll keep it wrapped for now. You get Lorne to show you how to change the bandages."

"Okay," I said, wincing as I looked at the oozing hole in Ace's foot. Now that the nail wasn't there, the pressure must have been released and the stinky liquid was leaking out.

The vet squirted the syringe on the bottom of Ace's hoof to

clean it up and then focused on fitting the tip into the nail hole and flushing out what was in there, too.

"It's not a perfect solution, we run the risk of shooting bacteria up higher into the hoof capsule but it's the best we can do right now. I'll flush it a few more times and then we'll wrap it."

He repeated the process with the syringe and pretty soon there was no more foul material coming out of the hoof.

"Hand me that open jar and a couple squares of that gauze," he said to me.

With one hand, he scooped out a dollop of the yellow cream, smeared it on the gauze, and then stuck the gauze–cream-side down–onto the area where Ace's wound was.

"Okay, now hand me that cotton pad there and the white roll of gauze."

I obeyed instantly, watching in fascination as he placed the thick cotton pad over the medicated gauze on Ace's hoof and then expertly wrapped the whole thing up, first with a roll of thin fabric, and then with a layer of brightly-coloured stretchy wrap.

"Always use the cotton layer under the elastic wrap," the vet said, looking up briefly, "you can control the tension better that way and it lets the skin breathe. You have to make sure it's on securely but not so tight that it cuts off the circulation. Got it?"

"Got it," I said, hoping I could remember everything.

"You'll soak his foot in a medicated solution every day and change the bandage. He'll be on antibiotics and also an anti-inflammatory for pain control. Hopefully, it ends up just being a simple infected puncture that clears up in a few weeks. But we'll have to monitor it closely. There are quite a few moving parts inside the hoof capsule. Nothing looked compromised on the X-ray, but it's hard to tell if there are more pockets of infection brewing. We'll have to cross our fingers for luck, okay?"

"Okay," I said, swallowing hard. There seemed to be a lot of ways things could go wrong.

"Cheer up, you're giving him a good chance to heal."

"I feel bad about his foot, though. How could he even walk around with that nail in there? He was only a little lame when we got him home, but it's gotten so much worse since he's been here. The man who brought him from the mainland said he hadn't even been lame when he got off the trailer."

"Hmm," the vet said, rising to his feet. "Well, sometimes people aren't always truthful. But, actually, I've seen these hidden nail punctures quite a few times. If it goes in at just the right angle and misses everything essential, sometimes they're not even lame. It could have been in there for weeks without causing an issue. I don't think it was the nail itself causing the inflammation so much as the bacteria brewing in there. It's the swelling from the infection that brought on his sudden lameness."

He expertly packed up his gear, gave Ace a final pat, and me a friendly wave. Lorne followed him out to his truck to pay and get the pile of medications and bandaging materials for Ace.

Julie grabbed the wheelbarrow, and I stood at Ace's drooping head, waiting for him to wake up. I glanced down the aisle to where I could just see the truck outside. Lorne and the vet were deep in conversation and I felt a twinge in my gut; a mixture of guilt and fear. I felt bad about Lorne having to pay a huge vet bill just a few days after bringing the horses home. He hadn't even *wanted* to buy Ace; it had been all my idea. He'd only wanted Dragon. And I didn't have the money to pay for anything a horse needed like feed and medical bills.

Maybe I could get a part-time job and find a way to buy Ace, I thought, considering my options. *Maybe I could get a night shift somewhere to at least help pay for his vet bills.*

I loved spending all my days with the horses, I didn't want to give that up, and I'd already agreed to work for Julie around the farm in exchange for lessons anyway. But there might be other jobs I could do after-hours, there were night time receptionists at the hotel where my mom worked.

My thoughts broke off as Ace raised his head and snorted

loudly, and then rubbed his nose up and down my sleeve, smearing it with slobber.

"Oh, great, thanks buddy," I said, "are you waking up?"

"His stall is all cleaned," Julie said, giving his shavings a final fluff before stepping aside so I could lead Ace in. "But don't give him any hay for another hour or so. Not until he wakes up fully. He might choke if he eats while he's still half-asleep. I'll leave Bear inside today to keep him company."

Ace didn't look like he wanted to eat yet anyway. As soon as I slipped off his halter he wandered back to the far corner of his stall and stood there with his head about an inch above the shavings, snoring softly.

I rolled the door shut carefully so I didn't wake him up.

"You really like him, don't you?" Julie asked, glancing over from the next stall.

"Yes. From the moment I saw him at the sale I just knew there was something special about him. The way he looked at me was so kind and smart and trusting."

"Well, you have a good eye for them. I like him, too. He's very mellow for just getting off the track. Not like her highness out there."

"Oh yeah, Dragon, I definitely did *not* have the same feelings about her. That was all Lorne's doing."

"Well, don't write her off yet. Lorne and Gretta had a solid reputation for picking out fantastic horses. Some upper-level horses are pretty feisty, you know."

"Ugh." I shuddered. "I hope I never have to ride at the upper levels then."

Julie laughed. "Well, you might not feel that way once you get there. Now, I'll finish the last of these stalls while you start on getting that tack room cleaned and organized. It looks like it hasn't been used in a century. Pull everything out into the aisle and I'll sort through it and see what's salvageable."

And that was the rest of my afternoon.

Trying not gag at all the dust and spider webs coating everything, I hauled all the dirty blankets, tack, old brushes and assorted junk out of the tack room and piled them outside the door. I hung the clean tack we regularly used over one of the unused stall doors and heaped the rest of the old, dried-out leather together below it. I had no idea what half that equipment was for.

I also discovered a plastic tub full of bits of all shapes and sizes.

What on earth is that? I wondered, holding up a twisted piece of metal with two long cheek pieces. *It looks like a torture device.*

I didn't have time to stop to examine them all, but one day in the future I would have to take pictures of them all and look up their uses online.

Julie came over to deal with the things I'd piled in the aisle and then she helped me sweep, dust, and scrub. The windows had about ten years'-worth of grime and dead flies attached to them and it took all my willpower to force myself to deal with them.

It was worth it in the end though, because with the sun finally able to shine through the freshly-scrubbed windows, the space looked like a million dollars once it was all cleaned up.

"Wow," Julie said, stepping back to study our handiwork. She was covered in dirt and dust just like me, and a smear of brown ran across her cheek. "This is just like the old days."

"Were there lots of boarders back then?"

"Oh yeah, it was always full with a wait-list a mile long. We used to trailer down the road to Orchard Brook to use their indoor for lessons. We had to do three trips to get everyone accommodated. We pretty much took over the place some nights. It's a wonder they put up with us."

"Was it your parents who owned this place first?"

"My parents?" She looked at me blankly. "No, they thought horses were a complete waste of time; they still do, actually. I took years of lessons and then bought my own horse with my saved-up birthday money. I kept him in a farmer's field and I used to ride past this place and dream of taking lessons here. Somehow I conned them into giving me a job cleaning stalls. Then I groomed and rode for them. I guess I've been here off and on my whole life."

"Lucky," I said wistfully, wishing I'd done something like that when I was little. It had never occurred to me as a kid to get a job and find my way in the world on my own like that. I wondered how she'd ended up being able to buy the farm in the end. It seemed like a dream come true to me.

"I was a pretty stubborn kid." Julie laughed. "I was braver then; not much got in my way."

"Where did all the boarders and riders go?"

She gave me a strange look. "Didn't Lorne tell you the story?"

I shook my head.

"Well, you'd better ask him then. I can tell you that it's sure nice and peaceful just dealing with the horses rather than their owners."

"Don't any of the senior horses' owners come and visit?"

"Sometimes. Sleet's mom is travelling around Europe right now, but when she's home she visits her on the weekends. You'll like her. As for the others, they do drop in from time to time just to make sure their horses are still standing."

"I can't imagine not wanting to visit my horse every day if I owned one."

"People's lives change," she said with a shrug. "At least they didn't dump them at auction or let them starve. They pay for me to take care of them properly so that's pretty responsible."

"I guess so," I said doubtfully.

By the end of the afternoon, I was yawning and weary with exhaustion. Every muscle in my body cried out for a hot shower and bed. I'd completely forgotten that I was supposed to drop

Lorne off at his home and then drive his ancient car back to my house.

"You'll be fine," Lorne said briskly as he got out of the car in front of a fancy-looking condominium block. I hadn't thought of him and Gretta living in a condo. I'd pictured them in a cute little bungalow somewhere with a beautiful garden and a swing on the front porch. This building looked posh but sort of sterile, too. He didn't invite me in.

"See you tomorrow," I said to his departing back but he waved without turning around. I was faced with navigating that boat of a car out of the tiny parking lot and out into the street by myself.

I'd been doing a fair bit of driving since Lorne had first forced me into the driver's seat, but this was different. It was easy when I did the exact same route from my house to the barn every day with Lorne there right beside me if anything went wrong.

Pull yourself together, I told myself sternly, *you're practically an adult. You know how to do this*. But, I still felt like a guilty little kid who'd stolen her parent's car and had no idea what she was doing.

After a few wrong turns and a moment of panic at one of those roundabout traffic circles that peppered that part of town, I somehow made it home, which was a complete miracle.

I eased the car into the driveway, silently congratulating myself.

"What is Lorne's car still doing here?" my mom asked the second I opened the door. "Doesn't he want to come in?"

"He's not here," I said. "I'm driving his car today."

Her eyes widened and I could practically see all the arguments forming in her mind.

"I have my license," I reminded her before she could say anything, "and I'm a good driver." This last part was a blatant lie, but it was best to just lay all her worries to rest all at once so she would stop hovering.

"But the insurance," she said finally. "You're not on his insurance, are you? He'd be liable if something happened to the car while you were driving it. What if you run someone over?"

"Thanks for the vote of confidence, Mom."

"You know what I mean."

"Fine, fine. I'll talk to him about it tomorrow."

"I'm sorry to sound negative. I just don't want you to get hurt. First, the horses, and then the driving—" she broke off suddenly, probably realizing how ridiculous she sounded.

"Yeah, I'm pretty high-risk," I said sarcastically. "At least I don't day-drink, do drugs, and sleep around with other people's boyfriends."

She inhaled sharply, her nostrils flaring

"Sorry," I said quickly, feeling a stab of guilt. It wasn't *her* fault Angelika was the way she was.

"I'm going to shower now and get changed. I'll try and do it safely." I said, unable to resist a small dig.

She didn't respond but I heard her muttering under her breath as I climbed the stairs.

Poor mom, she has the worst luck in daughters, I thought ruefully. It was true that I wasn't willfully destructive like Angelika, but my illness had put them on a financial and emotional roller coaster that had aged them significantly over the last year and a half. It was a miracle that they hadn't gotten a divorce.

After dinner, I spent the night sitting cross-legged on my bed, working on my blog.

I hadn't decided if I was going to publish it or not, but I liked playing around with the layout and uploading the photos just to see how it looked. I'd written about that first day at the sale when we'd picked up Ace and Dragon and I'd even done a story about meeting Gretta in the hospital. It was a tribute to how much of an impact she'd made on me in just the short time I'd known her, and I teared up every time I re-read it.

"Mind if I come in?" my dad asked, standing in the open doorway.

"Sure," I said, reaching out to shut my laptop.

"The October Horses?" he said, catching sight of my blog title. "What are you working on?"

"Oh, just a silly project. I probably won't even publish it."

"Can I take a look?" he asked quickly as I went to close down the program.

"Fine, but it's all rough draft; I'm sure it's not any good."

He was silent the whole time he was reading and scrolling through my photos of the farm and the horses. I'd had quite the time trying to photoshop all the mud out of the pictures and trying to make the barn look less run-down but the final result had been very nice.

"Wow, Bree, this is very well done. You should definitely publish the blog. But can I ask what the title means? Why October horses?"

"Oh, it's sort of an inside joke that Lorne and Gretta had together. She used to get her side-project sales horses in early October so that's what she called them."

He stared at the photo of Ace on the screen with a faraway look on his face.

"There's another meaning for that phrase, though," he said slowly as if he were sorting through the storage room of random facts he kept in his head.

"Right, I read about that. The gross Roman thing about sacrificing the winning racehorse and parading its head through the city; this is totally not that."

"Right, Rome," he said, nodding, "during the chariot races at the Campus Martius."

He snapped his fingers together in a sudden burst of enthusiasm. "Actually, Bree, that is a great idea. Brilliant, in fact."

Huh? What was he even talking about?

He stood up and rubbed his hands together briskly. "I've been commissioned to do a project for a travelling installation. Only, I was out of ideas on what to make for them. You've given me some inspiration. I'll be downstairs if you need me."

"Glad I could help," I said laughing as I heard him thud down the stairs. Were other people's parents as crazy as mine?

Still, it meant a lot that my dad had liked my blog.

What harm could it do to publish it? It's not like anyone I knew would be reading about horses anyway. And it gave me something to do.

I hesitated only a moment more before I took the plunge and hit publish.

Chapter Thirty

❧❀❧

The next morning was Sunday and I woke up in the dark with a throbbing headache.

Five a.m. Part of me wanted to stay in bed but the other part of me knew that the horses were depending on me. I took some ibuprofen and played around with my phone for a while, waiting for the medication to kick in.

Wow, Ace's personal page had somehow managed to get thirty new followers overnight, most of them from people posting as ex-racehorses like himself. Despite the pain in my head I had to laugh. Apparently there were other horse people out there as nuts over their horses as I was.

Finally, I forced myself to get up, get dressed, and go downstairs.

It was pretty much my parent's only day to sleep in so I tip-toed around, making myself a real breakfast of oatmeal, nuts, and fruit. I needed something more substantial to get me through the day if I was going to be working like yesterday. It had nearly killed me and my sinuses still felt full of dust.

I brewed coffee and filled two travel-mugs, and then bagged up some of my mom's homemade muffins. I also packed a lunch of sandwiches, fruit, and trail mix for both Lorne and me. We couldn't keep getting fast food every single day. There were better, healthier, ways for me to put on weight.

I stuffed everything into a backpack, along with apple slices for all my favourite horses, and then headed out the door.

The crisp, fresh morning air made me feel instantly better. There was something peaceful about driving by myself in the early morning, especially since it was Sunday and the roads were mainly empty.

I found Lorne's condo without getting lost too many times and was happy to see that he was waiting for me out front.

"Well, how did it go?" he asked gruffly, clambering stiffly into the passenger seat. "Have you stopped being such a coward about driving?"

"Ha ha," I said sarcastically. "Yeah, I'm fine. My mom did ask about insurance, though. She said that I should be on your policy if I'm driving your car."

"Bah, she worries too much. You're just doing me a favour. We don't need to overcomplicate things."

"Okay, it's your car. I'm just telling you what she said."

"Well, maybe I'll ask Julie what she thinks. You're going the wrong way, though; the drive-thru is down the next street."

"No drive-thru today. There is your coffee and some muffins. And I made us a healthy, balanced lunch."

"Oh no. You sound like Gretta. She was always going on about me not eating too much junk food. I never cared about that sort of stuff, though. Fast food never hurt me."

"The body is a machine," I said, quoting an article I'd read about athlete fitness. "If you don't take care of it then eventually it will break down."

"Yeah, and sometimes you take perfect care of it and it breaks down anyway," he said sharply, turning abruptly to look out the window.

I bit my lip, knowing that he was thinking about Gretta.

Gretta the athlete, the health-nut, the one who nagged him about junk food. The woman who'd done everything right and still gotten old and died anyway.

"Sorry, Lorne, I shouldn't have said that. We can go to the drive-thru if you like."

"No, no," he said finally, "you're right. I should eat better. Thank you for breakfast ... and for packing me lunch."

He was quiet the rest of the way to the barn, but when we arrived, he seemed back to his old self.

We were early enough that the horses hadn't been turned out yet; they were inside munching their hay. I noticed that Julie had hung up hay nets for Ace and Dragon while the other horses had only a smaller flake tossed in their mangers.

"Most racehorses are used to having food in front of them all the time," Lorne said. "They rarely have access to turnout when they're at the track so if they're not working or hand-walking then they're stuck in their stalls. Having a net full of hay gives them something to do and if they have hay in their belly they're less likely to get ulcers."

"Oh," I said, "I didn't know horses got ulcers."

"Yep, from stress, or pain, or too much grain and not enough hay. Or sometimes it's a reaction to medication. It could be anything, really. It's not just racehorses that get them; ulcers are fairly common across all riding disciplines, although they're often not noticed until the problem is out of control. We used to give all our prospects coming off the track a round of ulcer medication just in case something was brewing."

Lorne's diet plan for Ace and Dragon was really simple. Unlimited access to hay or pasture and a small scoop of soaked alfalfa pellets, mineral pellets, and ulcer-guard fed twice a day. Plus, now Ace had his medication to be given at meal-times, too.

I had been scared to look at his leg that morning, worried that the swelling would be worse or that he'd be crippled with pain, but he actually looked much happier. The bandage was still in place and the swelling that had been creeping up toward his hock had gone down.

"Are you up for a short trail ride today?" Lorne asked. "Bear could use some very light exercise."

"Of course," I said. Bear hadn't seemed very enthusiastic in the ring last time so maybe an easy trail ride would do him good.

Dragon was back to her usual obnoxious self that morning. Apparently running away and joining the herd hadn't soothed her restless soul because now she paced up and down her stall, grabbing a mouthful of hay each time she passed her net.

"Why is she like that?" I asked Lorne in frustration. Her constant pacing was irritating. The barn was supposed to be a quiet, peaceful place.

"Oh, you know, these top athletic horses are funny. When you give them a purpose, they can be the most focused, talented horses on the planet. But when they don't have a job, when they're at loose ends, it drives them nuts.

"You have to remember that Dragon has been fed and trained and conditioned to win for the last four years of her life. She had a routine she understood; she had a job and an outlet for her excess energy. She is a trained, sculpted athlete. Now she's lost. Once she has something to focus on again, she'll settle down."

"Well, she looks nuts," I said darkly, moving into Ace's stall with the grooming tote.

"You should have seen Gretta after a big win. You'd think it would make her happy, and it did for a few days, but the minute the celebrations were over she'd get restless. If she didn't have an upcoming event, competition or project to focus on then she'd become crankier than an upside-down porcupine. She was a lot like Dragon. She'd pace, she'd pick fights over stupid things with anyone who crossed her path. She was awful. But the second she had another goal in front of her, she was sweet as pie."

"Oh." I thought of Angelika, who always needed a challenge, whether it was auditioning, preparing for a concert, or seducing some poor guy, or she'd fall apart. The similarity didn't make my opinion of Dragon any better.

Ace turned to gently nuzzle my arm, his upper lip moving in circles across my skin.

I scratched the spot under his mane and leaned against his shoulder, marveling at how warm and solid he felt. He was a very comforting presence to be around.

"Are you ready for your lesson?" Julie asked, appearing in the doorway.

I blinked at her in surprise. Instead of her usual outfit of tattered jogging pants, rubber boots, and a plaid jacket, she was dressed in a pair of clean grey breeches and a fitted black winter jacket. She looked like a different person.

"Oh, Lorne sort of said he wanted to go on a trail ride."

"Did he now? Well, how about a lesson first and then a quiet trail ride to cool Nipper down. We can't have him cantering off with you whenever he gets the urge."

Ack, of course she'd seen that. She'd probably sat up at the house and watched my every ride on Nipper with a pair of binoculars or something.

"Right," I said, sighing, "we can't have that."

My sore muscles from yesterday contracted painfully when I gingerly eased into the saddle but after Julie adjusted my position slightly, and I'd walked a few laps around the arena, I felt much better.

"We are building muscle memory as well as strength and flexibility," Julie called, "someday you will be able to do all this without working so hard."

Well, today is not that day, I thought ruefully as she again corrected my floating hands and wobbly position. Instead of staying low near the front of the saddle, my hands wanted to rise up to somewhere near my chest whenever I felt unbalanced at the trot. I hadn't even noticed I'd been doing that when I'd ridden with Lorne.

And what was wrong with my feet? One toe kept turning out and, on the other side, my heel kept curling up so I was practically riding crooked.

"Don't worry about getting it all perfect at once." Julie said patiently. "You're doing just fine. You have more body awareness then you did last week so it feels extra frustrating. But our goal is to patiently, gently, teach your body what the correct position is for all the movements. That's how we train the horses, too. We don't get mad at them when they are physically or mentally unable to perform something. We patiently educate them. You must allow this same kindness toward yourself and your own body. We're not in a rush here."

"There's just so much to think about," I said, drawing Nipper to a halt and reaching down to scratch his neck.

"Yes, trying to coordinate all the moving parts of our body is hard enough. Now you add an animal into the mix and you can see why riding is a lifelong pursuit. You'll get it, though. You're a good student. Now let's try that again."

By the end of the lesson, I felt like I'd made a few accomplishments. My leg position felt steadier and when I concentrated on using my protesting abdominal muscles to stay in balance I didn't tip forward so much. I could only keep it up for a few minutes at a time, but at least I could now *feel* when I was out of alignment and fix it.

I was puffing with exertion when we were done, but Nipper didn't seem tired at all.

"Okay, go and enjoy your trail ride," Julie said when Lorne appeared at the edge of the ring already mounted on Bear.

Despite his age, Lorne looked like such a natural on a horse, like he'd been born in the saddle. Bear resembled a much younger horse too, with his neck arched and his eyes bright and eager. It made me realize how much he enjoyed getting out.

"How are you liking your lessons with Julie?" Lorne said as soon as we'd left the farm behind.

"I love them, I'm learning so much." I stopped, worried that I'd offended him.

"Good, good," he said, not looking upset at all. In fact, he looked relieved. "I was never a fan of all that fiddly stuff. In my day, you just got on and rode and figured things out as you went along. If you ran into something you couldn't solve, well, then you asked someone to help you with it, but until then you were on your own."

"Wouldn't it have been easier to just learn properly from the beginning?"

"Bah, in my day most people didn't have spare money for lessons or trained horses. You learned to be tactful so the animals didn't buck you off, and you learned to have a solid seat from hitting the ground dozens of times first."

"Sounds painful," I said with a shiver.

"It made you stronger," he insisted, "riders in those days were tough as nails and didn't back down from any challenge. I won't deny that there may have been a fair bit of drinking ahead of time to build courage, but the point is that they went out there and did it. Now it's all about safety and positive feelings, and all that *namby-pamby* stuff."

"But I thought Gretta liked dressage."

"Well, she did. Not at first maybe, but later she met this coach, Lars, who changed her mind. Once she started to train with him, her scores improved so much that she was hooked. It changed her whole way of riding. She was still fearless, but her aides became much more subtle and finessed. That's when she really hit her stride and her career took off."

"I wish I could have trained with her," I said, sighing. The Gretta I'd met had been still so full of vitality. "She must have been an amazing teacher."

"She was. But, you know, Julie was Gretta's working student and apprentice for many years, so having lessons with her is the next best thing. They were both a lot alike when it came to dressage. Although they didn't always see eye to eye on everything else."

He laughed under his breath and navigated Bear over to the easier side of the trail where there weren't so many roots for the older horse to trip on.

Nipper was happy to stay beside Bear today. He was tired after his lesson and was content to just saunter along. I relaxed in the saddle, absorbing his swaying motion and listening to the trees rustling gently in the breeze around us.

Nipper snorted and let out a big sigh, dropping his neck and stretching down so that I was only holding the reins by the buckle on the end. His ears flopping gently to the sides and I didn't think I'd ever seen him so mellow.

In a second Bear followed suit, shaking his head from side to side like a dog before dropping his head and ambling along on a completely loose rein.

"Don't get too relaxed," Lorne warned him, "we can't have you falling asleep and toppling over on the trail. I don't think either of us would survive the fall."

I laughed and watched the two of them ambling along together, thinking that their combined age must put the two of them somewhere near a hundred years old or more.

"You should have seen this boy in his prime," Lorne said, echoing my thoughts. "On his bad days, he would have made Dragon look like a child's pony."

"You're not serious," I said, looking dubiously at sweet, innocent Bear.

"Oh yes, he liked having things his own way. He was a monster on the ground when he was upset. Gretta wouldn't even go near him until we'd had him for over six months. He was always my boy right from the beginning."

I thought about what Julie had said about everyone having their own preferred horse personality that they gravitated toward. If I had met Bear in his younger years, I would have probably avoided him like I avoided Dragon. But now I loved him. Maybe in another fifteen years I'd love Dragon, too. Maybe.

The sun disappeared behind a bank of clouds and I shivered with a sudden chill. I'd left my heavier coat back at the barn and my sweater didn't do much to keep out the wind that had risen.

Lorne didn't look cold at all and it seemed rude to rush him through his trail ride but by the time we got back to the barn my teeth were chattering and a strange lethargy had fallen over me.

I pulled my coat on as soon as we got inside and fumbled my way through untacking Nipper, my fingers clumsy with cold.

"Here, you can do Ace's bandages today," Lorne said.

"Okay, sure," I said, just wishing I had a few minutes to rest.

I put Nipper back out in the pasture and we led Ace out into the aisle. I filled a low rubber tub with warm water from the inside tap and added a few squirts of betadine until the water was the colour of weak tea.

The smell reminded me of the hospital and I was sure Ace would object to me soaking his foot in anything so nasty. But, after I'd gently peeled the bandage off and wiped the sole of his hoof he let me carefully place his foot in the warm water. If anything he seemed to like the attention.

I groomed him while he patiently stood there, and carefully combed out his black mane and tail.

"He's not as flashy as Nipper," Julie said, passing by on her way to toss lunch hay to the horses in the field, "but he's a nice looking boy."

"I don't think he's plain," I said quickly, running a soft brush down his face and smoothing the little swirl in the center of his small white star. "He's perfect."

"Uh oh, you sound like someone in love."

"Well, he's a step up from my last boyfriend," I said laughing. "At least he won't sleep with my sister when I'm in the hospital."

Julie stopped and turned to face me. "Oh, wow, did that really happen?"

"It was a long time ago," I said quickly, regretting I'd brought the embarrassing incident up. "I'm over it." It was almost true. I didn't pine for Duncan or want him back or anything. But sometimes the hurt and betrayal I'd felt when I'd first found out came rushing back when I least expected it.

"You're a better person than I am then. I think I'd still be spitting mad if it had happened to me. Do you and your sister still see each other?"

I shrugged. "Not if we can help it. She travels a lot, so that helps. I'm sort of stuck living with my parents right now until I can get a place of my own, so once in a while we meet at family events."

"Your parents must have been furious."

"*Yesss*," I say slowly, "well, it's complicated. She's the youngest so my mom always thinks of her as the baby in the family. She's always gotten away with a lot."

Ace shifted in the water and I turned my focus back on him before he could take his foot out of the tub.

Lorne came over as soon as the timer went off and carefully dried and inspected Ace's hoof.

"It looks good so far," he said raising an eyebrow, "time will tell."

He held Ace's foot up while I applied the bandage in careful layers, finishing it off with a wrap of green elastic tape. It was bulkier and less professional-looking than the one the vet had done, but it seemed like it would stay put.

"Good job," Lorne said, surprising me.

I stood up and suddenly found myself swaying precariously. I put my hand out and steadied myself quickly against Ace's strong shoulder.

"Are you all right?" Lorne said, his face crinkled with concern as he stared at me closely.

"Yeah, I'm fine. I guess I just got dizzy."

"Well, it's been a long few days. I hope we haven't been working you too hard."

Despite my insisting that everything was fine, Lorne decided to cut our afternoon short.

Secretly, I was glad. By the time I'd dropped Lorne off and finally made it home, I was sniffling with cold and just wanted to crawl into my bed and sleep.

My parents had gone to some event in town so the house was quiet and dark when I got inside. I forced myself to take the extra step of having a shower before I fell into bed. I wrapped myself in my warmest pair of pajamas and crawled under the covers. I was asleep as soon as my head hit the pillow.

"Honey, are you all right? It's dinnertime."

I blinked awake, my eyes felt dry and irritated, and there was a burning feeling in my throat. I shivered and rolled over, mumbling something unintelligible.

I felt my mother's cool hand on my forehead and heard her sharp intake of breath.

"You're burning up," she said quickly, "you have a fever. When did this start?"

"I had a headache this morning," I said, sniffling. I felt like I was five years old again and just wanted to be taken care of.

She disappeared and then was back a minute later, tapping me briskly on the shoulder to wake me up.

"Put this under your tongue."

The thermometer poked the back my mouth uncomfortably and it took forever before it beeped.

"Low-grade fever so far. We'll need to talk to the doctor first thing in the morning. You are at extremely high risk for pneumonia you know. You shouldn't have been out working in the cold. I knew this horse thing was a mistake. It's too soon for you to be so active after you were sick for so long. You need to be resting. I blame your father—"

I kept my eyes closed and burrowed deeper under the covers. I was too tired to argue with her and there was a part of me, the sick and scared part, that wondered if she wasn't right. I hadn't been this active in years and maybe it *had* been too much of a shock for my body.

I must have inhaled tons of dust particles and spider webs when I'd cleaned out the tack room. Maybe my compromised lungs were clogged with dirt and brewing bacteria that was going to fester and—

I felt a stab of panic. I could *not* get sick again. I could not go back to the hospital. I had just started to live.

Tears pricked at my eyes and I sniffed loudly.

"What's going on here?" My dad's voice sounded unnaturally loud to my throbbing ears.

"She's sick," my mom said, her voice sharp and accusing.

"Fever?"

"Slightly. But I think we need to get her to Emergency. I have a feeling..."

"People get sick, Cecilia, they get colds and the flu, that's part of life," he said, trying to sound calm. There was a note in his voice that didn't sound entirely certain though, and that scared me more than anything.

"I'm not taking any chances. Not like last time. We thought she just had the flu then, too."

"Okay, I hear you. But I don't think we want her sitting around in the emergency room, exposed to who-knows-what-sort of diseases if it's just a cold that she can fight off with some rest and some soup."

"And I say that we can't wait. I want her to have the best chance—"

"Could you just stop fighting?" I said, as loud as I could, half-sitting up in bed. "I just want to sleep." The rest of my lecture cut off in a wheezing cough as my lungs contracted and I struggled for air.

That sealed my fate. My parents shot each other panicked looks and I was bundled into the car and driven to Emergency before I could even catch my breath to argue.

In the waiting room, wearing a blue cotton face-mask over my nose and mouth, I kept my eyes closed and half-listened as my mom explained loudly to the receptionist that I needed to be seen *that instant* or I would drop dead in their lobby and it would be all their fault.

They were used to people ranting at them but something she said must have worked because I was hustled into an exam room to wait. I barely even remembered talking to the on-call doctor but I was whisked off for X-rays and bloodwork, and then deposited in another room, on a different floor, to be hooked up on fluids and IV antibiotics for the night.

"Someone needs to call Lorne," I told my parents, "he'll panic if I don't show up tomorrow. I still have his car and Ace needs his bandage changed and—"

"I'm sure someone else will take care of it," my mom snapped. Her face was pale and lined with worry. "You just need to rest."

"But, Ace—"

"Don't worry, I'll call Lorne," my dad broke in, "I'll explain it to him and I can drop off the car too, if he needs it. The more you take care of yourself now the quicker you can be out of here and back at the barn."

He smiled down at me, ignoring the pointed glare my mom shot him.

I tried to smile back but sleep tugged at me hard, pulling me firmly downward until I finally gave in.

Chapter Thirty-One

M y first feeling when I woke up in the morning and found myself back in the hospital was pure panic. For one irrational moment, I thought that maybe I'd never left the hospital at all. Maybe meeting Gretta, Lorne, and the horses had been the dream and really, I'd been lying here all this time in some sort of coma.

My second thought was that I felt much better and that my breathing was barely laboured at all.

"Just a cold that turned into a mild lung infection," the young doctor assured me. He was blond and terrifyingly good-looking. "We'll keep you here for the rest of the day just for monitoring and then you can go home. Two weeks of antibiotics and then you should be fine."

"Thanks," I said, flooded with relief. So not a relapse after all. Just a normal thing that could have happened to anyone.

"We've already made an appointment for you to see Dr. Grace on Wednesday," Mom said, as soon as he was gone. "We can't take any chances. And the doctors here don't know anything about your condition."

"Stop worrying, Mom. You heard him; it was just a cold."

"Uh-huh. I heard him." She pressed her lips into a thin line. "Where's Dad?"

"He's with Lorne," she said darkly. "With the horses."

"Huh? What?" I wasn't sure I'd heard her correctly.

"When your dad called him to explain that you were sick, Lorne made him pick him up and take him to the barn to see the horses."

I burst into a laugh that quickly turned into a hacking cough.

My poor dad; that sounded exactly like something Lorne might do.

"I don't see how that's so funny. He should be here, with you, not ferrying some stranger around."

"Lorne's not a stranger," I said quickly, "he's a friend and he's done so much for me."

"Well, I'll leave you to rest then," my mom said, rising abruptly to her feet and walking out before I could say another word.

People are so complicated, I thought. *Horses are so much easier to be around.*

The hospital was busy and it wasn't until late that afternoon that anyone had time to discharge me. I was sent home with a script for antibiotics and an inhaler and given instructions not to exert myself too much for a couple of weeks.

Fine, I thought, *I can hold off on riding for a few days but I'm still going to the barn. I feel much better when I'm there than at home.*

When we got home, Lorne's car was parked in the driveway and so was an unfamiliar green Volkswagen that looked like it had seen better days.

When we opened the front door, there was the sound of voices coming from the kitchen. The smell of dinner cooking wafted out to meet us, and I was surprised when my stomach growled with hunger.

"What on earth?" Mom muttered but she put on her company face and smiled warmly at Lorne when she discovered him sitting at our kitchen table. Beside him, looking a little uncomfortable, was Julie's son Nicholas.

"Oh," I said, suddenly remembering that I was basically wearing pajamas and that I must look awful after a night in the hospital. He, on the other hand, looked perfect. "Hello."

"Sorry to drop in," he said quickly, half pushing back his chair, "I'm sure you weren't expecting guests."

"She's fine," Lorne said, beaming at me. There was a glass of what smelled like rum and Coke on the table in front of him and by the looks of him, it wasn't his first drink.

"What is happening here?" my mom said, her voice sharp despite her smile.

"Well, Lorne and I spent the day fixing broken fences and wrangling wild horses. Nicholas here is one of my students and, by coincidence, he *also* spent the day doing repairs at the farm and chasing animals. I thought we all deserved to have dinner and some drinks. He's brought Bree some books – her homework."

"I see. Dinner and drinks while your daughter was in the hospital."

"Mom, come on, it's fine," I said. "They're my friends."

"I guess we should probably go." Nicholas rose to his feet, looking awkward under my mother's glare. "My mom wanted to drop off your homework. She said that if you're not riding then you should be studying."

"Oh, thank you," I said, eying up the pile of books on the table beside him. They looked dressage-y. "But, wait, please don't go. I feel fine and you should both stay for dinner. I want to know about the broken fences and the wrangling. What happened?"

"Well, you know Dragon," Lorne said, picking up his glass and taking a good swig from it. "She decided she didn't want to be in the pasture today so she tried to jump out but the ground was pretty slippery so she sort of crashed through it instead."

"She took down a *lot* of fence," my dad added helpfully, "it almost looked like she destroyed as much as she could on purpose."

I could envision that happening perfectly.

"Were the other horses okay?"

"Oh yes, yes," Lorne said, shooting a look at my dad. "But they were very excited and they followed her as soon as they discovered the hole in the fence. It took a while to round everyone up. Everything is all mended now. No harm done."

I looked at Nicholas and he made a face. I could only imagine how their afternoon had gone. I was glad that I'd missed it.

"But I learned how to put a halter on a horse and lead it," my dad added. "Here, I have pictures to prove it."

He stopped stirring the sauce on the stove long enough to pull out his phone and show me a few selfies of him and Bear, and then another one of him standing with Ace.

"I like that guy," he said. "He's very gentle."

"Breanna picked him out," Lorne added, grinning at me.

I left them talking in the kitchen while I went upstairs to change my clothes into something more decent and run a hand through my hair before putting on a clean bandanna. It was growing fast now and was over an inch long. I couldn't wait for the day when I could put it in a pony-tail again. I swore I would never cut my hair again in my life.

I didn't bother with makeup. Nicholas had already seen me at my worst and I didn't want to look like I was trying to impress him too much. He was just a friend dropping by for dinner, that was all.

When I came back down, my mom was alone in the kitchen.

"Where did everyone go?" I asked, suddenly afraid that she'd kicked them all out.

"Downstairs, looking at your father's beloved models," she said, sounding tired.

"Is it okay if they stay, Mom?" I asked, moving to stand beside her at the stove. "I feel fine. I'll make sure to go to bed early."

"Sure, do whatever you like," she said, not looking up from the sauce she'd somehow taken over stirring.

"Okay." I turned to go downstairs and then hesitated. She looked so lonely standing there, like a stranger in her own house, and suddenly I felt sad for her although I didn't know exactly why. I turned suddenly and wrapped her in a tight hug, feeling how thin she'd gotten over the last year.

"Thanks for staying with me at the hospital," I said. "I'm glad you were there."

Then I turned and made my way quickly downstairs.

"Bree," my dad called as soon I appeared downstairs. "Come see what I've been working on."

I made my way over to the far end of the room to where he, Lorne, and Nicholas were standing around one of the model tables.

"She's the one who gave me the idea," he said proudly, waving a hand at the scene in front of us.

"Wow, Dad, you work fast," I said, staring down in amazement at the table. There was already an entire ancient city springing up around a huge open coliseum-type building that sat near the banks of a river.

"Well, I already had the base set up from the Julius Caesar scene I did a few years ago, and I had a few bits and pieces in storage. I'll need quite a few more horses for the races though, and everything needs a touch-up."

I leaned down to read the inscription on the display card. "*Ides Octobres*. That means just the middle of October, right?"

"Yes, October 15th was the date of the *Equus* October. It was a festival held at the *Campus Martius*, the Fields of Mars, right next to the Tiber river. It was basically a giant party that combined horse races, mixed with sacrificial elements. It sounded like a good time."

"Not for the horses who had their heads chopped off," I whispered under my breath, studying the half-built scene in admiration. It was amazing how someone as boring-looking as my dad, no offense, could be that talented. The models looked like they would spring to life at any minute.

"They were supposed to be sacrificing their most important, prized possession to Mars. A true sacrifice had to be something big, something worth losing."

"Huh."

"It's actually very interesting. The right-hand horse in the chariot was usually the strongest one so they would stab him with a spear and then chop off his head and his tail—"

"Nope," I said, holding up a hand to stop him, "I'm good. I do not need to know any more."

"But I'm getting to the most interesting part. They would stage this mock battle over the head, sort of like a football game, and whoever won the head earned the right to nail it up over their door."

"Fantastic. Okay, you can stop now. We've had all the history I need to know for one day. Thanks."

Nicholas laughed and I sent him a mock glare.

"That is exactly the reason why I never wanted to study history," I said, arching my eyebrows. "It is always full of the most gruesome details. Who wants to know about battles and sacrifices and stuff? It's depressing."

"Oh, there's plenty of boring stuff recorded, too," Nicholas said with a laugh. "I did this project on ancient exports once and had to go through like ten years' worth of shipping records. Endless lists of bags of barley, bags of oats, linen, metal bowls. It nearly made my eyes bleed. I would have taken a good battle to break up the monotony any day."

"What's this supposed to be?" Lorne asked, standing at a table on the other side of the room. He still held his drink in his hand and swayed a little unsteadily on his feet. We probably needed to get some food in him soon to sop up some of the alcohol.

"Oh, er, it's a work in progress," my dad stammered hurriedly, looking embarrassed. "It's not really ready to be looked at yet."

Nicholas and I followed him to where Lorne stood and I stared down at the mostly blackened surface in confusion. There were a few small, modern-looking cities scattered about but the rest was just dark, empty space.

"What time period is this set in?" I asked slowly. "And where is it?"

"Ah, well. It's just a little side-project for a friend. A bit of speculative futurism, if you will."

"The future? Like after some natural disaster?" Nicholas asked frowning. He reached out to gently touch one of the little buildings and then jerked back when it toppled over and fell. "Sorry."

"No, don't worry. It's not glued together yet. It's just, well, they wanted a model of what portions of the planet would look like after various disasters. This is, er, after a bomb of sorts."

Wow, that's depressing, I thought, looking grimly down at the scene of destruction. *Why would he take on such an unhappy project?* It felt wrong somehow that something like this even existed.

Beside me, I felt Nicholas's arm brush up against my own and felt strangely comforted.

"We should go upstairs," I said, "dinner smells like it's nearly ready."

The mood lightened considerably again once we were upstairs eating. Lorne filled us with stories of his eventful past, showing all over the world with Gretta, and even my mom couldn't help listening with interest.

I could tell that she was warming to both Lorne and Nicholas, and at the end of the night she packed up leftovers for both of them, including extra helpings of dessert.

"Now, into bed with you," she said as soon as they were gone. "I let your friends stay for dinner and now you need to keep your end of the bargain and rest. If you stay quietly at home for two days then I promise not to say anything when you decide you're healthy enough to go back to the barn. Deal?"

"Deal," I said, wrapping her in a hug.

The truth was that I really did need the rest. For two days, I did nothing but stay tucked in bed or on the couch and work on my blog. The stories were suddenly flowing out of me and, instead of being exhausting, it made me feel more alive. I went back and wrote about becoming sick the first time. About how hard it had been to be stuck in the hospital for all those months and the horrible toll it had taken on my family. It was like a whole year of emotion and experiences had been bottled up inside of me and now they came bubbling out.

I wasn't going to include it all in my blog, but in the end I decided that it wasn't just going to be about the horses, it was going to be about what it meant to be a survivor, too. What it meant to beat the odds when everything was against you.

Chapter Thirty-Two

I obediently stayed home for two days and on the third day, I had my appointment with Dr. Grace.

"Well, your lab work looks good," she said, after she'd listened to my mother tell the story of my latest trip to Emergency. "How are you feeling?"

"A little tired, I guess. I think that maybe I inhaled too much dust when I was cleaning out the tack room. I felt sick a few days after that."

"Aspiration pneumonia is a strong possibility. With your history, you do have to take extra care of your lungs. Next time you work in a dusty environment, you should wear a mask."

"Do you think she should even risk going back to the barn?" my mom asked worriedly, ignoring my outraged glare.

"I think she should do whatever makes her happy, but also take precautions. Do you wear a helmet when you ride?"

"Yes, always."

"Well, this is the same thing. You'll have to be proactive if you don't want an episode like this happening again. Got it?"

"Yes, definitely. I'll be more careful."

"Perfect. I'll see you in a couple of months for your check-up then."

My mom managed to stay silent all the way to the parking lot, but I could practically see the thoughts churning around in her head.

"Is this horse thing really that important to you, Breanna?" she said finally, the second we were trapped in the car together. "Is it worth risking your health?"

"Yes," I said firmly, "it is."

She sighed heavily and started the engine, guiding the car out of the crowded parking lot and back onto the road.

"Fine, well, then I guess I support you in it. Dr. Grace said it was okay so I guess I'll have to go along with that."

"Wow, really?" It wasn't like I was going to listen to her if she forbade me to go or anything, but it would be nice not to have to be constantly defending the horses to her.

"Yes. So I'm going to stop at the pharmacy to buy you some masks and then we can stop in and see this beloved barn if you like." She looked over and smiled.

"That would be great. You're going to love it."

I crossed my fingers, hoping that Dragon would be on her best behaviour.

Chapter Thirty-Three

I wouldn't say from that moment on that my mom exactly loved horses. But she learned to tolerate them, and would even pet Ace and feed him carrots although she didn't want to touch any of the others.

"No, I'm good just petting the one," she'd told me on that first day. "Just so I can tell the girls at work how brave I was."

By the next day, Lorne and I were back to our old routine. I had decided to be mature and put off riding for a few more days, but I was content to just be at the barn brushing Ace, Bear, and Nipper.

The swelling in Ace's leg had gone nearly back to normal and he was looking more chipper by the day. I had even started to take him out on very short hand-walking, grazing, sessions which he seemed to love.

Even the vet had been pleased by his progress.

"As far as I can tell, everything is healing up nicely. We might see something flare up once he starts on turn-out or goes back to work, but let's cross that bridge when we come to it. Keep soaking and giving him his medications for the next week. Hopefully, he'll be back to normal by then."

I was so happy with the vet's prognosis that I took Ace out to the long grass growing by the ring and did a little photo shoot with him, capturing his many handsome sides from all angles.

"I'll never understand you kid's obsessions with taking all these pictures," Lorne grumbled as I led Ace past him into the barn a half-hour later.

"It's fun," I told him, "and his fans like when I keep them updated on his progress."

"I can't believe that that scrawny horse has a fan club," he muttered, but I knew he didn't mean it. Even *he* had a soft spot for the little gelding. "Fine, put him away and then we'll have a little chat."

Uh oh, I didn't like the sound of that. Whenever people said they wanted to chat it meant that bad news was coming.

"Stop looking so worried," Lorne said, cracking a smile. "I wanted to talk to you about Dragon, that's all. We need to come up with a plan for her."

"Do we?" I asked cautiously. My plan was to avoid her as much as possible.

He shrugged. "Well, she's going to need some structure in her life pretty soon. Some horses are better to be turned out for a few months to decompress after they come off the track and some, like Ace, need to heal. But a horse like Dragon would probably benefit in going back to work right away. She's not the type to enjoy a vacation."

"Uh huh," I said cautiously, not liking the direction this was going. I could barely organize myself on kind, old Bear or Nipper let alone ride a dangerous horse like Dragon. I could clearly envision her bucking me off the second my seat landed in the saddle, then turning around and trampling me.

"We could start slow," Lorne said winningly. "You're progressing nicely in your lessons with Julie. I could start you on the lunge line—"

"No," I interrupted. "Sorry, but no. I've spent too much time in the hospital in the last year. I don't plan to go back there again if I can help it."

"She's not mean, Breanna, she's just spirited."

"Uh huh, well, if you like her so much then you ride her."

I instantly regretted it. His eyes lit up like he was imagining what it would be like to be mounted on her terrifyingly, swift back and then his expression fell again.

"I imagine that I might be too old," he said with a sigh, "but I would love to see her started in her new career. She's going to be something else for the right rider."

"There must be *someone* who would actually want to get on her," I said, "someone who is fearless like Gretta was."

He sighed and shook his head. "Kids just aren't like what they were in the old days. Even if they're brave, their parents always show up nattering nonsense about safety and concussions. But, I'll make a few calls and see what I can come up with. In the meantime, you get the rest of these stalls cleaned for Julie and I'll have a little nap."

It didn't take me long to finish the stalls. She'd only left me three of them to do plus I picked out Ace's stall to make sure his bed was fresh and clean.

When I was done, I went through to the back pasture and slipped through the fence heading down to visit the pastured horses.

Bear and Nipper saw me as soon as I crested the hill. Their heads lifted up and Nipper let out a little nicker of recognition before he started toward me at a brisk walk. Luckily, I'd filled my pockets full of molasses cookies. I gave one to each of them, taking a minute to scratch their necks and tell them how handsome they were before I headed down the hill toward the rest of the herd.

I hadn't spent much time with the other senior horses since they were usually out on pasture by the time Lorne and I got there. But now I stopped to admire how nice they looked, grazing peacefully down below.

Even though they were retired, Julie made sure they were groomed often and their fluffy coats shone with good health. Lorne had told me that older horses often had much thicker coats than younger ones, and seeing the senior horses beside the sleek, sinewy Dragon made me realize for the first time how true it was.

The difference wasn't just in their looks though, the older horses had a sort of calm serenity about them. They took slow, measured bites of the grass, snorting softly, their ears floppy and relaxed.

Dragon, on the other hand, grazed with small, angry bites, as if she were afraid her food were about to disappear at any second. Even just standing still, there was a tense, restless energy about her.

When I started down the hill toward the herd, she threw her head up and stared at me with wide eyes, a mouthful of browned foliage trailing from her lips.

"It's just me," I called softly. But my well-meaning words only agitated her more. Her long black tail rose in the air like a flag and she snorted loudly. A sharp, crackling sound that caused all the other horses to raise their heads, too.

Dragon began to trot slowly, her hoofs floating across the uneven ground like she was flying. Her neck arched and she swung her head from side to side. Was it in warning?

The other horses didn't seem to care. If Dragon's plan was to get them all running then she'd misjudged her herd-mates. After a moment, they dropped their noses back to the dying grass and went back to work.

Figuring they would stay put, I continued my way down the hill.

But Dragon didn't like it. Every second her energy seemed to build, her muscles bulged, her eyes white-ringed with excitement, or was it fear?

"It's okay, Dragon," I called out uncertainly, stopping twenty feet away from the herd. What on earth was wrong with her? Would she attack me if I came closer?

My question was answered when she suddenly dove toward me, ears flattened and teeth bared. I froze in terror, my heart seizing in my chest.

The hillside was bare; there were no trees to hide behind, and nowhere to run.

So this is how it ends, I thought.

There was a puff of warm breath in my ear and a gentle nudge on my cheek, and I turned to see that both Bear and Nipper had come up behind me.

Dragon was still coming though, and I shrank back, pressing myself into Bear's broad chest.

Was she going to kill us all?

A few feet away she slid to a stop, her hooves cutting long furrows in the earth. Her wild, rolling eye looked into mine, and then she spun around, galloping across the pasture, passing the herd and surging toward the fence. She didn't even hesitate before launching herself upward into the air and over. She was gone before I could even blink.

"Wow," I said out loud. "She's crazy."

Bear snorted beside me as if he agreed.

"I swear I will never, ever, want to ride something like that. I'll just stick with nice horses like you guys."

Bear and Nipper headed past me down to the herd and, after a moment to let my thudding heart go back to normal, I followed.

I went from horse to horse, taking time to pet them and hand out the treats I'd stashed in my pockets.

The huge, white mare Slate stood back until everyone else had had their turn and then gently stepped forward, her dark eyes huge and soulful against her snowy coat. She lipped the treat carefully off my palm then chewed it thoughtfully, her gaze fixed

somewhere in the middle distance as if her thoughts were somewhere else.

"You're so beautiful," I told her. "I wonder who owns you and
what your story is. Were you a champion like Bear?" I looked
down and noticed for the first time the thick, hairless scar that
ran across her chest and down one leg. I reached down to touch it
gingerly with one finger and she flinched slightly even though it
must have been years old.

"Was that your career-ending injury?" I asked her and fed her
the last crumbs from my pocket to make up for prying into her
past so rudely.

Once they were sure the treats were gone, they all gradually
drifted back to grazing, and I turned and headed back up the hill
toward the barn.

Chapter Thirty-Four

"What time is it?" Lorne asked for the fourth time in the last hour. He'd been fussing around the barn non-stop since we'd arrived. He'd brought Dragon in early from the pasture and had groomed her until she shone. He'd carefully wrapped her legs in blue polos and found a matching saddle pad in the same colour.

If you didn't know her awful personality, she looked quite stunning.

Finally, tires crunched up the driveway and Lorne fluttered out of Dragon's stall like he was on his way to a first date. Which I guessed it was; a blind date for Dragon.

"Hello," a firm voice called from the end of the aisle.

I turned around and smiled with surprise. It was the tough-looking, small-framed girl I'd met at the horse show; the rider of the horse, Monty, who'd nearly knocked me over.

"Oh, we meet again," she said, her face lighting up as she recognized me. "You're not in a wheel chair anymore."

"No, that was just for a short while," I said, not wanting to explain everything when Lorne was hovering so impatiently over my shoulder.

"I'm Chloe," she said, striding up to Lorne to shake his hand firmly. "It is so, so nice to meet you. I've read all about you and Gretta, and my coach said that I had to come right down and ride this horse. Monty's owner wants to ride him herself this year now that he's going well so I'm a little short on projects right now."

"Monty isn't your horse?" I asked in surprise

She made a face. "No, I wish. I was just leasing him for a year. I'm excited to meet your mare, though."

"She's a good horse," Lorne said, eyeing Chloe up and down speculatively as if weighing up her slight frame against the massive bulk of Dragon. "Well, you'd better come see her."

"Oh, she's nice looking," Chloe said, peering over the stall door. "I like how she's put together. Look at that shoulder. She's massive."

"She's been out of work for a few months to let her come down from track life," Lorne added, not mentioning the part where nobody here wanted to, or was able to, handle her. "She'll look even better once she's in full exercise."

"I'll bet. Can I try her out?"

"Er, yes," Lorne said, looking a little guilty for the first time. "You've ridden horses fresh off the track before?"

"Yep, and did training gallops for some trainers when we lived back on the mainland, too. I'm not afraid of her if that's what you're worried about."

Lorne's face lit up and I could tell that he'd met a kindred spirit. I tried not to feel too depressed at his elated expression. I was glad he'd found someone to ride Dragon, but part of me wished that I'd been brave enough to at least *try* to get on her. Maybe I was just being a coward and I would have been able to ride her perfectly if I'd had the nerve. Maybe not, though.

Chloe ran a brush over Dragon's glossy sides and tacked the mare up herself, talking to her quietly the whole time.

Both Lorne and I watched nervously but for some reason Dragon was on her best behavior. She picked up her feet politely and opened her mouth obediently to let Chloe slip the bit into her mouth and adjust the bridle over her ears.

"Right," Chloe said, looking eager, "let's go."

Dragon must have been thrown off her game by the disruption to her routine because she didn't offer to drag Chloe out of the stall and bolt. Instead, she arched her neck and high-stepped beside this strange new person handling her.

Dragon looked even more gigantic towering over Chloe and I almost couldn't watch them head to the ring because I was sure a disaster would happen at any minute.

It didn't, though; Dragon looked like she was seconds away from exploding but she somehow managed to keep herself together. Chloe led her into the ring and straight to the mounting block.

"Hold her head for me, would you?" she asked, looking at me. Luckily, Lorne stepped forward and gripped the cheek-piece of the mare's bridle.

There was about a half second where Dragon paused in her prancing and that's all it took for Chloe to leap lightly on board and nose her feet into the stirrups.

"Okay, let her go."

Dragon stood perfectly still while she considered this new inconvenience in her life and then she shot forward.

I'd had my money on her having a bucking and rearing fit, but she completely surprised me by breaking into a ground-covering trot instead.

Chloe kept a light but solid feel on her mouth for the first laps around the ring and then she gradually let the reins out so the mare had a chance to stretch down.

And that's all they did, just trotting and a little stretching in both directions for about twenty minutes until Dragon finally slowed down to a walk of her own accord.

"Okay," Chloe said, beaming. "I love her. I would love to ride her for you."

"But you only trotted her," I began but broke off as Lorne elbowed me in the side.

"She went forward nicely and didn't buck me off," Chloe said, laughing. "That's really all we can ask of her at this point. The ring's too slippery to canter her in when she can hardly bend in the corners, she's used to being able to stretch out."

"Julie teaches dressage lessons," I began.

"I doubt we'll need any of that," Chloe said dismissively, "I have my own coach and Lorne can help me with the cross country. This girl is going to be a super star. It's going to be too cold to ride outside soon. We'll need to trailer her to an indoor for lessons this winter, otherwise she won't be ready for the show season this spring and summer. Okay?"

And even though we didn't even *have* a trailer, Lorne nodded in delight, looking up at the two of them like he'd won the trainer lottery. I had the feeling that he'd do anything Chloe asked.

Chapter Thirty-Five

Day by day the temperature dropped, the horses' fur grew thicker, and the ground grew hard with frost.

Lorne and I had fallen into a familiar routine. I got up before sunrise each morning to pack our breakfasts and lunches, and then drove the old car to pick him up in front of his condo.

Julie would have already fed the horses their breakfast, and we would arrive just in time to turn them out and get to work on cleaning the stalls and refilling the water buckets.

Then, once the ring had had a chance to thaw out, I'd have my lesson on Nipper and then Lorne and I would go on a leisurely trail ride through the woods.

It was pretty much heaven.

As much as I loved riding Nipper, there was a part of me that couldn't wait to be riding Ace out there under the frost-tipped trees. I knew he'd love it. And then maybe I could convince Julie to come with us. I'd already started to research some adapted saddles that she might be able to use.

"So," I said casually as I was cooling Nipper out on a long rein after a particularly good lesson. "I did some research on saddles last night."

"Oh?" Julie said, raising an eyebrow. "What sort of research?"

"Well, someday I'm going to need a saddle of my own so I thought I should know what's out there." I paused and shot her a quick glance to see if she was listening. "And I just happened to come across this interesting website and I thought of you right away."

"Uh huh?" Julie said skeptically. "Why?"

"Um, I found these really neat saddles made out of super soft sheepskin. They look like those Spanish saddles you showed me but they're made in Germany or something. It's like a cross between a bareback pad and a saddle but the point is that they look very comfortable to ride in. Like a couch, really. I bet they'd be way more comfortable than a saddle."

I glanced over and saw Julie staring at me with her arms crossed.

"Where are you going with this, Bree?" There was a warning note in her voice.

I gulped and twisted a strand of Nipper's mane around one finger.

"You just seem like you miss riding and I thought that this might be a good solution—"

"I thought I told you that I didn't want to ride again. End of story."

"Okay, okay," I said quickly. "I'm sorry. I was just trying to help."

"I know. But, in the future, don't help."

"Fine." I drew Nipper to a halt and swung down from the saddle, running up my stirrups quickly so she wouldn't see my face flaming with embarrassment. "Thanks for the lesson. I have to hand-walk Ace now before it gets too dark."

Even though it was ridiculous, I felt very disappointed. I'd been so sure that I'd found the perfect solution so that Julie could ride. I should have just minded my own business. What if she was so angry that she stopped teaching me lessons or she stopped letting me ride Nipper altogether?

We'd decided to give Ace the winter off to just be a horse before we started him back in training in the spring. His gangly frame was still growing and it would be better for his health if we waited, even just for a season.

Also, then the ground would be softer and it would be more time to allow his injured foot to heal before we added the extra strain of a rider on his back.

I went home that night grumpy and out of sorts, but by the next day Julie was back to her old self and seemed to have forgotten the whole thing.

Every afternoon, Chloe drove up in her little commuter car for her ride on Dragon. Sometimes she rode in the ring and sometimes she took Dragon out for a gallop in the open fields behind the house.

It was bizarre to see the transformation in Dragon's attitude. She was still bossy on the ground, but her mood had been tempered by the daily exercise and attention. She loved her routine and would stand eagerly at the gate as soon as she heard Chloe's car pull up.

Chloe hadn't pressed the issue of Lorne not offering to trailer Dragon to an indoor arena yet. She must have realized at some point that we obviously didn't have a truck or a horse trailer, but she hadn't said a word about it so far. Maybe she just enjoyed riding Dragon too much to rock the boat.

The big mare still didn't like me very much for some reason, something I tried not to feel insulted about. She let me feed her without too much trouble but I still struggled to lead her anywhere.

No matter what I did, I couldn't keep her from dragging me out of her stall in the morning if I was unlucky enough to be the one to turn her out. And she'd just as eagerly drag me from the pasture back to her stall in the evening if she got the chance, too.

"I honestly think she knows that you don't like her," Chloe said tentatively one day as she watched Dragon slam me into the edge of the stall door on her way inside. "I know it's no excuse for her bad behavior. But you've probably noticed that she doesn't do that to everyone."

As embarrassing as it was to hear, Chloe was right. Dragon was like a slightly aggressive kitten in Chloe's hands. But the second I walked into the barn her ears would flatten and she'd get a sour expression on her face. And it wasn't fair; it wasn't like I'd ever done anything bad to her. I just didn't think she was a very nice horse ... not like Ace.

But, we couldn't go on like that forever. I had to find a way for us to become friends, or at least not enemies.

The idea came to me late one night when I was doing some research on an upcoming blog article.

For the last month or so, I'd started my Tai Chi practice up again as a sort of cross-training for riding. It improved my strength, flexibility, and my lung capacity, but it also had a way of keeping me calm and relaxed. Something Dragon could use, too.

One of the articles I'd come across had spoken of the benefit of practicing Tai Chi moves and breath work in the barn with the horses as a way to increase harmony. It sounded a little crazy, quite honestly, but it couldn't hurt. Anything was worth a try.

I had to wait until the next morning to put my plan into action. Lorne had gone up to the house to have coffee with Julie and the horses were finishing their breakfast inside, waiting for me to turn them out.

"All right, Dragon," I told her, as she eyed me up suspiciously, "today, we're going to try something different. We're going to be friends, right?"

She grabbed a mouthful of hay from her a net, a little more aggressively than necessary, and sent me a glare.

I felt a little silly as I set my phone on the small shelf across from her stall and pulled up the video I'd found especially for her.

I pressed the play button and suddenly the barn was filled with the gentle sound of pan-pipes echoing down the aisle. I glanced over at Dragon to see if there was any reaction but she just pretended to ignore me.

Right, let's do this. Trying not feel ridiculous, I set my legs into the familiar Tai Chi position called Horse Stance and mirrored the instructor's slow, flowing movements on the screen. I concentrated on controlling my breathing while I moved and gradually felt all the normal tension I felt when dealing with Dragon melt away.

She snorted behind me and when I glanced over she looked a little softer, a little less angry, while she ate her hay.

By the time I'd finished the twenty-minute video, all my muscles were loose and supple, and I was filled with a sort of serene energy.

When I turned around, I was surprised to see that not only was Dragon standing with her head over her stall door but her eyes were half-closed and she looked like she was having a good nap. I had never seen her so calm. She was usually always tense and full of movement, now her body was totally relaxed; she looked like a completely different horse.

"You're such a good girl," I said softly, "you are so pretty and strong and smart. I know we got off on the wrong foot but things are going to be different now, I promise."

Before I opened her stall door I pulled a carrot out of my pocket and showed it to her.

She looked at me in surprise and then tentatively reached out and lipped the treat from my hand, pulling back quickly like she thought I'd try and take it away from her.

I turned away to let her eat in peace and then opened her stall door again and stood there, patiently waiting.

And when she finally came over and put her nose in the halter with a heavy sigh, things all of a sudden felt different between us.

Instead of preparing myself for the battle of leading her outside, I just stood there petting her like we had all the time in the world.

She wasn't perfect when I led her out, she still pulled a little and was impatient while I struggled with the pasture gate, but the angry intensity wasn't there anymore. I had the feeling that we were on our way to a better relationship. I couldn't wait to tell Chloe about our breakthrough.

Another benefit of having Chloe around was that I suddenly had a new weekend trail riding partner. Our schedules didn't line up during the week but every Saturday morning, when the weather allowed, we'd bundle up and hit the trails together.

I'd been shy at first since Chloe was such a good rider compared to me, but she was easy to be around and her non-stop talking put me at ease right away.

She had pretty much become my biggest fan since the feature I'd written on her for my blog had been very popular and she'd immediately started her own fan page for Dragon. I had somehow over the last few months attracted over a thousand followers and every time I posted or shared a blog entry I seemed to gain a few more. It was a little surreal, actually, since in real life I could count the number of friends I had on one hand.

Chapter Thirty-Six

"I don't like you driving in this," my mom said ominously, looking out the window at the heavily falling snow. "It's not safe. You should stay home tomorrow."

"Oh, I'll be fine," I said, not glancing up from the video I was watching. In truth, I was more than a little terrified to drive on the icy roads again after my harrowing commute the day before. The car had spun out on a patch of ice and I'd nearly put me and Lorne in a ditch. But it didn't do any good to admit that out loud. The horses still needed to be taken care of and I wasn't about to spend the whole day cooped up at home just because of a little snow. I had had to miss one day already because of doctor's appointments. I wasn't about to miss another.

"How about I drive you and Lorne tomorrow?" Dad asked, appearing in the doorway. He'd been downstairs on the phone for the last hour and I hadn't even heard him come upstairs.

"Don't you have to work?" I asked, secretly hoping that he could, in fact, drive us.

"Exam week. I can spare a day out of the office."

"But you'd have to spend all day at the farm. Are you sure you want to do that?"

My dad had actually come out a few times to visit with Lorne and help do some light repairs around the barn. He seemed to like it there.

"Yes, I will be entirely at your service. I already called Lorne so it's decided."

"You did?" I asked, narrowing my eyes at him.

There was something in the way that he didn't quite meet my eye that made me sit up and take notice. He was definitely hiding something.

The next morning when we picked up Lorne, he seemed a little more agitated than usual. He was waiting at the end of the wide circular driveway instead of by his usual bench up against the grey wall of the condo.

I was already in the back seat so he opened the passenger side door and practically leapt into the seat before my dad had even had a chance to stop.

"Whoa, Lorne, where's the fire?" I asked, as my dad carefully pulled out into traffic. There weren't many cars on the road and the plows had already scraped the pavement clear so the driving had actually been fine so far.

"Oh, nothing, nothing," he said, "but we need to stop at the drive-thru to pick up some coffees."

"But I made us our coffee like usual—"

"Less back-talk from you, miss. We're going to be late. Let's step on it."

I could see my dad trying not to laugh as he obediently navigated to the drive-thru and relayed Lorne's half-shouted order to the attendant.

"Seven coffees and a jumbo box of donut holes," Lorne bellowed across my dad as soon as we rolled up to the order kiosk. "And assorted Muffins. But not all bran ones like last time. Chocolate chip."

It's finally happened, I thought, *Lorne had lost his marbles and has gotten dementia. I guess it was only a matter of time.*

I said nothing though, and when we got to the barn, I was shocked to see that there was a whole crew of people working on a structure halfway up the driveway to Julie's house.

"Drive us up there," Lorne said impatiently when my dad went to park in our usual spot in the barn driveway. "We can't be expected to walk all that way carrying coffee."

"Right, of course not," my poor Dad said, shaking my head in bemusement. "Whatever you say."

We pulled up the driveway and parked off to the side where Lorne's boat of a car wouldn't be in the way of all the big trucks.

Somehow, somewhere between now and two days ago, a section of the laneway had been transformed. An offshoot driveway had been plowed and bedded with gravel and lined with huge river rocks on either side. It curved to the right and led directly into what must have been an old orchard at some point. Right in between the trees, there was a huge square of black plastic on the ground and I could see that here and there concrete strips had been poured.

What on earth was going on?

Off to one side, two massive flat-deck trucks were parked nose to tail in front of the foundation strips and each trailer carried the entire half of a cottage, split neatly in two.

"What the heck is this?" I said in astonishment.

"My new home," Lorne said proudly, waving a hand toward the grey cottage.

"You're moving here? Lorne, that's fantastic."

"Yep, it was time to move back to the old homestead. I want to spend my twilight years looking over a field of horses and breathing in the good country air."

"And, he'll be close enough to do morning feeds when I want to sleep in," Julie said, appearing behind us. She looked at the cottage on the trailer with approval.

"That's so amazing," I said dreamily, turning to look out across the valley. The cottage wouldn't have the same commanding view of the faraway city and mountains that Julie's house had but it looked over the rolling hills of the farm to the woods and had a peek of the river beyond. It was almost better in a way, more peaceful.

"I figured it was time to give Lorne his farm back," Julie said with a laugh. "I've been freeloading far too long."

"Oh, nonsense," Lorne said gruffly, "you did us a favour by looking after it for us."

"Wait? What?" I stopped gazing dreamily over the farm and snapped to attention. "What do you mean *Lorne's* farm?"

"He didn't tell you?" Julie said innocently, taking a sip of her coffee.

"I was waiting for her to figure it out herself," Lorne said with a laugh.

"Well, how am I supposed to *know* anything if nobody tells me stuff?" I said, a little grumpily. I hated being left out of the loop.

"Lorne let me move into the house with Nicholas after the accident. I wasn't coping well on my own so he and Gretta took us in."

"We were happy to have you," Lorne said gruffly. "Katie and Lisa had already moved out and that big house was too empty without them."

He turned to me. "Early on, when Gretta first became ill, we had to move to town to be closer to the hospital, my eyesight wasn't so good even then, and I couldn't do all that driving back and forth in the dark and the rain.

"The doctors got her so she was feeling pretty good. She'd always wanted to travel so we kept the condo and left Julie and Nicholas in charge of the farm while we went to see the parts of the world we'd never been able to see."

He broke off, his mouth working up and down a few times as he struggled to contain his emotions.

"It was a good life," he went on, "a grand life. I only wish she was still around to spend this final part with me."

Julie reached out and put a hand on his shoulder. "Sometimes I really feel like she's still here with us, watching everything. She would have loved what you're doing here, Lorne. And she would have loved this cabin you're building."

I looked out across the valley below us and felt a pang of sadness. I would miss my drives with Lorne in the mornings. Come to think of it, I would probably have to give his car back since I wasn't going to be chauffeuring him around anymore. How was I going to get to the barn myself?

"And that brings us to the second part of our plan," Lorne said gruffly. "You tell her, Julie."

"Well, maybe I'll *ask* her rather than telling her," Julie countered. "We don't want to force her to do anything."

"Sure we do, it's the easiest solution for everyone."

"But maybe she doesn't want to—"

"Okay, okay," I interrupted, "I'm right here. Ask me what?"

"Lorne thinks you should move into the house with me, at least for the winter. With Nicholas gone, I would love help with the horses and that way your parents don't have to worry about you driving in all sorts of weather."

I looked over at my dad, and he grinned and nodded.

"It's up to you. I'd say you should go for it. Your mother and I will survive somehow on our own."

"Well, then yes, of course I will," I said, feeling a little stunned.

I loved the idea of living at the farm, especially of being closer to Ace and Nipper, but Julie wasn't always the easiest person to be around. What would it be like living with her full time?

You'd be able to see Nicholas more often, a little voice whispered in my ear and I blushed even though nobody could know what I was thinking. Nicholas had been too busy with school to visit the farm much but we texted sometimes and kept in touch online. I was secretly hoping I would see him more over the holidays.

We helped Lorne to hand out coffees and pastries to all the workers and then left him loudly giving advice to them on how to set up his new cottage while we went down to the barn to take care of the horses.

The snow had stopped falling the night before, and the sun was bright and cheerful overhead, making me feel like I was walking through some sort of happy dream.

I can't believe I'm moving out of my parent's house, I thought as I led the horses outside one by one and let them loose into the pasture. The ring was too snowy to ride in so everyone was getting turned out, even Nipper. It was a good thing I wasn't about to ride because there were so many thoughts swirling around my head that I couldn't focus properly on anything anyway. Dragon took advantage of my inattention to drag me an extra ten feet through the snow but she made up for it by gently nuzzling my cheek for a second before tearing off over the hillside in a series of bucks.

Well, she's a work in progress, I thought with a sigh, trudging back inside.

As soon as the stalls were done and the aisle swept, Julie waved to me from the driveway.

"Come on up to the house," she called, "you can pick out your room."

I gulped nervously and nodded, warmed a little by her reassuring smile. Everything was moving so fast, that I hardly knew what to think.

As soon as we'd climbed to the top of the hill, Julie ushered me inside. We dropped our boots off in the front entryway and I studied the interior of the big farmhouse with open curiosity. Despite my growing friendship with Julie, she'd never invited me up to the house so I felt a little out of my element.

The short hallway led to a large, open living room with a fire crackling away in the wood stove and three comfortable-looking old couches arranged around it. A fat tuxedo-coloured cat lay curled on the back of the nearest couch and he opened on eye briefly when we came in before shutting it firmly again.

There was a desk in one corner, piled with papers, horse magazines, and bits of leather, and an older flat-screened television on one wall. The remaining walls were hung with horse paintings and photos. I would have loved to have spent more time studying them but Julie hurried me on to the kitchen.

"Wow, it's huge," I said, staring at the long wooden table and the twelve chairs around it.

"Yeah, this place is pretty big for one person. I've started to feel a little guilty hoarding it all to myself. Originally, Lorne and Gretta had this place full of working students most of the time so that's why it's so oversized. I offered to move out so Lorne could have it back, or have him come live with me, but he said he much preferred to have a little cabin of his own. At least this way I can keep an eye on him."

Down the hall was a little two-piece bathroom with the faded blue wallpaper and sepia horse paintings on both walls. There was a library on the left and an office on the right. At the very end of the house, across from the stairs that led upward, was a big bedroom with a private bathroom.

"When I first got out of the hospital I couldn't climb the stairs for months," Julie said, "so Lorne and Gretta converted this area into a bedroom for me down here and I just never left. I honestly don't know how I would have survived without them taking me and Nicholas in. I owe them everything."

There was a sliding back door at the foot of the stairs that led to a snow-covered porch outside. Beyond it was a huge open field that seemed to stretch out for miles

"I didn't know there was this much pasture here," I said in surprise.

"Oh yes, the farm ends right at those trees you can see in the distance there. You can just see the neighbor's red roof if you look hard enough. They have horses, too.

"Come on upstairs; that's where all the bedrooms are. I'll apologize in advance for the general aura of neglect," Julie said, wincing at the dust motes that danced around us as we reached the landing. Sunlight drifted in from a few skylights overhead, lighting up the otherwise dark, narrow hallway. "I don't use any of this space, except for when Nicholas visits, so I tend to forget it's here. I think it will need a good dusting and airing out. That would make a good project for you."

The hallway was long and narrow with just rows of closed doors lining either side of the hall and one wooden table with a dust-laden plastic plant on it to break up the monotony. One of the skylights had clearly had a leak in the past and the flowered wall paper on the right had a brown stain running from ceiling to floor.

"Sorry, it does look a little grim right now," Julie said, "but I promise it will spruce up nicely. That leak happened years ago and there wasn't any real water damage except for the wall paper. I never bothered to replace it, but we can put something new up if you like. This first room on the left belongs to Nicholas when he visits, it was originally Gretta and Lorne's old room, but there are seven others to choose from so you take your pick."

"Okay," I said tentatively, wondering if there had ever been any ghost sightings in this place. It sure looked haunted.

"Right, well, I'll leave you to look around then. Just shout if you need anything."

She headed hurriedly downstairs and I wondered if this was the point where I disappeared into one of the rooms and was never heard from again.

"Come on, get a grip," I told myself. "This is a free place to live. And you get to sleep on the same property as Ace on a real horse farm. This is a dream come true."

I forced myself to march right down to the end of the hall and push open the last door on the left.

Huh, that's not too bad. It was a larger room with white paneling and faded blue curtains on the windows. As a corner room it had a view of the pasture from two sides plus a sky-light overhead and suddenly, I could envision what it would look like with fresh curtains and a matching duvet on the bed. The wooden floors creaked underfoot as I walked to the empty bookshelf and ran a finger through the thick layer of dust.

Leaving the door open so the room could air out, I crossed the hall to find a nearly identical room on the other side, only this one had the same view as from the kitchen window. I could see the lower pastures and the ring, and I could even see Ace out in the field with Bear.

I could get used to this, I thought with growing excitement. I went slowly from room to room, leaving each door open. The end rooms were larger than the ones in the middle and they all had connecting bathrooms between them that were split between two rooms. I still thought it was pretty luxurious since I'd grown up in a house that only had one bathroom shared between four people. Overall, the rooms were all in better shape than I'd originally thought.

I could hang pictures on the walls in the hallway to make it look more inviting, I thought, *and get rid of that gross plastic plant. I could price out new curtains for the rooms and there must be blankets and sheets for the beds around here somewhere.*

Sure enough, the room at the very end, across from Nicholas' room, was full to the brim with Rubbermaid tubs and cardboard boxes each carefully labelled with marker on strips of yellowed, peeling masking tape. *Queen sheets, Twin duvets, Pillow cases.*

It smelled a bit musty and moldy in there. And I wasn't sure if sheets and things had an expiry date after sitting in boxes for years but at least it was a start. I could try and run them through the laundry anyway and just throw out the ones that disintegrated in the wash.

"How did you make out?" Julie said when I finally came back downstairs, dusty but happy. She handed me a cup of coffee and looked at me a little anxiously. As if she were expecting me to back out of our agreement.

"Good," I reassured her, "I picked out a room."

"The one on the far end that overlooks the barn?" she asked, looking relieved.

"Yes, how did you know?"

"Lucky guess. That's my favourite view, too. Do you have any ideas for decorating?"

"Oh, it all looks fine," I said quickly, hesitating to criticize before I'd even moved in.

"Rubbish, it's a neglected mess and I know it."

"Right, okay. I'm not an expert or anything. But I think if we just took down all the old wall paper and painted the rooms instead that it would look so much better. And then if we cleaned everything and put up new curtains and hung some pictures, it would look really good."

"How long do you think it would take you?"

"Er, me? By myself?" I gulped. "I've never done anything like this. I'd have no idea where to start."

"Guess," Julie said flatly.

"Maybe a week or so to get my room ready?" I said slowly.

"Right," she nodded. "Perfect. Lorne's cottage will be ready for him to move into next week. You can start whenever you like and you can move in whenever your room is how you'd like it. Will that plan work for you?"

"Yes. I think so," I squeaked. This was all moving very quickly in an out-of-control sort of way. I hadn't even had time to think about things. Was this a hundred percent what I wanted?

But as soon as I walked from the house to the barn and saw Ace waiting for me at the pasture gate, I knew that my decision had been made. I was home.

Chapter Thirty-Seven

Things moved quickly after that.

First, of course, was breaking the news to my mom.

In one sense, she took it better than I'd expected. She'd gone very still when I made the announcement over dinner that night, and then she'd taken a drink from her glass of wine and shot a long, measured stare at my father as if she were blaming him completely.

"Fine," she said, looking down at her plate. "I can't stop you so do whatever you like."

I shared a look with my dad and he gave me a thumbs up, which I immediately felt guilty about. I wanted my mom to support me, not feel like we were against her.

"Mom, I—"

She stood up abruptly, and picked up her plate and glass without looking at either of us.

"I'm going to watch some television; you two enjoy your dinner."

"She'll come around," my dad said, once she was out of earshot.

I hoped he was right.

. . .

Lorne's cabin was finally assembled and then he had to impatiently wait for the city home inspector to check everything and give him the go ahead to move in.

I had thought that my family, Julie, and Nicholas would have been roped into helping him pack and move, but he waved me off when I suggested it, saying that he'd already hired a moving company to take care of things.

We were all there, even my mom, Julie, and Nicholas on the day that everything arrived.

Lorne didn't have many things and it hardly took the movers any time at all to ferry his furniture and boxes inside.

"Lorne, this is fantastic," I said, exploring his new, little house. It was the perfect size for him and the floorplan was open, making it cheery and bright inside.

The big picture-window in the living room looked over the lower pastures and had a small propane fireplace. The kitchen was compact but had brand new modern appliances and a pantry that I was sure he'd just stock with junk food. There were two bedrooms and a spacious bathroom.

"It's everything I need," he said with satisfaction. "Best of all, I can spy on you girls down on the barn to make sure you're doing all your chores."

"Ha ha," I said, rolling my eyes at him.

My mom insisted that we were all staying to help him to unpack the boxes, and my dad and Nicholas hung up the paintings under Lorne's critical eye. Julie and I helped put his kitchen in order, stacking the dishes and cutlery, and finding places to stuff his oversized toaster and a blender.

It hadn't seemed like that much to unpack, but it took us all afternoon to get everything just right, and then Lorne insisted on ordering pizza for everyone so that we could have a bit of a celebration.

"I'll just run and feed the horses their dinner," I said, putting on my coat and grabbing a slice of pizza for the trek down to the barn.

Nobody heard me, they were all huddled around a huge photo album that Lorne had set out on the table. They had gone through the horse album already and were on to the one of his children when they were babies so I thought it was a good time to slip away.

The ground was white with frost and the air was that startling cold that made your nose freeze the moment you stepped outside. It was beautiful, though; the night sky was completely cloudless and a million stars danced overhead.

"So, we're going to be roomies, are we?" Nicholas asked, trotting up behind me. He was still hastily zipping his coat up while trying to hold his own slice of pizza as well.

"Here," I said, taking the pizza quickly from him so he could at least keep from freezing.

"Thanks," he bundled up and then took his food back, falling into step beside me.

"Are you home for Christmas now?"

"Almost, I have a few more days at school and then I'll come home for the break. How are your renovations coming along?"

"I haven't really started yet. But I researched how to take down the wallpaper. It looks ... er, a bit complicated."

"Naw, I'm sure you'll be fine. I can help you once I'm back."

"Really? That would be great."

"Mom mentioned that we should really do all the bedrooms upstairs if we're doing yours anyway. We can save on paint if we buy in bulk. That is, if you're up for it?"

"For sure. That was sort of my plan for the winter, too."

We walked in silence for a few minutes. I suddenly wondered what living so close to Nicholas would be like. Would it be awkward? Would I discover that he had awful bathroom habits or something and I'd stop liking him so much? Or what if he stopped liking *me* or he brought home a girlfriend from school or—?

"Um, Bree, are you okay?"

"What?" I shook my head to clear it. "Of course I am. Why?"

"Well, you got this funny look on your face, like you were in pain or something."

"No," I laughed in spite of myself. Leave it to me to be imagining a future drama where everything went wrong with imaginary Nicholas when the *real* Nicholas was right here beside me, being ignored. "I'm fine. Let's get these horses fed."

The next few weeks I worked harder at renovating that stupid second floor than I had at anything in my life. Taking wallpaper down had to be the absolute worst chore anyone had ever invented.

Since I'd googled all sorts of how-to videos, I *sort* of knew what I was doing, but the reality was just so much worse.

Nicholas had been asked to visit a friend's place for a few days so he'd delayed coming. So for the first few days, I was on my own.

I'd started with my own room first. I'd pushed the few bits of furniture into the middle of the room and laid down old sheets across the baseboards to catch all the loose bits. Then I'd carefully started in one corner of the room, spraying the paper with the liquid solution that Lorne and Julie had bought me and letting it soak in for the recommended fifteen minutes.

That part had been easy enough, but when I'd started scraping, the paper didn't peel away in one nice sheet like the YouTube video had shown me. Instead, it came away in tiny strips and chunks, and some bits stuck stubbornly to the wall no matter how much solution I sprayed on it. What I thought was going to take me an hour ended up taking me three days to actually finish. And then I had to sand the walls where some of the paper had stuck and fill in the tiny holes my scraper had made.

And, after all *that* was done, I had to clean up the unbelievable, sticky mess I'd made and wash the floors and the baseboards and the window ledges. And only then could I actually start painting.

I'd picked a really pretty light bluish-grey color for the rooms, to go with the white ceilings and trim and when, after over a week had passed, my own room was finally done I had to admit that it looked amazing. Too bad I was too exhausted and blistered to really enjoy it.

"Don't worry, the rest will go so much faster now that you'll be living here," Julie assured me, "you can work right through the night now."

Great, I thought, *just great.*

The move-in had been pretty anti-climactic after all my worry. When my room was done I'd brought some things over to decorate with and then the next day I'd brought my clothes and then that was it; I'd officially moved.

"You can come back whenever you need a break," my mom said, "and we want to hear from you all the time. And we still want to be a part of your medical appointments ... if you'll let us."

"Of course, Mom. I'd love that. And you can come visit whenever you like. And we'll be together for Christmas anyway."

My dad had already become a bit of a fixture there and had busied himself doing small farm repairs for Lorne, and had spent a whole weekend helping me start tearing down the wallpaper in the room next to mine.

"It's a good break from grading papers or working on the models," he said, "it's nice to be physically active sometimes, and to get out of the house and give your mother some space."

I looked over at the wistful tone in his voice and frowned. I had guessed for a while that maybe not everything in their relationship was exactly perfect. They didn't spend that much time together except at meals and when they *were* together, they tended to fight.

"Is everything all right?" I'd asked cautiously.

"Of course, of course. Nothing for you girls to worry about. Just grown-up stuff."

Grown up stuff? What, was I four years old?

"Okay, Dad. Angelika and I are fully grown adults. We've had our own relationships and can handle real conversations. Or at least I can."

"Not today, Bree," he'd said, sounding tired, "let's just all have a nice Christmas together. We can discuss everything in the new year."

Hmm, that did not sound good at all.

He'd looked over and sent me a reassuring smile and I'd forced myself to smile back.

Chapter Thirty-Eight

✦

The following week, just a few days before Christmas, I had a different sort of surprise.

"Bree," Lorne said, his forehead wrinkled more than usual with concern, "you have a visitor. She said she's your—"

"Yeah, I saw her," I said grimly, bringing Nipper to a halt outside of the barn. We'd just been on a trail ride through the newly-fallen snow and my fingers were numb with cold. "I wonder what she wants."

"She didn't say. She brought a friend with her, though."

"Fine. This visit had better be quick, though."

I jumped down and drew Nipper's reins over his neck. Every muscle in my body was suddenly tense. Angelika and I had an unspoken agreement that we stayed as far away from each other as possible. Why was she going back on that now?

Nipper hesitated in the open barn doorway, probably sensing my agitation, and then bumped my arm gently with his nose.

Right, remember to breathe, I told myself, pausing to run a hand down his fuzzy neck. *She can't do anything to hurt me. I can just ask her to leave if she gets obnoxious.*

"Bree!" she squealed as soon as she caught sight of me. She

was standing right outside of Ace's stall like she belonged there and a tall, muscled man stood beside her. They were both wearing expensive-looking winter gear and matching hats with faux-fur trim, liked they'd stepped out of an outdoor magazine. Luckily, for them, they'd chosen to appear when there was snow and not the usual mud. "Eddie, this is my sister, Bree, the one I've been telling you about."

Her eyes were overly bright and her movements jerky. I couldn't tell if it was just nerves or if she was on something, but the guy with her didn't seem to notice. He strode forward smoothly with his hand held out for me to shake.

"Edward," he said, gripping my hand and looking me right in the eye as if he were trying to hypnotize me into thinking he was a good, trustworthy guy. I wasn't buying it. "I've heard so much about you from Angelika."

"Oh, really?" I extracted my hand with some difficulty. "What sort of things, exactly?"

"Your blog!" Angelika trilled. "I've been reading it to Eddie since we both *adorrrre* horses."

Adore horses? I restrained myself from bursting into laughter. *Since when?*

"You read my blog?" I asked, raising an eyebrow. I led Nipper into his stall and busied myself untacking him.

"Of course, silly. Eddie owns a lot of expensive racehorses—"

"You have horses?" I asked, suddenly re-evaluating my opinion of him.

"Yes, well parts of them anyway. We're a group, you see, some friends and industry professionals who got together to have some fun. We all chip in some cash and then we get to watch the races and cheer them on. And earn a little money sometimes, too."

"Sounds like fun." I said dryly, wondering why on earth someone would want to own a horse when they didn't even get to ride it or take care of it.

"Er, yes, well, it is, usually. But recently we've had a few problems in our group. One of our horses ended up hurting itself and couldn't run, so we had the trainer sell it and buy us a new one. We never thought anything more about it until, well, the animal turned up at a feedlot in the middle of nowhere six months later being fattened up for the meat market."

"Oh, gross. Seriously?"

"Yes, and some do-good rescue bought it and traced it back to *us* by its tattoo, and she went all public about how we were cruel murderers and all this nonsense. We have some young influencers and up and coming talent in our racing group. It was terrible for publicity and a few of them were on the brink of pulling out."

"I'll bet," I said, narrowing my eyes at him. I came out into the aisle and closed Nipper's stall door tightly behind me.

"That sounded wrong. We're not heartless, Breanna. It's completely illegal for racehorses to go for slaughter off the track but, like, how are we supposed to know what happens to every single one of our horses after they've been sold a few times? They could end up anywhere."

"That's true," I said slowly, thinking of where Dragon might have ended up if Lorne hadn't bought her. How many people wanted to take a chance on a homicidal mare like that? And how many people would have had the knowledge to handle her without getting hurt?

"Anyway, our plan was to quietly sell off all the horses and disband our group, and then Angelika here told me about your blog."

"She did?"

"Yes, and I think your October Horses program is completely genius."

"Uh, well, it's not exactly a program. We only have two horses and we're just casually—"

"Right. But, it's just the sort of place we need for when our horses retire. A sort of landing-spot where they could recover from any injuries and be retrained for future careers. We actually have two horses that could come here right now and there would be more in the future, I'm sure."

"But we're not set up—" I stopped. "How many horses do you own anyway?"

"There are ten right now. Our long-term plan is to get down to five good ones to keep the expenses and publicity manageable. And the ones that can't race would come to you and you'd put their retraining journeys on your blog so everyone can see that these horses are being cared for properly and that we're not monsters. We'd pay board and for the vet and everything. We could set up a non-profit to handle the details and deal with donations and things."

"Wow, this is—"

"Amazing!" Angelika broke in with a squeal. "It's like fate or something told me to bring you two together to help the horses."

"Uh huh, well, it's an interesting offer," I said slowly. "I'm going to have to talk to Lorne and Julie and see what they think. I really just work here."

"No problem, we'll be in town all this week. Just let us know when we can meet to iron out all the details."

Edward smiled his hundred watt smile at me and held out his hand for me to shake.

I hesitated, hoping that I wasn't accidentally agreeing to this crazy idea. Part of me wanted to tell them both to get lost. Anything that Angelika was involved with was bound to be full of drama and heartache.

On the other hand, wasn't this an amazing offer? Maybe it was the sort of thing that Gretta had in mind all along to help the horses. Maybe I was crazy to even be hesitating.

"I'll let you know," I said, slipping my work-calloused hand into his soft, manicured one.

"Oh Breeee, this is going to be so fantastic. It will be just like old times with us doing things together. That's what we did growing up, Eddie, we did everything together. We were as thick as thieves. Weren't we, Bree?"

"Yeah, just like thieves," I said, gritting my teeth.

Her smile dimmed and then the light drained out of her face like somebody had flicked a switch. To my horror, I could see tears brimming in her eyes.

"Actually, could I talk to you for a second?" she asked, sniffling.

"I'll just walk around and check out the facilities while you girls talk," Eddie said, turning on his heel and wandering out toward the ring. He pulled out his phone and I could see him taking pictures.

"What's the matter?" I asked cautiously. I wasn't cruel; I didn't want to see her cry, but I also knew that Angelika was an expert at playing on people's emotions and she could turn her tears off and on like a faucet.

"I just want to apologize for real, about Duncan and about abandoning you when you were so ill. I shouldn't have left town when you needed me. I was just so scared seeing you sick like that that I panicked and ran."

"You did?" I asked skeptically, wondering if it was true.

"Yeah, and I know that's not much of an apology and there's no excuse for how I acted; especially about what happened with Duncan. Believe me, I'm going to have to live with that for the rest of my life. I honestly never wanted to hurt you. I love you and I was selfish and stupid and ..."

She broke off and looked away, wiping her eyes with her gloved hand.

"Angelika, where is this all coming from?" I asked in astonishment. She had never said anything like this before. She sounded like a real person, not like she was acting or playing a role.

"I've been doing some therapy sessions now and then to try and get my life in order. I don't want to turn into an addict and I've had to learn a lot of hard things about myself. Look, Bree, I spent my whole life trying to make you love me. I know I went about it the wrong way but it's the truth. I always tried to follow you and join in whatever you were doing. That's the only way I could make you spend time with me."

"What do you mean?"

"You would never play with me. It was always you and Dad together doing fun things and you never wanted me around. It was awful. The only way I could be a part of your little unit was to sign up for the same things you did. And then you were so awful about it when I did that, yeah, I got mad and tried to outshine you. I kept hoping that one day we'd find something that we could actually do together."

I stared at her in growing distress, wondering how much of that was true. I did remember being jealous of her from a very young age. I didn't ever try and include her like other big sisters might have. I was always trying to get away from her.

"And you know what stupid thing hurt me the most? That dumb Chinese Checkers game you and Dad would play all the time. Did you know that that is a *four* person game? I didn't find that out until years later. You guys acted like there was never room for me or Mom, that it was a game for two, but that was bull. You could have made room if you wanted to."

And with that she burst fully into tears and before I could stop myself I'd wrapped my arms around her in a tight hug that was probably eighteen years overdue.

We stood that way for an eternity, both of us crying and sniffling and then breaking into laughter.

It didn't erase all those years of hurt or what she'd done with Duncan, but it did make it so that maybe we had a path forward. Maybe, if we were careful, we might be able to find our way to being friends.

They left shortly after that, leaving me to slowly groom Nipper and put his blanket on, my mind whirling in a million different directions.

"Good family reunion?" Lorne asked, appearing in the aisle outside Nipper's stall.

"It was ... interesting," I said. "Let's just say it could have gone much worse. I think we need to round up Julie and have a meeting. They sort of made us an offer you might be interested in."

In an hour, we were sitting at the battered wooden table in Julie's kitchen sipping her rich, percolator coffee and staring down at the notepad I'd been writing on.

"It sounds a little too good to be true," Julie said, rubbing the bridge of her nose like she always did when she was thinking.

"I know, and I don't love that Angelika is involved; she hasn't been exactly trustworthy in the past. But the guy seemed genuine about wanting to make sure their horses get good homes, even if it's just for the good publicity. If they dumped the horses here and didn't pay their bills I guess I could just write about that in my blog. I don't think they'd risk it."

Lorne didn't say much. He'd been beaming and rubbing his hands together gleefully ever since I'd told him what Eddie had wanted.

"That is exactly what Gretta had had in mind before she got sick," Lorne said in delight. His eyes shone and I could see that he was mentally filling the entire barn with racehorses.

"But Bree and I can't take care of all those horses on our own. And who is going to ride them? No offense," she added, shooting a look at me, "but you're not going to want to handle the spicier ones. I think Ace and Nipper are more your speed."

"None taken and I couldn't agree more. I just want to ride the slow ones. Would Chloe come work here full time or some of her friends?"

"Maybe, possibly. We could ask."

"And if Eddie's group paid full board for each horse then couldn't we hire someone to help with the stalls? Even part time."

"Potentially."

"Working students," Lorne said, "from overseas. Just like in the old days."

"You think people would want to come from other countries to work for us?" I said skeptically.

"Actually, I think he's got the right idea," Julie said. "Lorne still has a bit of a reputation in some circles. There are people who would come here to ride with him. If we had the right horses to offer them."

"So you guys think we should really do this? I can't tell you how little I trust anything that has to do with Angelika. It's likely to fall through at the last minute or the horses will turn out to be psycho or something."

"We should do it," Lorne said emphatically. "Even if this deal falls through and doesn't last long, we'll have made a beginning. That's what Gretta would have wanted. And you just make sure to write about everything in that blog of yours. Document everything."

"I like horse boarders whose owners live far away and never visit," Julie said, smiling at me over the rim of her coffee cup, "that sounds good to me."

"But, Julie, you don't want the house full of working students. You don't even like people."

"I like *some* people," she said, choking back a laugh. "I like your family and Lorne, and I'm sure the working students would be fine. Horse people aren't like regular people. Besides, it's too big a place for just the two of us. There would be plenty of room for everyone and we could split chores. You'll see, you'll love it."

"Wow, well if you guys are a hundred percent sure it's okay then I guess I'll call Eddie."

Eddie was delighted when I called him and agreed that we could start our partnership.

"Excellent. You won't regret this, Breanna. I'll let you know when the horses are coming. I'll send you some info on them ahead of time so you can start writing your first article."

Chapter Thirty-Nine

Nicholas, my dad, and I sped up our renovations and spent long hours sanding, painting, and decorating. After the rooms were done, we had to tackle the hallway and then, all too fast, it was Christmas.

My mom hadn't been feeling festive enough to put up a tree and decorations at home so Julie had invited them to spend Christmas at the farm.

It felt wonderful to have everyone crowded in the big house together, surrounding a crackling fire with Christmas music going in the background and the big, lopsided tree that Nicholas had chopped down glowing with lights and decorations.

That morning even Angelika and Eddie had dropped by. They'd been staying at an upscale boutique nearby instead of at my parent's house, and I could tell my mom was a little frosty about the arrangements.

I didn't blame Angelika one bit, though; the tension between my parents had been steadily growing and it didn't make them exactly a pleasure to be around.

To my surprise, I was actually happy to see my sister. She

looked really good; calmer and more like her old self before she became an overnight sensation. Her hair was pulled back in a ponytail and the designer clothes she wore were at least practical and didn't involve stilettos, exposed nipples or fishnet stockings.

Eddie went around shaking hands with everyone and beaming his mega-watt smile until Lorne finally barked at him to sit down and have a drink because he was making everyone nervous.

"Here," Angelika said, pushing a long, rectangular parcel into my hands, "it's for everyone, really, but you should open it."

She was beaming at me, excited like a little kid and I couldn't help but smile back.

"We'll get a bigger one for the driveway," she added quickly, "but we thought this would look nice on the barn. I hope you like it ... I hope it's not too ..."

She broke off as the paper fell away and I looked down at the beautiful painted sign in my lap.

October Horse Farms, it read in scrolling letters. Worked into the design were elegant orange and brown maple leaves.

"It's ... it's wonderful," I said, feeling my eyes prick with tears.

"Oh, good, I got the idea when Lorne told us that's what he wanted the new name for the farm to be. I was just hoping that you'd all love the design. We can change it if you don't like—"

"It's perfect," I said, leaning over to give her a hug. Then I got up and took the sign over so Lorne and Julie could see it.

"It's just how Gretta would have done it," Lorne said, wiping his eyes briskly.

"She would have loved it," Julie agreed, placing a hand on his shoulder, "and she would have loved what you're doing with the farm."

A sudden silence fell, and I could see Lorne struggling with his emotions.

"To the October Horses," my dad said suddenly, lifting his glass.

And we all joined in, ringing in our new future.

And to second chances, I added in my head, sharing a small, private smile with Angelika. From across the room I caught my mother watching us, her gaze full of love and hope. *And to new lives begun.*

Helping Horses

Would you like to help these amazing, talented horses find a second career?

Consider supporting organizations like:

Thoroughbred Aftercare Alliance www.thoroughbredaftercare.org

New Vocations Racehorse Adoption Program www.horseadoption.com

New Stride Thoroughbred Adoption Society www.newstride.com/adopt-a-horse.html

Thoroughbred Placement Resources
   www.goodhorse.org

Retraining of Racehorses
   https://www.ror.org.uk

Do you think you're ready to find a project horse of your own? Read this fantastic book, New Track – New Life, by Kimberly Godwin Clark and find out what it's all about. https://www.amazon.com/New-Track-Life-Understanding-Thoroughbred-ebook-dp-B01N2U7ULS

More Reading

If you enjoyed reading The October Horses, the Defining Gravity series, or any of my other books, I'd love if you'd take a moment to write a review on any of the platforms where they are sold.

Defining Gravity Series
    Defining Gravity
    Flight
    Freefall
    Riding Above Air

Greystone Manor mystery series (under G.M. Mckay)
    The Curse of the Golden Touch
    The Sting of the Serpent's Blade

The Wayfarer's End Series
    The Opposite of Living
    Good Bones
    Wayfarer's End

Short Stories and Collections
The Horses of Winter

Acknowledgments

Huge thanks to my editor, Jinxie Gervasio, for being my first reader and for all the good advice.

Massive appreciation to Mariko Brown, Helen Cartwright, Honey Johnston, Marti Oltmann and the rest of the Advanced Reading team. Your help is invaluable!

Fabulous cover design credit goes to *Cover Design by James, GoOnWrite.com*

Special thanks to a long-ago friend, Kidan, a thoroughbred with a troubled past but a huge, kind heart who graciously allowed so many kids to be part of his life.

About the Author

Genevieve is the author of ten books and numerous short stories. She lives on the wild West Coast with her family which also includes horses, dogs, cats, sheep and chickens. She loves all types of riding and all breeds and types of horses, especially the quirky ones.

You can follow her at:

Facebook www.facebook.com/authorgenevievemckay

Instagram @mckay_genevieve

Website www.genevievemckay.com

Printed in Great Britain
by Amazon